RINGSIDE WITH THE CELTIC WARRIORS

This book is dedicated to the six champions who are always in my corner, Betty, Jacqueline, Sinead, Ciaran, Colin and Vivian.

Thomas Myler

Ringside with the Celtic Warriors
Tales of Ireland's Boxing Legends

CURRACH
PRESS

CURRACH PRESS
55A Spruce Avenue,
Stillorgan Industrial Park,
Blackrock, Co. Dublin

Cover design by Bill Bolger
Cover images from the Thomas Myler Collection and
from photographs kindly supplied by Aidan Walsh
Origination by Currach Press
Printed by MPG Books Limited

ISBN 978 1 85607 787 3

All photographs in this publication are from the Thomas Myler
Collection except where stated.

CONTENTS

ACKNOWLEDGEMENTS

Writing this book was a sheer joy, allowing for all the hard work in researching, checking and re-checking all the facts and figures. The interviews and watching clips of the fights was a fascinating exercise. No work of this nature would be complete, however, without recourse to the many fine boxing books, all extensively researched and well written, which have enhanced and continue to enhance what the great American writer and author A. J. Liebling called the sweet science. The books are included in the bibliography but if any writer or publisher has been inadvertently left out, the omission will happily be rectified in any future editions.

The author is grateful for the many interviews granted by boxers, promoters, managers, trainers, matchmakers, publicity agents, referees, judges, officials, boxing writers and the many people who make up the tapestry of boxing. Without them, this book would have been much the weaker and poorer. Sadly, some who were interviewed over the years have passed on but they are remembered with affection.

Special thanks in particular are also due to publisher Fearghal O'Boyle and his hard-working and diligent team at Currach Press, including Patrick O' Donoghue, Shane McCoy and Michael Brennan. People like these are often the faceless ones behind a book but nevertheless they play the all-important part of putting it all together. Thanks again all.

Thomas Myler
Dundrum
August 2012

FOREWORD

Jimmy Magee, RTÉ boxing commentator

When Thomas Myler asked me would I consider writing a foreword for this book, I did not hesitate. I considered it an honour to be associated with this latest tome from the prolific Irish boxing writer and historian. Thomas and boxing go together like hands and gloves. He has been part of the boxing scene for as long as I remember. The big fights, the little fights, the professional shows, the amateur tournaments, the club cards, the media conferences, he is ever-present.

You get the feeling that he knows them all, even those who were boxing before he was born. That is because his love of the boxing game knows no bounds. He can write with fervour and talk with conviction about John L. Sullivan, Gentleman Jim Corbett, Jack Johnson, even the bare-knuckle fighter Dan Donnelly, whose right arm is remarkably preserved at the Curragh in County Kildare after nearly two hundred years.

As with his previous books, *Ringside With The Celtic Warriors* is well researched and clearly a labour of love. I like the idea that this Myler tome is dedicated to the Irish-born boxers and not a parade of Americans who claim Irish blood when their family names may be a collection of Italian vowels.

This book will take you on a colourful journey from Dan Donnelly, who linked the eighteenth century with the nineteenth, to the life and times of boxers like Tom Sharkey, Mike McTigue, Jimmy McLarnin, Jack Doyle, Rinty Monaghan, Barry McGuigan, Steve Collins, Wayne McCullough, Michael Carruth and right up to Bernard Dunne and Katie Taylor.

Myler was there on the night at the O₂ Arena in Dublin's docklands when Dunne rose from two knockdowns to win the world superbantamweight title from Ricardo Cordoba. He was in London on the occasion when McGuigan dethroned the legendary Eusebio Pedroza for the world featherweight title. He reported these great victories with joyous pride, just as he did when Steve Collins twice beat Chris Eubank in Cork in world supermiddleweight title fights. What great memories, and this book relives those memories. He also has a chapter on Katie Taylor and an assessment of the 2012 London Olympics. It's all here in these pages.

A boxing writer-reporter does more than cover a fight. He also makes sure that he seeks out the victor and the vanquished, congratulating one and consoling the other. Boxers like to know that the media likes them or at least cares. Thomas Myler does care. He is that sort of genuine person. Enjoy the journey in his company.

Jimmy Magee
Lakelands
August 2012

7

Boxing has an excitement, a drama, a charisma all its own. It's been like that since the sport came into its own with the framing of the Queensberry Rules in 1867, and which, incidentally, are basically the same as today's rules. Naturally a number of changes and modifications have taken place over the years by various controlling organisations and boxing commissions to bring them in line with conditions of the day, with greater safety always and solely the prime object.

These changes include the shortening of championships fights from forty-five rounds to twenty, then to fifteen and today to twelve. Other innovative moves were extra weight classes and bringing forward the weigh-in by twenty-four hours. Besides all this, the sport has remained basically the same.

My own love affair with boxing started in the 1940s when my dad brought myself and my brother Patrick, now a successful author in his own right, to the National Stadium in Dublin to watch the amateur shows, and cheer on the boxers. Dad was a very keen boxing fan and had a modest library of boxing books, an interest he retained up to the very end. We would also climb out of bed in the early hours to turn on the old BBC Light Programme, now incorporated with Radio 1 and 2, and listen to the big fights from America, particularly world heavyweight championship bouts involving Joe Louis.

In the immediate post-war years and into the 1950s and 1960s we would also listen in to big fights on the Light Programme, usually around nine o'clock in the evening or early morning, and follow the action from the first round in fights involving the likes of Sugar Ray Robinson, Randolph Turpin, Rocky Marciano, Floyd Patterson, Archie Moore and other big names of the day. Raymond Glendenning was the BBC's resident boxing commentator and was succeeded by our own Eamonn Andrews, himself a very useful amateur boxer and winner of an Irish junior title.

Encouraged by my early keen interest in the sport, in 1950 I joined Arbour Hill Boxing Club on the Northside of Dublin city to try my luck in the game. We were all coached by the resident trainer Mick Coffey, one of the best middleweights Ireland ever produced and whose all-action hard-punching style was a sensation in the US. Alas, I was not one of his star pupils, or anywhere remotely near, winning just one of my three bouts. One evening I sparred with one of the great amateurs of the day, the incomparable Dave Connell, and to nobody's surprise I simply could not land one single punch on him. Not that he hit me either, although he could have. All he did was block my punches, sidestep neatly aside or just glide around the ring in that effortless style of his.

RINGSIDE WITH THE CELTIC WARRIORS

When my rather brief boxing career ended, I decided the next best thing was to stay on the safe side of the ropes and write about the sport. I have been doing it ever since. It's been a thoroughly enjoyable journey, made all the better by meeting many of my idols. You will meet them yourself in this book. I hope you enjoy the journey as much as I have. There goes the bell.

1. BARRY MCGUIGAN

Man of peace in troubled times

The politicians may have brought about peace on both sides of the Irish border in the 1990s after many years of bombs, bullets and bloodshed. But a decade earlier, a young sporting hero christened Finbar Patrick McGuigan from County Monaghan and better known as Barry McGuigan became a beacon of hope as world featherweight champion and one of our finest boxers. Bono, lead singer with U2, would go on record as saying: 'At a dark hour in Ireland, Barry's spirit shone a light towards peace. He was not only a champion, and still is, but a hero.'

Boxing under the United Nations flag of peace rather than wearing Irish or British colours, McGuigan would have his father Pat singing a heartfelt rendition of 'Danny Boy' in place of a national anthem. Billed as the Clones Cyclone, Barry succeeded in bringing together north and south communities, Catholics and Protestants, and encouraged unity during the darkest days of the Troubles. As *The Ring* magazine put it, 'When McGuigan boxed, there was peace.'

It did not matter that Barry himself was a Catholic and his wife and former sweetheart Sandra a Protestant. Together they forged and strengthened the religious link. 'One of my first fights was in a Loyalist working men's club on the Shankill Road in Belfast,' he recalled. 'The Shankill was known at that time as a killing zone for Catholics. But extraordinarily, the Loyalist Ulster Volunteer Force guaranteed my safety and even gave me a personal escort. After that, the Loyalists formed a Barry McGuigan Supporters Club, making me welcome in areas where Catholics would have been terrified to set foot in. That had a profound effect on me, giving me a feeling in the ring that I could be a representative of the possibility of a united Ireland.

'The support I got from Catholics and Protestants was because the shadows run deep. And I think my fights felt a little like sunshine. Both sides would say, "Leave the fighting to McGuigan." You see, it was all entertainment. People loved to forget the troubles for a while. The fact that I wouldn't wear green, white and gold or put on a sign that said this is who I represent was powerful. It was a very mature and dangerous thing to do but I wouldn't choose sides. People appreciated that.'

McGuigan was undeniably a class act, a big hitter with a solid chin. The late Harry Mullan, former editor of *Boxing News*, remembered several years before his untimely death in 1999: 'I covered Barry's professional debut on a wet and blustery evening in Dalymount Park, Dublin in May 1981. Between then and the night it ended eight years later with a cut-eye loss in

11

Manchester, he established himself as the most explosive and consistently thrilling talent these islands have produced in twenty years. McGuigan, world champion at featherweight, was special, not least because he gave Irish men and women everywhere something to feel proud about at a time when that commodity was scarce enough.'

In his retirement years when McGuigan thought the tumult and the cheering was over, he would achieve one of the highest honours in the sport when, in June 2005, he was inducted into the International Boxing Hall of Fame in New York. It meant he was alongside greats he had grown up watching and reading about, such as Sugar Ray Robinson, Muhammad Ali, Henry Armstrong, Joe Louis, Carmen Basilio, Jack Dempsey, Gene Tunney and many more. Barry is the only Irish boxer of the modern era to be inducted. 'A truly great honour,' he remembered.

The third of eight children, McGuigan was born into a family of five girls and three boys on 28 February 1961 in Monaghan town, on the Republican side of the border, and not in Clones, as is generally believed. Clones is about fourteen miles from Monaghan town. His parents were Pat and Kate. Pat was a professional musician, later known as Pat McGeegan, who would come fourth in the 1967 Eurovision Song Contest with the appropriately named ballad 'Chance of a Lifetime'.

Barry was interested in boxing as a toddler and in 1978 he joined Smithboro Boxing Club in Monaghan. He quickly learned the rudiments of the sport and in 1976 travelled to Dublin and won the Irish junior bantamweight title. Two years later and nearer home, he won the Ulster senior title at the same weight at the Ulster Hall, Belfast. That year, too, Barry won the Irish senior bantamweight title and in August was a member of the Northern Ireland team for the 1978 Commonwealth Games in Edmonton, in the Canadian province of Alberta. McGuigan reached the final where he faced the tough Papa New Guinean hope, Turnat Sugolik.

'A customs officer, he was the biggest bantamweight I've ever seen in my life,' Barry remembered in his 2011 autobiography *Cyclone, My Story*. 'He wasn't tall, if anything he was slightly shorter than me, but he was massive, with huge arms. I don't know how on earth he made the weight but he did. I knew I had a real fight on my hands. Though I took two standing counts I felt I'd done enough to win. He may have landed the bigger blows but I hit him far more than he hit me. I got the points and won the gold medal.'

McGuigan was seventeen and his international career was really under way now. In 1979 he won a bronze medal at the European Junior Championships in Rimini, Italy but his real goal was the Olympics, scheduled for Moscow in the summer of 1980. An Irish boxer had not won an Olympic medal since 1964 when the classy Belfast lightweight Jim McCourt brought home bronze from Tokyo. Would it be different in Moscow? McGuigan, now a featherweight and captain of the Irish seven-man team, hoped so. Barry got a bye in the first series and stopped Issack Mabushi of Tanzania in the third round in the second series. Despite pain from an old injury to his left hand, he had Mabushi down twice in the second round and forced two standing counts before the contest was stopped.

In an attempt to safeguard the hand, McGuigan had to get an injection of anaesthetic before going into the ring in his third series bout with the tough Zambian, Winfred Kabunda. Despite subsequent reports that his frame of mind was not right, and that he was 'worried sick', he now says that the hand stood up very well. 'I had no problems with it,' he recalled. 'Kabunda was a tall, skinny guy and I thought I boxed well and clearly felt that I won the fight but it was Kabunda who got the four-one decision, which I thought was a bit harsh. I was gutted. The fight was only one of three I lost as a senior amateur.

'In Kabunda's next bout, he was outpointed by the eventual gold medal winner Rudi Fink from East Germany. This time it was Kabunda who got the raw deal. He beat Fink from pillar to post yet they gave the decision to the German. That's the Olympics for you. There was some consolation for the Irish, however, as Hugh Russell, the Belfast flyweight, finished up with a bronze medal. That was the year, incidentally, when Cuba finished on top of the table with six gold, two silver and two bronze medals, followed by Russia with one gold, six silver and one bronze.'

After returning home from Moscow, McGuigan reflected on his experiences in Moscow and decided that he'd had enough of amateur boxing, with its weird judging and bad decisions. He made up his mind to turn professional. 'The contrast between the professional and amateur worlds could not have felt starker,' he recalled. 'I was so disillusioned with what happened in Moscow that I actually thought about giving up boxing altogether. That's enough now, I thought, I have wasted enough time and have had too many raw decisions. My mind was made up to turn professional.'

Several leading British managers including big names like Mickey Duff, Eddie Thomas and Terry Lawless were anxious to sign the seventeen-year-old and offered him attractive contracts. Two years earlier on a visit to London, McGuigan had visited Lawless' gym and sparred with the world lightweight champion Jim Watt and Ray Cattouse, who was British champion at that weight. Terry told him if he ever thought of turning professional to look him up. However, it was nearer to home that McGuigan was now looking.

After being recommended by friends to contact Barney Eastwood's office in Belfast, McGuigan signed professional forms with the wealthy bookmaker and influential boxing manager. Barry felt Eastwood was the man to get him to the top. The youngest of eight children of parents who owned a hardware store in Cookstown, County Tyrone, Bernard Joseph Eastwood first came into contact with boxing through watching US soldiers at an army base near his home during World War II. Two decades later he would become more directly involved with the sport by drifting into small-time promotions in the tail end of the boxing boom in Belfast in the late 1950s and into the 1960s and the emergence of stars like the unrelated Kellys, Spider Billy and John, and later Freddie Gilroy and John Caldwell.

By the 1980s Eastwood had started to develop a chain of betting shops and became a familiar figure in the stockbrokers belt that is the County Down seaside village of Hollywood. He was considered 'a man of impeccable taste', becoming a knowledgeable and enthusiastic collector of antique furniture and clocks. He was now anxious to bring about a revival of professional boxing in the northern counties. The sport had been going through a rather lean period at the time and Eastwood felt that now was the time to try and revive it. 'We can make it big again, like it was in the 1960s when we had the Gilroys and the Caldwells,' he told boxing writers. 'Northern Ireland, particularly Belfast, has always been a great boxing area so let's try and bring back the glory days.'

With the Troubles still raging on the streets, it was a big gamble for anybody to even contemplate a return of professional boxing but Eastwood felt it would be achieved, particularly with the likes of McGuigan on his books. Eastwood suggested the knowledgeable Gerry Storey, one of amateur boxing's most respected coaches, as Barry's trainer but Storey had to turn down the offer as he was involved with the Ulster arm of the Irish Amateur Boxing Association. He was also a dedicated amateur man. Instead, a former professional boxer named Eddie Shaw was signed, and they would train at the Eastwood Gym in Castle Street.

McGuigan made his professional debut on 10 May 1981 at Dalymount Park soccer ground in Dublin. The scheduled six-rounder against Selwyn Bell of Manchester was on the undercard of the European lightweight title fight between the defending champion, Derry's Charlie Nash and his little-known Italian challenger Joey Gibilisco. Surprisingly, Nash was knocked out in the sixth round. It was left to the young Barry, then twenty, to give the stunned open-air crowd something to cheer about, and he did. After dominating the opening round, he floored Bell twice in the second round, first with a body punch and then a head shot before referee Bob McMillan intervened.

Barry did not have too long to wait for his second fight as, a month later, Eastwood got him a match on the world lightweight title card featuring defending champion, Scotland's Jim Watt against Alexis Arguello of Nicaragua at the Wembley Pool arena in London. The bout was little more than a gymnasium workout for McGuigan. In a bout set for six rounds, the Monaghan puncher stopped Gary Lucas in the fourth round as referee Bob Galloway stepped in to save the Liverpool boxer unnecessary punishment. It was a bad night for Watt as Arguello, one of boxing's all-time greats, won over fifteen rounds.

Things do not always run smooth in boxing, as McGuigan discovered in his third fight. Matched at the Corn Exchange, Brighton against the local Peter Eubank, whose more famous brother Chris would go on to win world titles at two weights, Barry lost the decision over eight fast rounds. The verdict was soundly booed even by the partisan fans. McGuigan had his man on the canvas and generally landed the harder blows but referee Roland Dakin marked it narrowly by seventy-eight and a half to seventy-eight in the days when fractions were still used in scoring bouts. 'A blatant miscarriage of justice,' said Eastwood. 'Still, it was a fight in which Barry will have learned from.' They were prophetic words. Three fights and four months later, they met again, this time in a thriller at Belfast's Ulster Hall, when McGuigan won after two minutes and forty seconds of the eighth round had elapsed.

A rogue bell incident probably cost McGuigan his chance of a knockout in the sixth round. Dazed and in trouble, Eubank was trapped on the ropes and taking heavy punishment when referee Bob McMillan pulled them apart and pointed the visitor to his corner. With twenty seconds of the round still remaining, somebody near the ringside had clanged something and McMillan naturally thought it was the bell. One glance at the timekeeper and the referee knew something was wrong and the contest was quickly re-started. However, the end was merely delayed and after a grandstand finish by McGuigan two rounds later, it was all over. The ring was soon showered by 'nobbins', a boxing custom going back many years, with coins thrown into the ring in appreciation of a very good contest.

McGuigan continued his good form with eleven consecutive victories before he was nominated to contest the British featherweight championship at the Ulster Hall in April 1983. But a fight a little over a year earlier came very close to bringing a sudden end to his career. It happened at a dinner-boxing show at the fashionable World Sporting Club in London. In his twelfth ring appearance Barry knocked out Asymin Mustapha in the sixth round of a fight that would have tragic consequences.

Mustapha, known to the boxing public as Young Ali, held the Nigerian and African bantamweight titles. Though he had yet to box in Britain, he was considered a competent professional and expected to give McGuigan a tough fight. He did, always coming in no matter what the Irishman threw at him. In the fifth round, McGuigan saw the openings he had been seeking from the start and fired combination shots. A final right hook landed on Ali's jaw and he sank to the canvas to be counted out by referee Bob Galloway after two minutes and forty-seven seconds into the round. Leaving the ring, he collapsed into the arms of his manager Guinea Roger and was taken on a stretcher straight to hospital. He never regained consciousness, and would die in his native Nigeria almost six months later to the very day.

The fight had a profound effect on McGuigan. As Ali hovered between life and death, Barry was distraught and was on the verge of quitting boxing. 'It was a terrible time, and incredibly difficult to deal with,' he recalled. 'I walked the streets and the countryside wondering if there was any point in carrying on. I hadn't taken up the sport to do something like that to anybody. Yes, I wanted to get the better of my opponent but I never wanted to hurt them, and certainly not permanently. The incident profoundly shocked me. I found out that Ali's young wife was pregnant and that he had come over from West Africa on his own, earn some money and go back to her, and then this happened.'

'Everybody thought I was a nice kid. People liked me, yet here I was, having almost killed somebody, and it was all legal and above board. Because of what I did when I was in the ring, I was legally allowed to almost kill someone. What must people have thought about me? I found myself asking why it had happened to Ali and not to me. I went to church and prayed. The people I always had faith in were those at the Poor Clare Monastery in Belfast because of their amazing dedication. I visited them a lot during that difficult time, and their words were a great support. 'There is nothing you can do, Barry,' they told me. 'Just leave it in the hands of God and just hope that by some miracle, he will recover. Sadly, he never did.'

McGuigan kept pondering the question: Was there was any point in carrying on? He had talks with his family and his team, and made the conscious decision to continue. Everybody told him it was an occupational hazard and that it could have been him. Barry's brother Dermot told him one day: 'Come on, Barry, try and get on with it. This is the reality.' It was then that Barry realised that he just had to do that, get on with it. He also decided early on that if he reached the top of his profession and won a world title that he would dedicate the victory to Ali – and that is exactly what he did.

McGuigan was back in the ring four months later with a victory, but for the first couple of subsequent fights, he kept getting flashbacks of knocking Ali down, the referee counting him out, and the Nigerian collapsing when he left the ring. But always he had his family and his team behind him. Barry knew, too, that if he wanted to make progress he would need to establish himself in Britain and attempt to win the British title. With that in mind, he took out naturalisation papers.

It was not a popular decision as he still considered himself an Irishman and always would, but if he wanted to qualify for a British title, and then hopefully go on to bigger championships, that was the way to go. He had been able to represent Northern Ireland at the Commonwealth Games because he boxed in the Ulster championships, which embraced the nine counties of the province rather than the partitioned six counties of Northern Ireland, but it was different with the professionals.

'When I took out British citizenship, I got a lot of stick from the Republican side who said I was letting them down,' he remembered. 'It used to get to me and cause me annoyance as there is nobody more Irish than I am. It was just a quicker way to get through the red tape and get to the top. Win a British title, then a European and then a world.'

McGuigan's manager Barney Eastwood was against McGuigan taking out British citizenship papers. Harry Mullan, the Derry writer who edited *Boxing News* at the time, recalled getting a call from Eastwood. 'I'm not in favour of it at all, Harry,' said the manager. 'Barry is so good that a British title would not really matter. He could go for a European title and win it without upsetting or alienating his own people.'

Mullan pointed out that boxers like the McCormack brothers John and Pat from Dublin had become British champions without encountering any problems. The same with Mick Leahy from Cork. But he stressed that the McCormacks and Leahy were limited to British titles anyway, whereas McGuigan was likely to go all the way and was showing such great potential. Eastwood relented, if reluctantly. 'Ah, sure it's only a piece of paper anyway,' he told Mullan. There was no more said about it, and McGuigan went about establishing himself on the international boxing scene.

The British Boxing Board of Control nominated McGuigan and Paul Huggins of Hastings to meet in a final eliminator for the British featherweight title. They met at the Ulster Hall, Belfast in November 1981 and Huggins turned out to be a tough opponent. A slugger in the mould of the former world heavyweight champion Rocky Marciano, he was one of those boxers who took four, five blows to land one.

Huggins handed out some solid shots to the head and body but McGuigan always got there first with his stronger punching. When referee Jim Brimmel intervened in the fifth, Huggins' corner protested, but Eastwood said: 'The kid was saved the humiliation of being knocked out and his corner should have been grateful for that. They should be thanking us.'

Five months later McGuigan won the vacant British featherweight title when he stopped Plymouth's Vernon Penprase in the second round at the Ulster Hall. Penprase lived fairly close to where the sixteenth century navigator Sir Francis Drake played and finished the most famous game of bowls before going out to face the might of the Spanish Armada. Against McGuigan, Penrose had little chance of bowling his opponent over, and after being floored twice in the second round, referee Harry Gibbs, one of Britain's most famous officials, called it off with just ten seconds to go in the session.

Now for bigger titles. The European featherweight championship was vacant and McGuigan was matched with Italy's Valerio Nati at the King's Hall in November 1983. This one really captured the imagination of the public. Nati was considered a strong opponent and had been European bantamweight champion so he knew his way around the rings. An hour before the card was due to begin, a five-deep queue stretched well up Balmoral Avenue and a crowd of eight thousand was in attendance to see McGuigan in his most important fight to date.

Barry had never boxed in the King's Hall before, and when he first saw the place he thought it was a big old barn with no atmosphere at all. All that changed when the fight got under way. Nati, with a solid chin, had never been on the canvas in twenty-eight fights so McGuigan's plan was to try and outbox him in the early stages and feel him out.

The Italian came in crouching all the time, and complained to the German referee Kurt Halbach that McGuigan was hitting him low. Barry would deny this, but at one time it looked as though Halbach was going to disqualify him. With McGuigan now mixing his boxing with solid body shots to the head and body, he hurt Nati with a big left hook followed by two blows to the midsection that put him on the boards. Thoroughly beaten, he made little attempt to rise as Halbach counted him out. Barry's father Pat sang the customary Danny Boy from the centre of the ring.

'There was great excitement afterwards and I really felt fantastic, having won the European title in the same ring where my idols Freddie Gilroy and John Caldwell had boxed,' McGuigan remembered. 'I felt very proud to be alongside them.'

Around this time, cracks were beginning to show in the McGuigan-Eastwood relationship. Barry claimed that he was entitled to more money than he was getting and that his manager 'was keeping him in the dark about business matters'. Eastwood denied this was the case. To this end, McGuigan hired his mother's brother, Leo Rooney, a chartered accountant living in London, to talk to Eastwood about: (a) having a full knowledge of his purse monies; (b) that he be officially paid by cheque; and (c) to also ensure that all his earnings were declared to the Revenue Commissioners. Eastwood agreed, but the relationship would fall to pieces in later years.

Meanwhile, the manager and the boxer were getting about the important business of furthering McGuigan's career. With the European title in his possession, Barry was now in the world ratings, and fast closing in on a fight with world champion Eusebio Pedroza of Panama. American promoters were beginning to take a keen interest in his progress. In an official world featherweight title eliminator, in April 1984 and again at the King's Hall, McGuigan took on the dangerous Dominican Republican, Jose Caba, who in his last fight six months earlier had taken Pedroza the full fifteen rounds in a title challenge in Italy.

As Jack McGowan of the *Belfast Telegraph* saw it: 'McGuigan made the unquittable quit in seven rounds, and with such textbook mastery of both himself and opponent that some boxing greybeards were lost for words. To have mixed it with a pit-bull like Caba would have asked for trouble, so Barry, for the most part, left his best punch, the left hook to the body, at home. For the first five rounds, you could have counted on the fingers of one hand how many times he threw that famed body punch, banking instead on an almost flawless exhibition of the noble art. He was a prince, whereas Caba looked a peasant.'

There was now the European title to defend. A match was made for the Royal Albert Hall, London against the Spaniard, Esteban Eguia in June 1984. It would be Barry's live TV debut in London at championship level, although it turned out to be a less demanding outing than it should have been. This was no fault of the promoters, Mickey Duff and Mike Barrett, but the European Boxing Union had ordered McGuigan to defend his title, and Eguia was apparently the best challenger they could come up with.

The Spaniard had a fairly respectable record, with forty-one wins, four defeats and two draws, but earlier in the year he had been beaten by a flyweight! The much harder-punching McGuigan at the time was considered one of the world's best at featherweight, two divisions higher, with twenty-one wins and just one defeat. Eguia was given little chance by British boxing writers, with most of them suggesting that it could well be over in five or six rounds, if the challenger was still around that long.

McGuigan had a scare when he injured an elbow in training and visited a Harley Street specialist, but it never affected him once the bell rang. He jabbed his way through an uneventful opening round and then got down to business in the second. Left hooks to the head and body hurt Eguia who was driven back to the ropes. McGuigan stepped in fast with lefts and rights as the Spaniard's body shuddered. The Monaghan puncher, sensing victory, dropped him in a neutral corner with a left hook for a count of six before a similar punch put him down for seven. Amazingly and bravely, Eguia rallied on rising but in the third, McGuigan moved in with two left hooks and a right which dropped him face down to be counted out after forty-five seconds by French referee Armand Krief.

Eastwood believed in keeping his promising boxer busy, and three weeks later McGuigan returned to competitive action with an impressive stoppage in five rounds over the New Yorker Paul De Vorce at the King's Hall. Barry softened up his opponent for four rounds before opening up in the fifth with smashing left hooks to the ribs as referee Sid Natan intervened.

The scheduled ten rounder introduced McGuigan to American TV audiences as it was shown live in the US to an estimated eighty-two million viewers by the CBS network. Mort Sharnik, their boxing consultant, was at ringside and told reporters: 'Your boy has everything – acceleration, intensity, personality and good looks. He's a real good fighter, the best I've seen in Europe for many a day.' The rival US network, HBO, were also impressed. George Kreiger, the chief fight buyer, said: 'McGuigan's got more movement than I've seen from any European boxer before, and I really liked the way he worked the punches up and down. There will certainly be bidding for him in future and there is no doubt that he is a real contender right now.'

McGuigan was now hot property on the international scene. America wanted to see him in the flesh. *Ring* magazine said he revived memories of the great Jimmy McLarnin in the 1930s and had him in their top three rankings. But Team McGuigan wanted to stay in Europe to see how the world title scene was panning out. There were rumours that world champion Pedroza was unwilling to come to Belfast for a title defence, and preferred a neutral US venue. 'We'll bide our time,' said Eastwood.

Meanwhile, Barry was keeping busy. The European Boxing Union pointed out that his six months' grace was up and nominated Londoner Clyde Ruan as his challenger. McGuigan's British title would also be on the line. They met at the Ulster Hall a week before Christmas, 1984 and Ruan was finished in four rounds. A swift left hook to the jaw sent the English challenger down to be counted out by Larry O'Connell as the Monaghan boxer, his arms stretched above his head, acknowledged the cheers of a packed crowd. 'McGuigan's a ghost,' said a bemused Ruan in the dressing room. 'He's a matador without his cloak, and his real strength is lightning reflexes. He's never there to hit when you're sure he will be. Did I see the punch that knocked me out? I didn't even feel it.'

McGuigan was now clearly closing in on a world title fight. At twenty-five, he seemed to be hitting his peak. His record stood at twenty-four wins and one loss, with fourteen of his victories inside four rounds. His win over Ruan was his eighteenth consecutive success either by countouts or stoppages. Could he continue his winning streak against his next opponent, Juan LaPorte, a Puerto Rican based in New York and expected to provide the toughest test of his four-year career?

LaPorte, with a knockout wallop, tremendous heart and durability plus, was a former world featherweight champion, and had taken the reigning king Pedroza the full fifteen rounds to lose on points. He had also knocked out the current world junior lightweight champion Rocky Lockridge so he was one to be totally respected.

They met at the King's Hall in February 1985, and after ten rounds of exhilarating boxing and hard punching, McGuigan won on points. With the chant of 'Here we go, here we go' ringing in his ears, the Irishman kept up a relentless succession of jabs and hooks to add up the points. In a thrilling last round, the Puerto Rican matched McGuigan punch for punch against a crescendo of noise but it was Barry's fight. LaPorte had never been on the canvas before but he came close to it in the final minute when McGuigan ripped punches to the head as the yelling crowd stood on their seats.

Referee Harry Gibbs scored it 99–97, giving McGuigan six rounds against two for LaPorte and the remaining two even. Sugar Ray Leonard, who was there to commentate on the fight for CBS television, visited McGuigan's dressing room later and told him: 'It was a pleasure to watch you. That was one of the best fights I have seen, and you are on the way to a world title fight.' McGuigan knew he had been in a fight, a war. 'Being hit by LaPorte sent tingles all the way down to my feet, shock waves of pain through my body,' he said in later years. 'A big spark went off in my head, and it felt as if there were goose pimples inside me, pins and needles right down to my feet.'

Here is how Harry Mullan saw it in *Boxing News*: 'Winning the world title looks no more than a tiresome formality for the brilliant McGuigan, who gave a performance of astonishing maturity. His display was as close to perfection as I have ever seen in a ring, ten rounds of exhilarating quality and variety. We knew he could box and hit, but wondered how he could take a top-quality punch himself. Now we know. He was hurt in the fifth and ninth rounds but he kept his composure and came roaring back. That is the mark of a champion.'

Ring magazine accredited Barry with their Fighter of the Month accolade, and reported: 'McGuigan is a throwback to the old style of fighting. He comes forward, bobbing and weaving, gloves held high and, having made an opening, is not content to jab and move away. He stands his ground and having got within range, punches away hard and accurately.'

A war of the promoters was now really declared. America desperately wanted a McGuigan-Pedroza fight, with the widely-read Associated Press boxing writer Ed Schulyer reporting in the US: 'A McGuigan fight would make Irishmen out of a hell of a lot of Americans.' Bob Arum sought it for Las Vegas and John Condon was prepared to put it on at Madison Square Garden, New York. Stephen Eastwood, Barney's promoter son, sought to have it for the King's Hall. There was also a new promoter on the scene, an ambitious Londoner in his early thirties named Frank Warren, who was anxious to put it on in the British capital. Warren would in time become not only Britain's number one promoter but a leading one on the world stage, matching his American rivals.

A dropout from grammar school at fifteen, Warren had, in succession, taken on a range of jobs that included a clerk in a solicitor's office, a runner for an on-course bookmaker, a porter in a meat market, a partner in a London restaurant, a pool-hall owner and a slot-machine operator. At the age of twenty-seven, he took his first tentative steps into professional boxing when he was approached by a cousin who had lost a fight and wanted a rematch.

The problem was that the cousin could not find a promoter, and Warren agreed to become an unlicenced promoter. Getting his boxer a trainer, he put on the show at a theatre in North London. Encouraged by the show's success, he put on more unlicenced shows but incurred the wrath of the British Boxing Board of Control. Later on, he was given an official promoter's licence by the board, and put on a show at a London hotel in 1980 headlined by two unknown American heavyweights. However, although he had arranged TV coverage, he was blocked from broadcasting the fight by the board on the rule preventing promoters from televising their first fights. Warren lost heavily on the show.

Undeterred by the disaster, and his finances boosted by the sale of his slot machines, he subsequently secured his first TV date with the BBC for a British lightwelterweight title fight. With that initial success, he set about taking on, and eventually smashing, the established promotional and managerial hierarchy of British boxing, a virtual monopoly consisting of Jarvis Astaire, Mickey Duff, Mike Barrett and Terry Lawless. Today, Warren is the leading promoter in these islands, and has promoted and managed some of Britain's best boxers of the last twenty-five years, including world champions Naseem Hamed, Nigel Benn, Joe Calzaghe, Ricky Hatton and Amir Khan.

In early 1985, Warren made an audacious bid to stage McGuigan's world featherweight title challenge against Pedroza in an open-air promotion at Queen's Park Rangers soccer ground in London. He agreed terms with the Panamanian and his manager Santiago de Rio, after McGuigan's manager Barney Eastwood and his American agent Mickey Duff had apparently given up on them, saying they were 'just impossible to do business with'. Pedroza and Santiago both intimated to Warren that they had no hesitation in putting the title on the line in London. A provisional date was set for May.

'I just couldn't do the deal with the Eastwoods, Barney the manager and his son Stephen the promoter,' Warren recalled. 'Even though I had done all the groundwork in getting Pedroza's signature, the proposal never got off the ground. The fight would cost a fortune to stage so naturally I wanted two options on McGuigan's services if he won. I didn't think that was unreasonable, and the options guaranteed would have earned half a million, at least. I was prepared to negotiate a joint promotion with the Eastwoods but they would not even discuss the idea. From then on, whenever I read about how impossible it was to get Pedroza, I took it with a pinch of salt.'

Stephen Eastwood told a magazine: 'I'm fed up with people like Frank Warren trying to jump on the bandwagon. I have developed McGuigan from novice to world title contender, and if anybody puts on his world title fights it will be me. My father, who is Barry's manager, and myself, the promoter, are the only people who control McGuigan's future. After his win over LaPorte, McGuigan is the hottest fighter in the world and we are certainly not going to tie him in with another promoter when he could be earning more than that as a free agent. We would naturally prefer to have the fight in Belfast but if Pedroza will only fight in London, that's fine. I'm a licenced promoter and there is nothing to stop me running the show there.'

The big fight eventually went ahead on a Stephen Eastwood promotion at the QPR ground on Loftus Road, West London on 8 June 1985. Soon after the announcement, all twenty-five thousand tickets were sold, such was the interest in the fight. Could McGuigan pull it off, and become the first native Irish boxer to win an undisputed world title since Rinty Monaghan in 1948?

Pedroza was one of the great champions, and had nineteen title defences to his credit, a record that still stands. Born in the poor Maranon district of Panama City in March 1953, he started out as a professional bantamweight at twenty years of age with a knockout in four rounds. A tall, rangy boxer with sharp   reflexes and a punch in both gloves, Pedroza's first fifteen bouts were all in Panama, and for bout number sixteen he went to Mexico in April 1978 to challenge world bantamweight champion Alfonso Zamora, El Toro, in his home territory but was knocked out in the second round.

When Eusebio was again knocked out in the next fight three months later, he decided to move up to featherweight. In his new division he achieved his greatest success, winning the world title from the Spaniard, Cecelio Lastra in Panama in thirteen rounds and began the longest nine-stone reign in history, one that would last seven years. He became a household name in Latin America, his face appearing on posters and the covers of glossy magazines. It made no difference where the location was.

To paraphrase the title of the TV series, with Pedroza it was Have Gloves, Will Travel. He risked his title in Puerto Rico, Japan, New Guinea, Korea, Venezuela, Panama, Italy and across the USA to give new significance to the term 'world champion'. His stellar achievements put him up there with all-time greats like Willie Pep and Sandy Saddler. Pedroza had a reputation, too, of being a master of the black arts of boxing, with the occasional hook straying below the belt and the 'unintentional' elbow often in evidence, although he never lost a fight on a disqualification.

A crowd of close to twenty-seven thousand, including an estimated twelve thousand Irish fans, filed into the Loftus Road venue to watch the fight that had received massive advance publicity. BBC would reveal later that the fight had a live TV audience of 20 million, and 200 million worldwide saw the action. Pedroza's greater experience was expected to be the deciding factor, with his record of thirty-eight wins, three losses and one draw against McGuigan's twenty-six victories and one defeat.

But this was going to be Barry's big night, and Ireland's. He injured his left elbow in training but kept it a big secret. From the start, the Clones Cyclone kept the pressure on his man, and while both were warned for infringements by South African referee Stanley Christodolou, it was never a dirty fight.

For the first six rounds, it was fairly even, with McGuigan getting through with his strong jabs and hooks, and the moustachioed Panamanian using his skill at long range and inside. But gradually, Barry seemed to be getting on top, especially after putting Pedroza on the canvas with a hard right for a count of three in round seven. Twice more, in the ninth and thirteenth rounds, the

Pamanian was desperately hurt by right-hand shots but a combination of heart, defensive skills and sheer refusal to go down kept him in the fight.

The decision was a mere formality. The two judges had it for McGuigan, Fernando Viso of Venezuela marking his card 147–140 and Denmark's Ove Oveson calling it 149–139. Referee Christodolou gave it to the Irishman by 148–143. The announcement that McGuigan was the new featherweight champion of the world set off scenes of wild enthusiasm and sheer pandemonium.

'McGuigan became surely the most rapturously acclaimed winner in the history of European boxing when the intensity of his aggression wore down the magnificent resistance of Pedroza,' wrote Hugh McIlvanney in *The Observer*. 'McGuigan's father Pat had sung Danny Boy before the start but there was no possibility of a singing celebration. What came from the dancing, back-slapping throng was a blurred tumult that foretold a party which would last for a week at least and spread from the Irish pubs here to every corner of the island across the water.

'McGuigan had lived up to all the promise of an astonishing career. He had refused to be frustrated or diminished by the wonderful talents and unbreakable spirit of one of the finest champions the featherweight division has ever seen. No one now is entitled to oppose very strenuously the claims some of us have made that this young man is the most dramatic fighter to emerge from these islands in many years.'

Harry Mullan in *Boxing News* wrote: 'McGuigan's performance was the greatest in a British ring since Randolph Turpin took the world middleweight title from Sugar Ray Robinson thirty-four years ago, and unquestionably the finest ever by an Irish boxer. McGuigan didn't merely outpoint Pedroza, he swamped him with punches, and won as he pleased.'

The scenes that greeted McGuigan's victorious arrival home were unprecedented. A crowd of over seventy thousand greeted the conquering hero on Royal Avenue in Belfast, and three days later, an estimated four hundred thousand gathered on O'Connell Street in Dublin. 'It was amazing,' Barry recalled. 'Looking back on photographs, all you see is a mass of people, Thomas. I suppose that was when I realised how much the victory meant to the Irish people. The papers said I was re-uniting north and south, Catholics and Protestants, on both sides of the border. I think that when I'm pushing up the daisies, the Pedroza fight is the one they will remember me for.'

McGuigan promised he would be a fighting champion, and he was. In any event, he had agreed to take on the formidable American, Bernard Taylor if he won the world title. They fought before a packed and passionate crowd at the King's Hall in September 1985. Known as the B.T. Express, Taylor from North Carolina and the number one contender was undefeated in thirty-three fights after compiling an incredible amateur record of four hundred and eighty-one wins and just eight losses. He was a former US amateur champion and missed out the 1980 Moscow Olympics because of the US withdrawal over the Soviet invasion of Afghanistan. In his previous fight before meeting McGuigan, he had boxed a controversial draw with Pedroza which many felt he should have won.

In the opening three rounds Taylor boxed a beautifully controlled fight, well balanced and fine defensive action, using every foot of the ring and scoring with fast jabs as McGuigan chased him without landing any effective punches. The American's plan was to frustrate Barry and it was working. The fourth round was even but by the fifth McGuigan was beginning to connect with left hooks which slowed Taylor down. The American was now having to fight on the Irishman's terms and a booming right in the sixth shook him to his bootlaces.

In the seventh McGuigan's fierce body shots were beginning to slow down the challenger and he took a pounding in the eighth as Barry's punching was draining the last of his strength, which had already been reduced by having to shed nearly a pound at the early morning weigh-in. The end came dramatically, with Taylor sitting on his stool at the end of the eighth, utterly spent. He had not been off his feet but defeat had become inevitable and his manager Ace Millar acted compassionately in announcing his retirement. 'He was the most awkward man I've ever met, and I was glad to get him out of the way,' said McGuigan in the dressing room.

America was now crying out for the Clones Cyclone. First, however, McGuigan and Eastwood would fulfill an early promise to box in Dublin for the first time in three years, and this time as world champion. The challenger would be the Argentinian, Fernando Sosa, and the fight was set for 15 February 1986 at the Royal Dublin Society grounds, known as the RDS and mainly used for showjumping and the annual Dublin Horse Show. The fight would also be the first world title bout in the capital for sixty-three years, recalling distant memories of Mike McTigue's successful challenge against Battling Siki for the world lightheavyweight championship at La Scala, later the Capitol Theatre.

Seventeen days before the fight, Barry got a call to the gym in Belfast to say that Sosa had broken a finger in training and was out. Danilo Cabrera of the Dominican Republic was the new opponent. Cabrera was a good all-rounder with just two losses in twenty-three fights but was not expected to give the world champion too much trouble. It did not turn out quite that way. The twenty-two-year-old from the Caribbean provided McGuigan with the toughest fight of his thirty-bout career. Cabrera was gritty, durable and determined, taking all the Monaghan man's punches without flinching, although never looking likely to win.

Going out for the fourteenth round, McGuigan had swellings around both eyes and a cut on his left cheek which would later require six stitches. Cabrera's strength, however, was now gradually fading because of the champion's constant aggression. About a minute into the round McGuigan went on the attack and put Cabrera down for a count of six, taking the mandatory eight count on his feet. Another big left hook sent his gumshield flying, and as he fumbled around trying to find it, McGuigan looked to Florida referee Eddie Ekert before landing the final left hook to prompt a stoppage after one minute and forty seconds of the round. Even if Cabrera had completed the course, he was trailing impossibly on points.

With America still calling, Team McGuigan answered the call, and his US debut was scheduled for Caesars Palace, Las Vegas on 23 June 1986 on a Bob Arum promotion. His opponent would be Fernando Sosa, the Argentinian who had pulled out of a previous fight with the Monaghan boxer through injury. Now, four weeks into training, the ill-fated Sosa had to withdraw again. After complaining about problems with his eyes, he was examined by a local doctor who discovered 'probably detached retinas in both eyes, with the right one being far more severely threatened'. In came Steve Cruz, from Fort Worth, Texas and a stablemate of world welterweight champion Don Curry.

Cruz, known as Super Kid, was a part-time plumber. He had an impressive record of twenty-five wins and one defeat following an amateur career of one hundred and ninety-five wins and five losses. Ranked number eight in the world, he was not expected to provide very serious opposition and entered the open-air ring as a prohibitive nine to one on outsider. It looked like a comparatively easy title defence for McGuigan, although Barry knew that the intense heat in an open-air ring in the late afternoon sun could be an issue.

It turned out to be 110 °F outside the ring, and with the TV lights blazing down, probably around 130 °F between the ropes. While Cruz would also be affected by the conditions, he was living in Las Vegas and would be better equipped than McGuigan, or any Irishman or western European for that matter. Irish and British writers would be unanimous in their view that the fight should have been put on later in the evening when the sun was not so hot. Yet Barry made a great start, winning four of the first five rounds on most writers' cards, jabbing and hooking effectively and keeping up his constant aggression, with the American looking in trouble.

But Cruz stormed back in the middle rounds, dropping McGuigan with a big left hook in a thrilling tenth round and there were roars from the crowd of ten thousand two hundred, including two thousand Irish fans. Barry regained the initiative in the eleventh but a low blow in the twelfth, for which he was deducted a crucial point, would have a direct bearing on the ultimate result.

The thirteenth and fourteenth rounds were thrilling ones, with McGuigan coming out on top but he strength was being inexorably sapped in the intense heat. Still, all he had to do was to stay on his feet through the fifteenth to win on points but this proved beyond his capacity. Cruz sent him down for two more counts. Another knockdown in the round and the fight would have been stopped on the automatic three-counts rule. On rising, McGuigan grabbed the American and held until the bell before his legs betrayed him and he fell into the arms of his seconds.

The verdict was unanimous for Cruz. Judge Angel Tovar of Venezuela made it 143–142 and judge Medardo Villalobos of Columbia scored it 143–139. The third judge Guy Jutras of Canada had it 142–141. It meant that had it not been for that warning for the low blow in the twelfth, the result would have been a draw, allowing the Monaghan boxer to retain his title. 'I wasn't hurt by Cruz's punches but I lost because of dehydration and that incredible heat out there,' he said in the dressing room. 'Not many people know either that I hurt my ankle and had to miss eight days training. Look, it's blown up like a balloon.'

Richard Hoffer wrote in the *Los Angeles Times*: 'No disgrace to McGuigan, he gave as valiant a battle as boxing has known, staggering through a fifteenth round that he probably shouldn't have been in. He seemed devastated by the heat, and was suddenly unable to move his feet. His body, tilting all over the ring, seemed to dictate the action, dragging him one way or another. How did he stay upright?'

It was McGuigan's last fight for almost two years. With his father dying of cancer in the summer of 1987 and a prolonged court case around the same time with Barney Eastwood over financial matters to contend with, the fight game was the last thing on McGuigan's mind. When he returned, it was as a super-featherweight under his new promoter Frank Warren. In a London ring in April 1988 he stopped the Mexican Nicky Perez in four rounds.

In June he beat Francisco Tomas Da Cruz of Brazil in Luton, also in four before going in against the rugged and courageous Argentinian Julio Miranda in London just before Christmas. Miranda gave him a tough fight, and cut McGuigan over both eyes, but Barry was in control, with referee Larry O'Connell intervening in the eight. The South American had been floored in the previous round and stood little chance of victory. Barry also finished with a damaged right hand.

With the realisation now creeping in that his glory days were coming to an end, McGuigan decided he would retire if he lost his next fight. On 31 May 1989 before a full house of eighteen thousand one hundred at the G-Mex Centre in Manchester, Barry's glorious career came to an end when he was stopped in four rounds by the lightly-regarded Londoner Jim McDonnell. Referee Mickey Vann intervened after making a close inspection of a severe cut over Barry's right eye. The fight was over, and so was McGuigan's eight-year career between the ropes.

In his retirement, Barry has been one of the busiest ex-boxers. He makes frequent appearances on television shows and is a boxing analyst for Sky TV. He writes a regular newspaper column as well as being a promoter and manager, and was involved in the movie *The Boxer*, with Daniel Day-Lewis. In 2011 he had his autobiography published. Any regrets about making boxing a career? 'None whatsoever,' he said. 'I would do it all again. If you are a young person thinking of going into the game, or a parent whose child is interested in boxing, go for it. There's the chance to travel and get excited about something. I really hope in the years ahead that boxing continues to blossom and get better, and safer too.

'We need to find a way though to have more clarity in the sport, more simplicity and less clutter. There are too many titles and organisations, junior champions and champions emeritus and what have you and it has got to be sorted out. This is going to take time because it means cutting people out who at the moment are earning money. But it needs to be done. There is competition from the Ultimate Fighting Championship or mixed martial arts, whatever you want to call it. However, I don't think the UFC involves the same level of skill as boxing. That is because in boxing you are only able to strike with your upper body, not your legs. For me, boxing at its best is the greatest skill of all. It is an art.'

2. DAN DONNELLY

A nineteenth century folk hero

The rain was falling steadily on the early morning of 13 December 1815 with no sign of a break in the dark clouds. But the weather did not deter the brave souls who were making their way to the rolling hills and gorseland of the Curragh in County Kildare. They came from all over the country, in every horse-drawn vehicle that could be found and that would groan and creak all the way to the battle scene. Many came on horseback.

Others who could not beg, borrow or steal a lift had to trudge their way on the long journey by foot. The big occasion was the eagerly-awaited battle between Dan Donnelly, the Irish champion and something of an early nineteenth century folk hero, and his great English rival George Cooper.

Donnelly was a Dubliner so naturally most of the fans came from the capital, with its dingy streets and narrow alleyways. With their ragged clothes and dirty faces, they were convinced that Dan was unbeatable and that no Englishman, Cooper or anybody else, could come near matching his prowess. They thought nothing of making their way from the city to the Curragh, thirty miles away. 'Dan will finish him off in no time,' said one. 'Let nobody here even think of defeat,' yelled another. 'Otherwise, they'll have me to contend with.' And he seemed ready to start a fight there and then with any doubters.

By ten o'clock, a noisy crowd estimated at twenty thousand had packed every available inch of space and the surrounding high-vantage points to see the battle which had captured the imaginations of a nation. They were convinced that Dan Donnelly, the pride of Dublin's Fair City, would turn back the challenge of this brash Englishman who had dared to question his ability. Dan the Man would show Cooper and his supporters who travelled over from England that there would be only one man in it, and that would not be Cooper.

Anti-British feeling was running high at the time. The Ireland in which Donnelly was born was a land characterised by colonial oppression and burning patriotism. The country seemed leaderless and completely broken down in spirit. They struggled with injustices like the payment of some of their income to the so-called 'established church', which was Protestant. No Catholics could be a Member of Parliament, although four-fifths of the population were of that faith. They were also forbidden to hold any public office, even at local level.

While still at school in 1798, Donnelly remembered the rebellion of that year to rid the country of British rule. The frustration of the public had boiled over into an uprising led by the Society of United Irishmen, inspired by Theobald Wolfe Tone, an iconic Kildare-born lawyer and a political theorist. Tone was strongly influenced by the events and philosophies of the French Revolution. He held the view that Ireland should be a non-sectarian republic. An avid supporter of Catholic rights, even though he was a Protestant, Tone published a pamphlet, An Argument on Behalf of the Catholics of Ireland, in 1791.

In the classroom, Donnelly learned that Tone went to Belfast and joined the Society of United Irishmen before returning to Dublin to establish a branch of the organisation there. While the government appeared to be dragging its feet about reform, Tone and the United Irishmen began to consider military options. Tone sought military help from France but the agent he dealt with was compromised by an informer. The Dublin branch of the organisation was suppressed and Tone was forced to flee to America to avoid arrest. From America he went to France where he continued to lobby for a French invasion.

French involvement in the planned rebellion turned out to be of a minor nature, however, as Napoleon needed his armies against Egypt. The small force arrived too late, as the main rising had already been ruthlessly suppressed. Tone sailed from France to Lough Swilly in County Donegal, but was arrested along with French officers and taken to Dublin where he was found guilty by court martial and condemned to death. He cheated the executioner by cutting his throat in his cell.

There was another failed revolution in 1803, also remembered by Donnelly, when Robert Emmet, who passionately believed in Irish freedom, failed to get promised French support from Napoleon. Emmet was captured, found guilty of high treason, hanged, drawn and quartered and then beheaded once dead.

More than ever, Ireland was now a land in desperate need of somebody to come along and give the hated British a lesson. Ireland looked to their fighting hero Dan Donnelly to do that. The abortive rising led by Emmet had a particular effect on Donnelly, as one of his workmates at a timber yard in Dublin was the brother of Anne Devlin. She had played a central role in the 1803 Rising as she was Emmet's housekeeper and she too was arrested, tortured and jailed.

Donnelly felt deep down that his country now needed him in these hours of peril and he would take care of the cocky Englishman. 'Things have gone far enough,' he was quoted as saying in a contemporary report. 'Indeed, too far. I will give our downtrodden nation a lift by beating Cooper.'

Born in 1788 in Dublin's Townsend Street in the city centre, with the River Liffey flowing nearby, Donnelly was the ninth of seventeen children, including four sets of twins. His father, Joseph, was a carpenter but suffered regularly from chest problems and was frequently out of work. In those days there was no pay if you did not work so it can be gleaned that it was a tremendous struggle to bring up a large family. To Donnelly, like most kids of his time, this was the life he knew and was not particularly aware of the poverty around him.

A naturally quiet mannered boy, he was often picked on by bullies but he was strong and fought back. This was a time of regular pitched battles on the streets between rival gangs and young Dan usually had to take on bigger and heavier kids but it was always the survival of the fittest. Sometimes he would finish best, other times he came out the worst but he was always standing at the finish, which could not always be said for most of his rivals.

School held no great attractions for Dan and many a time his mother had to abandon her heavy household chores, go out, locate him and take him by the hand to the classroom. He left school at an early age and went to work as a carpenter to bring in some much needed money for the struggling household. On the tough streets of Dublin, Donnelly had a reputation of being a hard man to provoke, a man who would go to great lengths to avoid settling an argument in the traditional manner. Yet when the need arose, usually when the old, the feeble or females were being mistreated, Dan was known to be handy with his fists and he soon became the district's new fighting hero and one to right any wrongs.

On one occasion he heard the screams of a young woman down at the nearby docklands. On investigation he found two burly sailors molesting the lady and he soon went to her rescue but he could not overcome the two-against-one situation and he ended up lying on the pavement, nursing a badly damaged arm. A passer-by saw him lying on the ground and took him to the premises of Dr Abraham Colles, a noted surgeon. At first the surgeon thought he might have to amputate the arm but managed to fix it up.

On another occasion, a local neighbour, an old lady, had died of a highly contagious disease in poverty-stricken circumstances. Dan went up to her room, hoisted the body up on his shoulders and went off to a local cemetery where he found gravediggers at work. 'Put the old lady here in that grave you are digging,' he told them. When they refused on the basis that the grave they were digging was for a person of distinction, Donnelly said: 'If you don't, then both of you will go into the grave, live!' The two diggers looked at each other and agreed to give Dan the use of the grave.

Donnelly was a tall, strapping man of nearly six foot and weighed almost fourteen stone. His strongest trait was his outgoing, sociable personality and he was fond of the company of others, and this was reciprocated. He could also well hold his own at hard drinking.

News of Dan's fighting exploits with Dublin's feuding gangs spread fast. He gained a reputation of keeping the city's undesirables in check. The message was: 'If you want to sort out trouble, or break up a row, get Dan Donnelly.' One local boxer who was recognised as 'the city champion' became jealous of Dan's reputation and took to following him around the bars demanding a fight. Donnelly did not really want to fight him, preferring to keep the peace, but his rival insisted. Eventually Dan relented and the fight was arranged for the banks of the Grand Canal.

The event attracted a good deal of attention and a large crowd turned up. At the beginning it was fairly even but gradually Donnelly got on top and in a furious attack in the sixteenth round, beat his man to the ground. Dan was now hailed as the new champion of the city.

Meanwhile, an Irish aristocrat Captain William Kelly was sitting in an English tavern with his companion and overheard two English pugilists mocking Ireland's reputation as a nation of fighting men. 'They've nobody over there worth anything,' said one. 'You're right,' said his companion. 'We'd take two of them on together and beat them easily. It'd be no trouble at all.' Captain Kelly, nor his companion, said nothing as they did not want to engage in a row but vowed to find an Irishman to take up the challenge.

Captain Kelly was a talented performer on the uilleann pipes, which he played before King George IV on the monarch's visit to Ireland in 1821. A keen sportsman with a consuming interest in boxing, he owned a prominent horse-racing establishment in Maddenstown, County Kildare. His companion, a Scotsman named Robert Barclay Allardice, better known as Captain Barclay and a keen follower of boxing, agreed to help Kelly in his search.

They travelled to Dublin where they were told about a promising fighter named Dan Donnelly. After making enquiries, they located Donnelly in his local bar and put their proposition to him. 'You are the man to bring honour and respect to the nation, Dan, and make a bit of money for yourself too,' said Captain Kelly. Barclay made a similar suggestion, and told the Dublin fighter of the conversation in the English tavern between the two English pugilists.

Donnelly was silent for a few minutes and replied: 'I appreciate what you are attempting to do for me, and the nation, kind sirs, but I am a man of peace. I do not want to fight.' Kelly said: 'Well, tell you what, Dan. You think it over and we'll meet here again this day week and you can give us your final verdict. Is that all right?' Donnelly nodded. When they met as arranged the following week, Dan told them he had talked the matter over with his family and friends and decided to take up their offer. Holding up his right fist, he declared: 'You are both right. I will attempt to bring honour and respect to my nation. I owe nothing to England and I will do my level best to live up to your confidence in me.'

Delighted that they had convinced Donnelly of their plan, Kelly and Barclay promised Dan he would receive the full benefit of their experience and teaching. Kelly installed the fighter at his brother's residence in Calverstown near the Curragh in County Kildare where he would be taught the rudiments of boxing skill, with Kelly's friend Captain Barclay looking after Donnelly's physical fitness. Barclay was a patron of two of the best English bare-knuckle champions Tom Cribb and John Gully and was regarded as one of the foremost trainers of the day. Donnelly earned his keep by looking after Barclay's cows at Calverstown Demesne.

Donnelly's first fight under his new patronage was staged at the Curragh on 14 September 1814. The spot was known at the time as Belcher's Hollow, a natural amphitheatre at the Athgarvan end of the Curragh. Regularly used for big prize fights, it would later be the site of his most celebrated battle, against George Cooper (the fight that introduced this chapter and which will be returned to later on). Donnelly's opponent was a prominent English fighter Tom Hall, who was touring Ireland at the time, giving sparring exhibitions and boxing instructions. A crowd of over twenty thousand made their way to the Curragh by every available method of transport, many on foot, to see the encounter and cheer on their hero.

It should not be forgotten that boxing at that time was very different to what it is today. There were no gloves and very basic rules. Nor was there any boxing organisation to oversee the sport or lay down regulations or procedures. In 1743 Jack Broughton, a former English champion, drew up a set of rules for governing behaviour in the ring. They were very rudimentary, however, though one innovation was that 'no person is to hit his adversary when he is down, or seize him by the ham, the breeches and any part below the waist, and a man on his knees to be reckoned down.'

Broughton's rules, while not always adhered to, were in existence until 1838 when the British Pugilists' Protective Society introduced the London Prize Ring Rules, one of which was that 'kicking, gouging and head butting is ruled out' and that 'if a fighter goes down deliberately without being hit or thrown, he is disqualified'. These rules were revised in 1853 and again in 1866 before being superseded by ones drawn up by an Englishman John Chambers and published in 1867. These were sponsored by the Marquis of Queensberry who agreed to give his name to them. These rules, with some modifications, are still in use today around the world. Back in Dan Donnelly's day, though, it was very much a case of anything goes.

For a few rounds, Hall's skill was paramount. He scored first blood, which was an important fact in bare-knuckle boxing as there were bets on who would first draw the claret. However, as the rounds went by, Donnelly's strength was beginning to tell. Hall's tactics were often to slip down on one knee, without being in any danger, but to get a thirty-second rest and come back refreshed. He was doing this a bit too often for the Dubliner's liking. At one stage, Dan was about to lash out when Hall was down but Captain Barclay shouted: 'Don't do it Dan, or you might be disqualified.'

Eventually he did lose his temper, in the fifteenth round, and as Hall slipped down, Dan lashed out and caught him on the left ear, causing the blood to flow and bringing an end to the round. Hall's seconds refused to allow their man to continue, bringing the round to an end and claiming he had been blatantly fouled and that Donnelly should be disqualified. Barclay and Kelly insisted that Hall's people were just looking for an easy win and that their man was always the superior of the two. Contemporary accounts would seem to support this view, with Donnelly described as being the harder and more effective puncher.

The neutrals in attendance suggested that a draw would be the fairest result and that the purse money of £100 should be split evenly, instead of the original arrangement which called for sixty for the winner and forty for the loser. Hall and his backers agreed with the even split, with the stipulation that a rematch be arranged as soon as possible.

In the end, it was decided that the winner was Donnelly on the basis that Hall did not want to fight on, and all bets were called off. Donnelly got the bigger share of the purse, as agreed, but they never fought each other again. Dan was now a greater Irish hero than ever before but after all the celebrations, he was now broke, having spent his entire purse on drink for himself and his friends. He now had no choice but to go back to his job as a carpenter while his mentors Kelly and Barclay looked to England for another opponent to test their hero. They found one in the English champion George Cooper.

Cooper was known as the Bargeman because, when not engaged in ring activities, he worked as a labourer on canal barges. A native of Stone in Staffordshire, and with a gypsy background, he had a fearful reputation in the ring and when the fight was announced, he was ten to one on to win. While Donnelly was the sentimental favourite among every man and woman in the nation to give Ireland hope and beat this sporting representative of the oppressors, the betting people just could not see Cooper lose.

Bets were made in those days not alone on the result of the fight, but on who would draw first blood. Or on who would score the first knockdown. There were limited rules, but they were designed to accommodate gambling, the public, and those who organised the fight. The fighters themselves were really of no consequence.

Cooper was touring England, Scotland and Ireland on an exhibition tour with a black American boxer named Tom Molyneaux, who was born a slave and raised on a plantation in Virginia. When they came to Dublin, they were told of Ireland's best fighting man Dan Donnelly and made arrangements to meet him in a local tavern. Cooper, who had just beaten Molyneaux in Scotland over fourteen rounds, suggested that Donnelly take on the American, who was nearing the end of his career and that there would be good money in the fight, as well as prestige if he were victorious.

'We have been led to understand that you are the best man in Ireland and here is your chance to prove yourself against a well-known American,' said Cooper over drinks. 'We are looking for good men to fight and provide some sporting entertainment for the people of your country. What do you say to taking on Tom Molyneaux?'

'No, I have no intention of meeting somebody who has been conquered,' replied Donnelly. 'What would I have to gain? Okay, so I beat Molyneaux but what would that prove to my supporters and the wider audience out there? They would say that George Cooper beat Molyneaux too. It would do absolutely nothing for my prestige.'

Directing his gaze at Cooper, he went on: 'I will take you on, nobody else.' Molyneaux was visibly hurt by the blunt dismissal of his abilities and he started to hurl abuse at Donnelly, raising his fists as if to take him on there and then. After all, Molyneaux was one of the first black boxers to achieve fame in the ring, even if he was now somewhat past his best and his only two losses previous to Cooper had been to the Englishman, Tom Cribb. Cooper cooled him down and turning to Donnelly, grabbed his right hand and said: 'Ok, that's settled. I will fight you.'

The big fight was on, and as described at the outset of this chapter, over twenty thousand fans made their way to the Curragh in County Kildare on 13 December 1815. Excitement was intense. In the minds of the populace Donnelly had come to epitomise the national struggle, championing their seemingly hopeless cause against the intransigent representatives of the Crown. As recounted, the site of the fight was originally known as Belcher's Hollow, named after the victory of Englishman Tom Belcher over Dan Dougherty, an Irish fighter, the previous year but after Donnelly's win over Tom Hall, it became Donnelly's Hollow and so it remains to this day.

Before the fight got under way, there was a dispute over the purse monies and for a time it looked as though it might be called off. The original agreement was that the winner would receive £100 and the loser £20. When Cooper and his backers arrived, they were told that there was not enough money to cover the original terms. It would now be £60 to the winner and nothing for the loser. 'I cannot go through with this arrangement,' said Cooper. 'Call the fight off.' He refused to budge and stayed put for nearly an hour.

It was only when news of this dispute spread through the big crowd and there were fears of a riot that he relented. Quite wisely, he reckoned that with over twenty thousand Irish in attendance and in the interests of his health and safety, he had no real choice but to face Donnelly.

It was a bare-knuckle fight to a finish, and bloody one, that would fluctuate one way and then the other. Certainly that was what happened in the opening round. After some preliminary sparring, Donnelly connected with a strong left hook to Cooper's neck but the Englishman came back with solid lefts and rights to the head and body.

So it went, though the Irishman's greater strength was beginning to show as the rounds progressed. In one of the early rounds, Cooper used a cross-buttock tactic that severely winded the local. The cross-buttock was more of a wrestling manoeuvre than a boxing one. One of the competitors would get, more or less, in front of the other and throw his adversary over his hip, causing him to land with great force on the ground. As it happened, it was legitimate under the rules of the sport at the time.

If one popular story is to be believed, Donnelly, who was being hammered in the fifth round, was saved by the allegedly magical powers of a piece of sugar cane slipped to him by Captain Kelly's sister. She had been pleading with him to win, telling him she had bet her entire estate on the outcome. When Donnelly looked like he might be falling behind, she gave him the sugar cane and said: 'Now my charmer, give him a warmer!' It seemed to work because Donnelly was rejuvenated and the course of the fight changed.

In the seventh round, the Dubliner sent his man flat on his back with a powerful right cross and then jumped on him, winding him so badly that he could hardly rise. He did rise for the next round but Donnelly was now getting on top, the cheering of the crowd being 'likened to the sound of artillery going off,' according to a contemporary report.

Bravely, Cooper battled back and more or less held his own during the ninth round in hard, gruelling close-quarter exchanges, but in the tenth Donnelly started to get back on top. The English bargeman was now beginning to lose ground and seemed to be fighting on sheer raw courage. His punches were lacking power and Donnelly was able to brush them off while countering with his own powerful blows. He threw Cooper down to finish the round.

The brutal battle ended in the eleventh round. Cooper made a strong, brave rally with both hands but the Dubliner now had victory in his sights. Donnelly brushed Cooper off and knocked him down with a tremendous right to the jaw. The Englishman was already senseless when he hit the tuft and it was discovered later that his jaw had been broken. Donnelly's victory was greeted by an almost deafening roar from the ecstatic crowd, and the cheers could be heard in villages for miles around. His followers invaded the ring and congratulated their national hero. The battle had lasted twenty-two minutes.

As Donnelly strode up the hill towards his carriage, several of his supporters dug out the imprints of his feet. These became known as 'The Steps to Strength and Fame' and are preserved to this day in Donnelly's Hollow, leading from a monument commemorating his famous victory up to the rim of the hill. They look like the marks of a monster out of the Jurassic period.

Donnelly politely declined all invitations to celebrate his great victory in the taverns of County Kildare as he had promised his friends and family that he would return to Dublin straight away. 'I can't go back on my word, and that is it,' he said. 'In any event, there will be plenty of parties all over.' Balladeers have described in colourful detail the wild scenes of enthusiasm and adulation that greeted him as he was chaired through the streets of his native city.

In an article in the *Dublin Penny Journal* of 25 August 1832, the newspaper looked back seventeen years to the eventful day: 'We remember well Donnelly's triumphal entry into Dublin after his great battle on the Curragh. That indeed was an ovation. He was borne on the shoulders of the people while his mother, like a Roman matron, leading the van in his procession and with all the pride of a second Agrippina, frequently slapped her naked bosom, exposed for the occasion, and exulting, exclaimed: "There's the breast that suckled him." Was the pride of a mother ever more admirably expressed?'

Meanwhile, as word spread of Donnelly's triumph across the Irish Sea, the fancy (a nineteenth century English term for followers of boxing and where the word 'fan' originated) were forced to revise their earlier view that the Irishman was simply 'a big, clumsy rough'. *The Sporting Magazine* wrote: 'Since Donnelly fought Tom Hall, we think there is no man could improve more than he has in fighting, and if we may judge from his conduct to this day, he has also improved in his temper.'

By now, however, Donnelly had gained a reputation as a gambler and a drunkard. Following his win over Cooper, he became the landlord of several Dublin taverns, positions set up by the owners. It was the custom of the day to have 'celebrities' as front men for their popular establishments, mixing freely with the customers and spinning yarns about their various exploits, usually wildly exaggerated.

Unfortunately for the owners, Donnelly helped himself to most of the profits and would be dismissed before moving on the next one. With his luck finally running out, and with not a penny to his name, Donnelly turned to what he knew best, the ring. He boxed some exhibitions in England, and while he was well paid, he spent money as fast as he made it. A fight was arranged against the Buckingham fighter Tom Oliver at Crawley Downs in Sussex for 21 July 1819. Oliver was a fast and scientific boxer who represented the English nobility and gentry, and was very confident he could emerge victorious.

Donnelly trained hard, in between downing bottles of beer at every opportunity but he was satisfied that he would be successful in his first fight on English soil. However, his case was not helped when, a week before the fight, he fell from the top of a stagecoach and so damaged his right arm that it was extremely doubtful if he could use the arm. Rather than request a postponement and disappoint his many followers who were crossing the Irish Sea to watch him, he went through with the fight.

By the day of the contest, there was an improvement in the arm but it was still sore, and he found it difficult to put his full weight behind his rights. Nevertheless, there was little between the two antagonists in the early rounds, both gaining an advantage at different stages. Donnelly, who was a seven to one on favourite, was mainly using his left as he wanted to preserve his right as much as possible.

Oliver had Donnelly down several times, nevertheless, with solid punches but the gritty Irishman refused to give up and let his faithful countrymen down. The punches flew hard and fast as the rounds went by with Dan gradually getting on top, although there was a lot of wrestling, with each man guilty of pulling the other on to punches. The thirty-fourth round proved to be the final one. Donnelly crashed through a tremendous right to the jaw and then threw the dazed and dispirited Oliver down with a cross-buttock, a common practice at the time.

After being picked up by his seconds, Oliver looked all in and when the half-minute interval passed, with the Englishman's head on his chest, 'time' was called. Donnelly had won again in a gruesome battle that had lasted an hour and ten minutes. To ecstatic cheers from his supporters, Dan strode arm-in-arm with his seconds to a nearby farmhouse to rest, but not before consoling his beaten opponent 'who gave me a hell of a fight, and no man can do more'.

The celebrations in Ireland and London went on for days, and while there was great praise for Donnelly in England, not everybody was impressed. Pierce Egan, the leading boxing writer and foremost authority of the day, wrote in *Boxiana*: 'The Irish champion has not turned out as good a fighter as was anticipated.' Apparently not aware of Donnelly's injured right arm, he continued: 'He is not the decisive, tremendous hitter with the right hand as calculated. Had he used it earlier, it would have probably ended in half an hour. He is not lacking in gameness and coolness, however, and is a dangerous man in a fall.'

Donnelly took the comments to heart, and started drinking more than was good for him, especially whenever he crossed the Irish Sea. A married man, he also started to acquire a succession of girlfriends. As the ring historian W. Buchanan-Taylor recalled in his book, *What Do You Know About Boxing?*: 'London night life and the "hells" of St James's put a quick end to the Irishman's career. He stepped on a toboggan of good living and bad company.' The 'hells' referred to were a series of nightclubs of the period; worse indeed than most of the haunts of recent years. One of the things missing was the knowledge of hygiene.

'The total ignorance aided the acquisition of a disability that laid him low. Yet he was still a hero – possibly a victim of ignorance and, far worse, an amateur in pseudo-love. Donnelly "could not take it" as we now know the praise. Donnelly admitted it was a bad fight, that he acted like a wooden man and could not account for it. He frequently hit with an open right hand. He showed little sign of the punishment taken, except that his right ear was slightly marked and his body was reddened and bruised.'

Donnelly made a good deal of money in England by touring in exhibitions. While there, he was introduced to the Prince Regent, later King George IV, and who, on meeting the famous boxer, remarked: 'I am delighted to meet the best man in Ireland.' Donnelly corrected him by replying: 'I beg to differ, your royal highness, I am the best man in Ireland and England.' The royal subject laughed and the meeting led to a strong friendship between the pair.

It was said that the Prince Regent, an ardent boxing fan, later conferred a knighthood on Dan, making him the last man to be so honoured during the Regency period. This claim has been strongly disputed by historians and there is no official evidence of it in royal records.

Nor is there any reference to 'Sir Dan Donnelly' on his tombstone in Kilmainham, Dublin or on the monument later erected in his honour in Donnelly's

Hollow, on the exact spot where he had beaten Cooper and Hall. But the boxing writer Pierce Egan always insisted that there was no reason to believe the fighter was never knighted. 'The Irishman is king in England,' he used to say.

Donnelly moved back to Ireland, and with the money he had left after continuous drinking sessions, plus his reputation in his native Dublin still intact, opened four bars in succession. Unfortunately, he was the bars' best customer. One after the other they lost money, with Dan either drinking the profits or buying drinks for his wide circle of friends, often both. He was also carrying on with his womanising, with his patient and long-suffering wife Rebecca fully aware of his romantic liaisons.

Eventually Donnelly's health suffered and he died on 15 February 1820 in his Dublin home, penniless, while cradled in his wife's arms. He was thirty-two. On the day of his funeral, thousands of his grief-stricken admirers lined the streets, and carriages loaded with flowers forlornly followed the hearse. Shops, bars and business premises closed as a mark of respect as the cortege wound its way to the Bully's Acre cemetery in Kilmainham. The graveyard, said to have gotten its name because of the number of bullies buried there, was the only free cemetery for the city's poor, a final resting place for paupers.

Within days, his body was stolen by grave robbers, a common practice at the time. The body snatchers, known as 'sack-'em-ups' or 'dead watchers,' would steal the corpses and sell them to surgeons and anatomy teachers for experimental purposes for as much as £40, more than most people earned in a year at the time. It was a practice conveniently ignored by the authorities, whenever they knew about it. On this occasion Donnelly's fame and well developed muscular structure was a prize catch.

The body was bought by a Dublin surgeon, a Dr Hall, but fearing any repercussions, returned the body to the grave, though not before cutting off the right arm to have it studied. Later on he had the arm transported to Edinburgh University where it remained undisturbed for several years. Eventually it was purchased by a travelling circus and exhibited in a peep show. It was then procured by an Ulster bookmaker and local politician Hugh 'Texas' McAlevey, a keen boxing fan and collector of memorabilia.

On McAlevey's death, the relic came into the possession of Belfast wine merchant Tom Donnelly, unrelated to the fighter. Donnelly subsequently presented it to the Byrne family who displayed the arm in their premises, the Hideout, in Kilcullen, County Kildare. Though the family later sold the pub, they held on to the arm and it now travels the world as the main attraction in an exhibition, The Fighting Irishmen: A Celebration of the Celtic Warrior.

'It is one of the oldest and most unique pieces of sports memorabilia in the world,' said James Houlihan, a New York businessman and curator of the exhibition. 'People who are knowledgeable about boxing have heard about the arm, but to the uninitiated, they think you are joking until you explain the full story of the great Dan Donnelly.'

RINGSIDE WITH THE CELTIC WARRIORS

Donnelly's early death prompted an outburst of poems and verses about him. The following verse by Joseph Halliday was the original epitaph chosen for his memorial at Bully's Acre graveyard in Dublin. It remained intact for several years until targeted and damaged by members of a Scottish regiment supposedly on guard at the adjacent Royal Hospital. It was later replaced by a plain unmarked stone. The original epitaph, with the initial letter in each line spelling out 'Daniel Donnelly', read:

> Dan rests beneath, still hold his memory dear,
> Around his tomb let fall the pitying tear,
> Now mingled with his kindred dust he lies,
> In silence sleepeth – never more to rise.
> Except on that fateful day when all,
> Living and dead, shall hear the trumpets call.
> Death, Tyrant Death, that fell relentless foe,
> Our champion levell'd by a mortal blow,
> None else in single combat could him harm,
> No human foe resist his mighty arm.
> Erin lament, bear in record his name,
> Lament the man who fought to crown your fame.
> Laid prostrate Cooper, Oliver and Hall,
> Yielding to none but Death, who conquers all.

3. JACK DOYLE

Gorgeous Gael who 'coulda been a contender'

He may not have been the greatest Irish heavyweight of all time but Jack Doyle was certainly the most colourful, and the most controversial. Although the big Corkman, known as the Gorgeous Gael, never held a professional title or attained the fistic heights attained by others, he was certainly not the worst in an era of good foreign heavyweights in the 1930s. To use Marlon Brando's line from *On The Waterfront*, he 'coulda been a contender'.

Certainly had he taken the sport more seriously, Doyle would have made further progress. He received more space in newspapers and magazines of the day than many of the world champions, though very often the coverage was because of his often crazy antics outside the roped square which made headlines around the world.

Hugely popular with fight crowds and the 'darlin' boyo' of women who thronged to his fights due to his innate charm, impressive physique and striking good looks, the 6 ft 5 in Doyle more importantly possessed the big wallop, particularly in his right hand, to make him one of boxing's major attractions of his era. Also dubbed the Playboy Puncher by the press when his reputation as a ladies' man got around and his career began to take off, he won seventeen of his first twenty-three professional bouts, thirteen by countouts and three on stoppages.

Doyle was the toast of London, New York and Hollywood and he was as much at home in the company of royalty as he was with the movie colony and stars like Errol Flynn, Clark Gable, Robert Taylor, Barbara Stanwyck and Marlon Brando. He went through money as though he had a printing machine at home and could turn out cash whenever he needed it. Jack's problem was that he could never hold on to it.

Nor could he keep his head in the ring, or put his mind down to hard training. Jack threw away fights he could well have won had he kept his cool and prepared better. One exasperated English promoter in the 1930s offered the opinion that the word 'impulsive' could well have been created with Jack Doyle in mind. That was the tragedy of Doyle. Sadly, he preferred the bright lights too much. It is generally agreed, and it is a view shared by this writer and expressed in an RTÉ television documentary on his life, that his was a genuinely wasted talent.

The sheer grind of hard, disciplined training in what would quite likely be spartan gymnasiums, and pounding the lonely miles of roadwork early in the morning was simply hard graft, not to mention utterly boring. He reckoned that his big right-hand would do the job, but he never realised, or wanted to face up to the fact, that there is more to boxing than a hefty wallop, whether with a right or a left. All the great boxers put down their success to hard training. Having said that, were he around today in this age of fragmented titles with more belts to be won than there are TV cooks in the world, he could have arguably won at least one of them.

Michael Taub, Doyle's biographer, wrote: 'Jack was a giant in stature and with a giant appetite for life. He lived his life like a hell-raiser, and by the time he was thirty, he had earned and squandered three-quarters of a million pound fortune.' Boxing historian and author Gilbert Odd observed: 'Doyle, for all his potential ability, could never quite dedicate himself to boxing and all that goes with it.'

Outside the ring, Jack was a real charmer. It was often said that he got his eloquence as a child when he kissed the Blarney Stone, the inscribed stone at the fifteenth century Blarney Castle in Cork and said to impart the gift of words – especially of flattery, persuasion or even deception – to anyone who kisses it.

Certainly it was never too difficult to realise why people liked Doyle, especially the ladies. Besides his good looks, he was the ultimate flatterer. This writer got to know him quite well in the 1970s when he was long into his retirement years. He was living at the time in a dimly-lit, cramped basement flat in the Paddington district of London, one of the poorer areas of the city and a far cry from the luxurious hotel suites he once stayed in. He was also fighting a serious drink problem.

Yet Doyle was friendly, chatty and outgoing, and simply very good company. Our acquaintances were renewed later when he was in Dublin to prepare for a singing tour, as he still had a good, resonant tenor voice and could easily have had a successful singing career had he not chosen boxing. He was also still the charmer and the gentleman, and he always referred to the author as 'Mr Myler' never 'Thomas'.

Doyle was born on 13 August 1913 in Queenstown, now Cobh, from where the *Titanic* sailed on its ill-fated maiden voyage the previous year. He was one of six children born to local sailor Michael Doyle and his wife Anastasia. A strong, solid youngster, Jack grew fast and at the age of sixteen he was a husky six-footer who got employment as a bricklayer on a building site to add to the family's modest income.

Jack got into lots of street fights, mainly against bullies, and it was in these battles that he discovered his right-hand wallop. However, it was not until he joined the Irish Guards, a regiment of the British army, when he was seventeen that he realised his full potential as a boxer. An admirer of the former world heavyweight champion Jack Dempsey, who had recently retired, he knew he would get nowhere fast by staying in Ireland and made up his mind that Britain would be his base.

Based in Windsor, outside London, Doyle began to learn the rudiments of boxing in the Irish Guards developed his fine physique even more. Jack tried out his limited boxing abilities in army tournaments, and while he enjoyed the fancy stuff, he always finished up by tossing his right with lusty abandon. On one occasion he knocked an opponent into the lap of his commanding officer at ringside. 'No problem, Jack,' said the top brass, 'but you should take up boxing seriously when you leave the army. You would do well.'

Doyle took the advice and made his debut as a paid heavyweight on 4 April 1932 at Crystal Palace, London by flattening Chris Goulding in thirty seconds, including the count. Big Jack was on the way to what he believed would be fame and fortune. Winning his first eleven fights, all inside two rounds, he qualified for a crack at the British championship, held by the stylish Welsh heavyweight Jack Petersen.

The big fight was scheduled for 12 July 1933 at the White City Stadium, a large London arena normally used for greyhound racing. Petersen was a slight favourite as he had won all his twenty-five professional fights, thirteen by the short route, and while Doyle was also without a loss, it was considered that the Welshman had met stronger opposition and was therefore expected to retain his title.

By fight night, interest was high for the biggest fight Britain had for many years. The fight was promoted by Jeff Dickson and a crowd of over 60,000 passed through the turnstiles, including many society women who just wanted to be there to stare at Doyle's classic features. Even though Petersen was champion, the handsome Corkman was the main attraction. Who else would pull in the crowds against Petersen? Hadn't he the explosive punch in his right hand? The nagging question, though, was: Could he land it on the chin of the clever champion?

As it happened, the fight turned into a brawl. In the opening round Petersen shook Doyle with a stinging right that buckled the Irishman's knees and made his eyes roll like dice on a roulette wheel. But Doyle hung on, wrestled his opponent halfway around the ring as referee Cecil 'Pickles' Douglas warned Doyle for holding and pulling his man. Two rights landed just on Petersen's beltline, with the champion wincing and Douglas issuing another warning.

In the second round, both men engaged in two-fisted rallies in the centre of the ring as the big crowd roared. Petersen was first to break away but Doyle followed him like a greyhound chasing the mechanical hare and staggered the champion with another big right. Petersen tottered to the ropes on unsteady legs as Doyle rushed in but the Welshman hit back with a powerful right that made the Corkman blink. This stung Doyle into action.

He began throwing punches from all angles, with one of them landing well below the belt, causing Petersen to wince and prompting Douglas to issue another warning: 'Watch those low punches, Doyle. One more and you're out!'

The Corkman, however, would not be denied. One more good body shot would probably finish Petersen, and this time it would be above the belt. But it didn't work out that way.

Doyle threw a long left to the chin that staggered Peterson but the follow-through right uppercut landed well below the belt causing the champion to double up on pain, and raising his left knee. Today, certainly in the US, Doyle would have merely lost the round and Petersen given time to recover but at the time, particularly in Britain, it was different.

Douglas immediately dashed between the two boxers and shouted: 'Go to your corner, Doyle, you're disqualified!' When the large crowd realised what had happened, a storm of booing broke out. They were unable to believe that the contest which promised so much had ended in such ignominy. It had lasted just 213 seconds. Now it was all over, and as the two men left the ring, there was no sign of the unrest abating. The booing continued into the following contest. Never had a crowd been so angry, and felt so cheated.

In the dressing room, Doyle adopted a couldn't-care-less attitude, which was typical of the boxing playboy. 'I did my best and no more,' he said. 'There'll be another day, mark my words. I wish we had gone another round because I would have won as I had him out on his feet and he knew it. I just sailed in, knowing so many of the folks back in Ireland were listening in on the radio. I made up my mind to finish it quick. Yes, I suppose I did hit low because everybody says I did but it will never happen again. Before the fight I had a telegram from Jack Dempsey and he wanted me to go to America so I may well do that.'

Then, as if to convince himself that the defeat was just a temporary setback in his quest for greater things in the ring, and before bursting into song, he declared: 'I was disqualified because I was so young and inexperienced but I can beat anyone alive and I shall be champion of the world someday.' In the other dressing room Petersen said: 'It's true I was disappointed at the sudden ending and I thought Jack and I were going to have a really good fight.'

The respected boxing writer and author Gilbert Odd, former editor of *Boxing News*, recalled in later years: 'I'm convinced that if the referee had been anybody but 'Pickles' Douglas, Doyle would not have been disqualified. He was a bit unfortunate in that respect. He just happened to have the wrong referee. Douglas had obviously taken after his father John Douglas, who was the strictest and fussiest referee I have ever seen. He would think nothing of disqualifying a boxer in the last seconds of a twenty rounder.'

Doyle's carefree mood and attitude changed dramatically the next day after being informed by the British Boxing Board of Control that a fine of £2,740 was being deducted from his £3,000 purse and that he was being suspended for six months. The verdict was strongly attacked in the press as being very unfair. Doyle took the board to court and won, but lost when they appealed, with the original fine and suspension still standing. In an interview with this writer in his retirement years, Doyle admitted: 'All I got from the biggest fight of my career was a paltry £260, which was a mere pittance, and as you can readily imagine, a disgraceful amount of money for a championship fight.'

Now discouraged with the boxing set-up in Britain, Doyle had just one more fight across the Irish Sea, knocking out Frank Borrington of Derby in eighty-three seconds at London's Royal Albert Hall in March 1934. He would take Jack Dempsey's advice and go west. America was the land of opportunity. He would also continue with his singing career over there. Possessing a fine tenor voice, Doyle had toured halls and theatres in Britain, including shows at the London Palladium. He also cut his first record, a single with 'Mother Machree' on the A-side and 'My Irish Song' on the B-side. As well as the boxing and the singing, perhaps he could even break into the Hollywood movie scene as well.

First, however, was the not inconsiderable matter of celebrating his twenty-first birthday in August 1934. This notable event took place in a Dublin hotel where several hundred guests got through over a hundred gallons of champagne. Not surprisingly, with Doyle's large circle of friends and acquaintances, many coming from his native Cork, it went on for several days, with more than a few lingering hangovers.

With that out of the way, Jack finalised plans for America, and returning to Cobh, he packed his bags. A large crowd gathered outside the Atlantic Hotel to bid farewell, at least temporarily, to their favourite son. Jack spoke from the balcony and proclaimed that he would not return to Ireland until he was heavy-weight champion of the world. He would then settle down and marry 'a sweet Irish girl'. Just before boarding the S.S. Washington he sang 'Mother Machree' to tumultuous cheers.

Doyle's personal style of showmanship and charisma made him an instant hit in the US. As he waited for fights, his singing kept him in demand in concert halls, theatres and on radio. Jack also found love, in the shape of movie starlet Judith Allen, a divorcee. They married in passionate haste in a registry office in Ague Caliente, Mexico in April 1935. At the time Judith was the regular girlfriend of the reigning world heavyweight champion Max Baer but Doyle tended to ignore such trivialities.

It was a romantic occasion but, sure enough, the judge who performed the ceremony obviously did not think so. Omitting the normal routine of asking the groom and bride to kiss each other, instead he handed Jack and Judith a couple of business cards on which was printed the name of a lawyer, with the words 'Legal Mexican Divorces Secured'. Quite clearly the judge was looking ahead.

Meanwhile, although still married, Doyle's name was linked with several Hollywood stars and socialites as well as businesswoman Libby Holman who, apart from being a successful singer, was heiress of a major tobacco company. Doyle had the lead role in an adventure movie in 1935, McGluskey The Sea Rover.

He hoped it would make him a celluloid swashbuckling hero, a new Douglas Fairbanks, but reviews were abysmal, one critic writing that whatever success Doyle had at boxing and singing, he would be better advised to leave movies alone. He took the advice, though he would make two more films, in supporting roles this time, in later years.

Doyle's eagerly awaited American ring debut finally arrived. He flattened Phil Donato with a tremendous right to the chin in the first round in June 1935 in New York. A few weeks later, in Newark, New Jersey, Jack Redmond took the full count in the fourth round from a roundhouse right to the side of the head. This was followed by a knockout in the second round at the end of July, in Elizabeth, New Jersey, over Bob Norton with a fusillade of lefts and rights, after sending his luckless opponent out of the ring earlier in the round.

Though the opposition was not of top calibre, the manner of Doyle's executions impressed the tough American press. Jack's big American invasion was really under way now. Max Baer had just lost his world heavyweight title in a stunning upset to James J. Braddock so Doyle now turned his attention to the new champion. 'Get me Braddock,' he bellowed to the boxing writers and anybody else who would listen at a press conference to publicise the continuing tour. 'I came to your country to become champion of the world and I intend to keep that promise. I'll even take on Max Baer first to prove I deserve a title opportunity.'

When this news reached Baer in California, Max suggested that Doyle first take on Baer's younger brother Buddy. Standing 6ft 6 ins and weighing over seventeen stone, Buddy had compiled a series of quick wins with only one defeat. He claimed he had the punch to match anything the Corkman could throw at him. Jack scoffed at this cockiness and the match was scheduled for the Long Island Bowl in New York.

Doyle now wanted more than anything else to be taken seriously as a heavyweight contender, especially after his three early victories on American soil. He became depressed when a freak rainstorm caused the fight to be postponed for a week and switched to the indoor Madison Square Garden. The new date was 29 August 1935. Doyle, at twenty-two, was two years older than his opponent, two inches shorter and nearly two stone lighter, but both were heavy hitters and an explosive fight was anticipated by the capacity crowd.

It was explosive, while it lasted. Doyle started fast and shook Baer with one of his big rights to the jaw but Buddy quickly countered with a thumping right hook to the body that put Jack on the canvas. Doyle tried to rally when he got up but Baer shrugged off the right-handers like a dog shaking itself after coming out of water. Another big right from the American, this time to the ribs, followed and Doyle slithered down the ropes to the floor.

He got up on decidedly shaky legs, eyes glassy, before Baer moved in fast with a combination left-right to the chin and Doyle sank down again, this time like a puppet when its strings have been cut. The game Corkman climbed to his feet again, groggy and unsteady, at the count of six as Baer landed a strong right to the head just on the bell. Referee Billy Kavanagh then waved his hands wide to indicate it was all over. The time of the finish was two minutes and thirty-eight seconds.

A controversy arose when Doyle's corner pointed out that the bell had sounded a second or two before Baer landed the finishing punch and that the American should have been disqualified. 'I was robbed,' protested Doyle, but even had the fight gone into the second round, the outcome would hardly have made any difference. There was only one boxer in it, and that man was not Doyle. The sad result was that Jack's big American dream of world heavy-weight domination was at an end. He never boxed in the US again although he would continue to make headlines outside the ring. Baer would go on to fight Joe Louis in two world heavyweight title fights, once knocking the Brown Bomber out of the ring.

Doyle went to Hollywood in the hope of reviving his stalled, if brief, movie career but nothing came of it. However, he fell for actress Carole Lombard and aimed to take her away from the star known as the King of Hollywood, Clark Gable, who was living with Lombard at the time and would subsequently marry her. Doyle had met Lombard on her own at several Hollywood parties and had long fancied her, even telling Gable once that the feeling was mutual.

Gable just smiled, and said in that familiar husky voice well known to moviegoers: 'Kid, don't fool yourself. Carole loves one man, and that man is not Jack Doyle.' But Jack would not be put off and he used to drop her name into the conversation whenever he met other Hollywood stars, including the notorious hell-raiser Errol Flynn, for drinking sessions.

At one party Gable warned Doyle off his future wife, and Jack took this as a challenge, like a kid being dared to rob an orchard. One night at a party, Doyle saw Lombard across the room, and without Gable. They got into conversation and at the end of the night, or rather early morning, Doyle escorted her to her home and went in.

The next morning Jack was awoken by somebody hammering on his door. It was Gable and he wanted to know what went on the previous night between Carole and Jack as he had heard both were at the party. 'Nothing happened,' insisted Doyle but apparently the jealous Gable did not believe him. Soon, the two men exchanged blows, with Doyle sending the Hollywood star sprawling across the room with his finest right hook, smashing a chair and knocking over a lamp.

When Gable regained his feet, he rubbed his jaw reflectively, smiled, offered Doyle his hand and said: 'You have a mighty kick in that right hand, you boyo,' before inviting the Corkman for a drink in the bar. From then on, Doyle wisely decided the leave Lombard alone for Gable and they became close friends.

Clark would marry Lombard in 1939, the year he made his most famous movie *Gone With The Wind*. Three years later she would die in a plane crash.

Doyle spent the rest of his stay in California and as well as Gable and Errol Flynn, became friendly with the likes of James Cagney, Bing Crosby, Pat O'Brien, Frederic March and Johnny Weissmuller, the former Olympic swimming champion who became famous as Tarzan. Doyle got a small part in a movie called *Navy Spy* but he admitted that he had not really enjoyed working on the film. For a man who liked action, particularly in the ring, he found the hours of delay between takes extremely irksome and the learning of lines rather monotonous and tedious, even though he had very little to say.

On the domestic front, things were no better between Jack and Judith, going from bad to worse. Doyle's dangerous liaisons with the opposite sex were obviously getting in the way of a lasting, happy marriage. They had many rows in public and private, between his philandering and his heavy drinking, before Judith finally filed for divorce. She later changed her mind, delaying the split in the hope that Doyle would change his ways but the last straw came when Jack became involved very publicly with the rich Dodge family who ran the motor car empire. His marriage to Judith Allen was over, having lasted less than two years.

Doyle had struck up a friendship with Horace Dodge Junior, son of the company's founder. Before long he had not only captured the affections of Horace's sister Delphine but also their 66-year-old mother Anna and even Horace's wife Mickey. There was nothing the bould Jack would not do for love or money, and it came as no surprise when Doyle was handed a cheque by Horace, said to be in the region of $10,000, with the stark warning never to contact Mickey or any of the family again.

Now a free man as far as romantic entanglements were concerned, Doyle vowed to move away from the bright lights and the entertainment scene and to move closer to home and return to his first love, boxing. His first ring appearance after being inactive for the whole of 1936 was in January 1937 against Alf Robinson, a Manchester greengrocer in his other life, at Wembley, London.

Looking as confident and as cheery as a student who has just received good results in his exam, he dropped Robinson with a succession of hard blows in the opening minute of the first round. As Robinson started to rise, the Corkman's impetuousness got the better of him and, rushing across the ring, struck his opponent, whereupon he was promptly disqualified for the second time in his career.

Undaunted, Doyle continued what was essentially a comeback in London rings with a win in six rounds one month later against the Dutchman, Harry Stall, at Earls Court. This led the way clear for an important ten rounder against the tough American, King Levinsky at Wembley in April. Levinsky was from Chicago and had gone the twenty round distance with Max Baer, taken the giant Primo Carnera the full ten rounds and had beaten Jack Sharkey, all former world heavyweight champions.

Here is how Peter Wilson described the fight very colourfully in his book *Ringside Seat* in which he made the point that this was the only contest in which Doyle took part that went the full scheduled distance, in this case twelve rounds. 'The fight was not without incidents,' he wrote. 'Outstanding among them was the occasion when Doyle, trying to call attention to the fact that he thought the 'King' was holding him, allowed his arms to be pinioned and then whirled round and round with Levinsky still holding on like a strap-hanger in the rush hour.

'The referee duly intervened but the "King" had enjoyed this slight terpsichorean interlude, and at the first opportunity he grabbed Doyle again. Once more the Irishman started to circle and this time Levinsky joined in with abandon, cavorting around the ring in a kind of elephantine waltz and taking Doyle with him, to the astonishment of the cash customers who were unused to beholding nearly a fifth of a ton of raw beef on the hoof cavorting and galumphing around the hempen square which was designed for sterner stuff. Generally speaking, a good time was had by one and all, not excluding the fighters.'

Doyle won the decision, and there was a story, confirmed in later years by Jack to the author, that one of the Corkman's supporters, anxious to encourage him to box rather than fight and risk yet another disqualification, promised to pay him £1 for every left he landed on Levinsky's somewhat battered features. Doyle came out of that little arrangement with over £100.

Instead of following up his win, Doyle returned to his singing engagements around the halls, an indication that he may have been growing tired of the fight game. Indeed, he might have abandoned boxing had it not been for an offer from promoter Sydney Hulls to take on the former British lightheavyweight champion Eddie Phillips at Harringay Arena, London, set for September 1938. Phillips would be a tough test as he had been around the rings, having had three wins over Tommy Farr, the gritty Welshman who had taken Joe Louis the full fifteen rounds for the world heavyweight title in New York a year earlier.

Doyle prepared for the contest at the invitation of Billy Butlin to work out at his holiday camp at Skegness on the English coast. It seemed an ideal arrangement, especially as it would offset the normally heavy cost of training. In addition, filling his lungs with that bracing sea air each day was considered the perfect tonic to such an important fight which could propel Jack back into the title picture if victorious.

Doyle delighted in the surroundings and the adulation he received from the camp's two thousand five hundred holidaymakers. He rode out each morning on horseback, and the open-air sparring sessions with the camp's resident conditioner Phil Fowler, who could also well handle himself in the ring, attracted in excess of a thousand people daily.

Jack's brother Bill acted as his valet and was responsible for his large wardrobe. This included eight trunk loads of clothes, with twenty-five suits, twenty-five pairs of shoes and dozens of sweaters. There was a story emanating from the camp that Doyle had injured two ribs in training but it was denied in turn by Jack himself, his manager Dan Sullivan and trainer Frank Duffett. At the pre-fight medical in London, the British Boxing Board of Control were satisfied that he was fully fit.

On the night of the fight, Doyle once again looked after his own financial matters rather than leaving that sort of thing to his manager. Glancing over his contract in the dressing room, he noticed a clause which stated that he would not get a penny of his £2,000 purse were he to be disqualified. This would not be beyond the bounds of possibility, considering what happened in the past.

Doyle locked the door and, turning to promoter Hulls and board officials who were in the dressing room making sure everything was in order, declared: 'Gentlemen, this contract is invalid.' Explaining about the disqualification clause, he pointed out to Hulls: 'Now, either you change this contract here and now and agree to pay me my full purse of £2,000, or I won't walk into the ring. I'm tired of being kicked around. In fact, I'm fed up with boxing too and I plan to retire. So if I don't get my cheque now, and hand it to my brother Bill here, there will be no fight.'

Before anybody could say anything, Doyle went to his locker and pulled out his jacket. Looking in the mirror, he patted his hair into place and prepared to leave. Hulls was the first to speak. 'You're crazy, Doyle,' he said. 'You cannot hold us to ransom like this. You can't walk out just like that. There is a full house out there expecting a fight between you and Phillips. You'll get your money but you'll first have to put up a decent fight for the paying customers and give them full value.'

Doyle was adamant. No money, no fight. Eventually, Hulls produced a cheque for £2,000 which he handed to Bill Doyle. That was not enough for Jack, however. He insisted that the newspaper cartoonist Tom Webster, who was in the dressing room, act as guarantor in case the cheque bounced. With that, Doyle thanked Hulls and said: 'Now gentlemen, if you excuse me, I have a job to do out there.'

Jack had promised everybody that he was really serious about the boxing business now, and in the first round he chased his smaller opponent around the ring, trying to nail him with his big right. But Phillips proved to be as slippery as a wet fish. In the second round Doyle managed to back the Londoner against the ropes and flailed at him with everything he'd got, hurtling himself forward and tossing a right that started from the floor.

Phillips neatly sidestepped like a bullfighter and Doyle stumbled clean through the ropes and out of the ring, his legs shooting up in the air and crashing down on the press bench. Several typewriters were swept to the floor and ringside telephones were scattered in all directions. Timekeeper Joe Palmer's stopwatch was also in pieces. The scene was described by one ringsider as boxing's comedy of errors, though the boxing writers and the timekeeper certainly did not regard it as amusing.

While all this was happening, referee C.B. Thomas had already counted out Doyle, as under the rules, a boxer is expected to get back in the ring unaided and inside ten seconds or be counted out. Doyle did not, or could not, and Thomas announced that Phillips was the winner by knockout in two minutes and twenty seconds of round two.

Doyle eventually scrambled to his feet to a mixture of cheers and boos, even some laughter, but he did not climb back into the ring for the official result. Merely forcing a smile and apologising to the boxing writers and the time-keeper for all the trouble, he strode back to the dressing room more like a conqueror than a conquered. Jack may have not been the winner but the short-lived fight, if it could be called that, managed to gain entry into the Guinness Book of Records as 'probably the only time in ring history of a boxer knocking himself out'.

Questions were asked afterwards: Was the fight, or rather the fiasco, a fake? Did Doyle take a dive, in this case, out of the ring? After all, he had his £2,000 cheque in advance and had already declared he was tired of boxing. Years later, when the author put those questions to him, he was adamant that the fight was on the level. 'Look, Mr Myler, I was just unlucky to miss Phillips and fell out of the ring,' he explained. Could he not have climbed back sooner, as some writers had suggested at the time? 'No way,' he said, 'because by the time I had freed myself and got my bearings, it was too late and I was counted out.'

Phillips admitted to Doyle's biographer Michael Taub many years after the fight: 'I saw his punch coming, caught him with a left and he went sailing out of the ring. I was a good gymnast, and I know something about that side of things, but I don't believe a man of sixteen stone or more could have thrown himself like that. I can't see that Doyle would have suffered a defeat against me willingly.'

At a press conference the next morning Doyle again apologised for all the trouble when he fell out of the ring. He said he hoped to get another chance to avenge his loss. It came in July 1939, this time at the White City where Jack had fought Petersen for the British title six years earlier. Topping the bill was a fight which promoter Sydney Hulls was billing as being for the vacant world lightheavyweight championship between the skilful Len Harvey and big puncher Jock McAvoy. Jack promised he would beat Phillips this time.

While interest in the Harvey-McAvoy fight was high, the fact that Jack Doyle was on the bill was in itself a tremendous draw and an enticing added attraction. War clouds were gathering over Europe and it seemed only a matter of time before hostilities would break out, even if the British public had been assured by Prime Minister Neville Chamberlain that Adolf Hitler had person-ally promised him 'peace in our time'.

A crowd of over one hundred thousand pushed and jostled their way through the turnstiles on what was a glorious summer's evening. Crash barri-ers were knocked over and the main gate subsequently stormed. It was later ascertained that twenty-five thousand people literally gate-crashed as police reinforcements fought to restore some kind of order.

All roads leading to the White City were blocked and cars abandoned where they stood. People were alighting from buses and taxis which could go no further through the dense crowd. Even the four principal boxers had to abandon their cars a mile from the stadium and make their way by foot through the heaving crowds.

The ringside was packed with high society, and as with any Doyle fight, there was a strong presence of women. After Harvey won his fight on points, it was close to eleven o'clock but nobody wanted to leave. Jack Doyle was the man they wanted to see and it did not really matter what time he was getting into the ring. With the crowd chanting, 'We want Doyle, we want Doyle,' the spotlight picked out the tall and resplendent figure of the handsome man from Cobh as he strode across the turf.

Doyle climbed into the brightly-lit ring in an otherwise darkened arena and a mighty roar went up. He waved to stars and celebrities at ringside, as well as friends he recognised. Jack seemed in a cheerful mood, unlike Phillips who was sitting quietly in his corner, staring at the canvas. The Londoner looked anything but a confident fighter about to go into battle, even if he had beaten the Irishman in two rounds just ten months earlier.

It was all over in 144 seconds of the first round. Doyle simply walked through Phillips' guard and landed two rights to the chin which sent him down on one knee. The Englishman was up without a count but Doyle charged with lefts and rights and Phillips was down for the second time. This looked easy. As Phillips regained his feet, Jack again stormed in but with his man at his mercy, he left himself open. Phillips took his chance and landed several hooks to the head that sent Doyle flat on his back, his legs in the air and his head strik-ing the canvas with a resounding thud. The full count was a mere formality.

It now looked like Doyle's ring career was finally over, and he turned his attention to resuming his singing career. By now Jack had acquired a new wife, a fiery Mexican actress named Movita he had married in a registry office in California and who could also sing. Together they travelled around Ireland and Britain on singing tours, often with 'Two Ton' Tessie O'Shea, the much-loved music hall star.

Tessie would remember in later years: 'In my opinion Jack had the greatest personality, both on and off the stage, of anyone I knew. He was a real lady-killer. We were all crazy about him. I suspect that apart from his handsome looks and his fine physique, it was his Irish blarney that really got through. I wish there were more Jack Doyles in the world. In my remembrance of him, he was a leprechaun, and a charmer.'

Trouble was looming on the matrimonial side, however. Surprise, surprise there were reports of Doyle having affairs with a succession of women. He was also drinking and gambling heavily, and there were constant rows, with crockery thrown on many occasions. In a bid to save the bond, he and Movita decided to get married officially in a Catholic ceremony in Dublin in February 1943, a day that brought traffic to a standstill in the area of the church.

Gerald Egan, a Cork promoter, approached the groom at the wedding and asked if he wanted to box again. 'Why not,' Doyle replied. 'I could do with the extra money.' Jack was now approaching his thirtieth birthday and had been out of the ring for four years but he announced he was fully fit and raring to go.

The comeback fight was held at Dalymount Park, a soccer ground in Dublin, in June against the Mullingar boxer Chris Cole and it was a disaster, at least as far as Doyle was concerned. He was swinging so wildly that one of his rights nearly struck the referee Harry Hanley. Cole got his chance early and smashed Doyle with a powerful right to the chin in the first round. He followed through with more lefts and rights that had the Corkman floundering before Hanley mercifully intervened after two minutes and thirty-five seconds.

Doyle had one more fight two months later, again promoted by Egan, and managed to knockout a Cork journeyman named Butcher Howell in the third round. The crowd's enthusiasm was poor and Jack decided to finally call it a day on his ring career. There were talks of another comeback but Doyle was through and realised he risked permanent injury by continuing. He made occasional appearances as an all-in wrestler, the last resort for a former boxing star, but the roar of the crowd was no more.

Gone forever were the champagne parties, the luxurious hotels, the array of Savile Row suits. Gone too was Movita. After seven stormy years with constant rows, reconciliations and more rows, she walked out on him one day in 1945. Doyle had not heard from her for ten years when he got a letter saying she wanted a divorce. Jack replied that it was not possible as they had married in a Catholic church. He heard no more from Movita until one day he read in a newspaper that she had married the movie star Marlon Brando, a marriage that would also end in divorce. One later quote from Movita remained in his mind: 'The only true love of my life was Jack Doyle but we just couldn't live together.'

Doyle's singing career also dried up. By 1947 he was sleeping rough in Dublin, often in the back of a taxi in a city back street. Jack later moved to London where he would live out the final years of his life. He struck up a friendship with an Irish woman, Nancy Kehoe, who seemingly put up with his drinking and his womanising. Doyle's name was being linked with the blonde English movie star Diana Dors around that time.

Jack divided his time between his small, modest flat in Paddington and his local pub where he would often buy a drink for his cronies, or more often than not, get somebody to buy him one. The former boxing star hit rock bottom in 1966 when he was hauled up in court for stealing a packet of cheese from a supermarket and was fined £5. A Sunday newspaper paid the fine amid allegations that they concocted the whole affair to make a front page story, and had paid Doyle handsomely for his co-operation.

When this writer met him in a Paddington pub for an interview in the early 1970s, he was extremely courteous and friendly, although his views on the losses might have needed a bit of scrutiny. On his two summary defeats to Eddie Phillips, first in the second round when he was knocked out of the ring and then in the first, he said: 'Well, that's what the record books say but in truth, he landed a lucky punch in the first fight, and by the time I got back into the ring, it was too late. As for the second fight, I had him down twice before leaving myself open and he caught me, again with a lucky punch.'

What of his loss in one round to Buddy Baer in the US? Again, Jack turned a blind eye to contemporary ringside reports which showed that the big American was clearly the better man and finished Doyle with a right and left to the jaw, although the final punch was on the bell. 'Look, Baer's people made a big issue of that result,' he said. 'What they ignored is that Baer fouled me as the bell had sounded and he should have been disqualified.'

The loss on a foul to Jack Petersen for the British title? 'Now there has never been a greater injustice to an Irish boxer than what happened in that fight, and its aftermath,' Doyle explained. 'Ok, I may have hit him low in the excitement of the big occasion but the punches were really body shots. Don't forget too that at one stage I nearly had him out. If being disqualified was not enough, the British Board fined me £2,740 and banned me for six months. It was just disgraceful.'

What did Jack think of the contemporary heavyweights? He waved his right hand dismissively: 'Look, boxing has taken a turn for the worse. The men of my day, the 1930s, would have mopped the floor with the current crop. There simply are not enough good men around today, no hungry fighters, and the game needs hungry fighters. Life is too soft for them today. In my day you had the likes of Joe Louis, Max Schmeling, Max Baer, Tommy Farr, Len Harvey and so on. Where are the likes of those men today?'

Doyle had little regard for the two leading heavyweights of the 1970s, Muhammad Ali and Joe Frazier. 'Neither were in the same class as Louis or Rocky Marciano,' he pointed out. Asked what would have happened had Jack Doyle fought Ali and Frazier, he said: 'If I had caught Ali in the right spot, and I would have, he would have gone down in the same way that Henry Cooper put him down. As for Frazier, it would have been a case of who landed first, and don't forget that Jack Dempsey used to say that I had the best right-hand punch in the business.'

Had he any regrets? 'I'll tell you now,' he replied. 'None at all. I saw a bit of the world. Yes, I was a playboy, and enjoyed the company of beautiful women, living the high life. Yes, I should have taken myself more seriously but so what? I had a good time. What more can anyone say?'

Doyle died of cirrhosis of the liver at St Mary's Hospital in Paddington on 13 December, 1978. He was sixty-five. He used to say he would die a pauper and he seemed destined for a pauper's grave had it not been for a photographer friend he had once befriended in London. Joe Faye set the wheels in motion for Doyle's emaciated body to be taken home to his hometown of Cobh. On the day of his funeral, thousands lined the streets to pay their last respects and a wreath in the shape of a boxing glove was laid on his grave by members of the Cork Ex-Boxers' Association. Jack Doyle, the Gorgeous Gael, had not been forgotten.

4. BERNARD DUNNE

Rise and fall of the Dublin Dynamo

When Sugar Ray Leonard first laid eyes on the twenty-two-year-old Bernard Dunne in a Connecticut ring in the summer of 2002, the American ring legend was instantly impressed. A former Olympic gold medallist who went on to win world titles at five weights, Leonard was by then a promoter, and turning to his partner Bjorn Rebney, said: 'You know, Bjorn, this kid's got tremendous ability. He is something special and even at this early stage, I would see him going on to win a world title.' Rebney nodded: 'Yes Ray, he has all the moves and I think you are right.'

It was the beginning of a story that saw the Dubliner box and punch his way to the superbantamweight championship of the world. In defeating Panama's Ricardo Cordoba in the spring of 2009 in the O_2 arena in his home town after one of the most sensational fights in Irish boxing history, Dunne became the first Liffeysider to win a global title in his native town. He was also only the second Dubliner to win a world championship, following Steve Collins who had captured the world middleweight title in Sheffield and the world supermiddleweight belt in Cork.

Dunne, nicknamed the Dublin Dynamo, was responsible, along with Meath businessman-turned-promoter Brian Peters, for reviving professional boxing in Dublin after the sport had been in the doldrums for years. Boxing people used to refer to the city as 'a graveyard for an extinct sport'. Amateur boxing was big but the professional game was a pretty hard sell. In 1996, it took three open-topped bus rides and a sparring session in the middle of the city's fashionable Grafton Street laid on by promoter Frank Warren to get rid of tickets for a card topped by world champion Naseem Hamed.

A year earlier, promoter Frank Maloney almost gave away tickets on the street when past-and-future world heavyweight champion Lennox Lewis boxed in the city. Another top UK promoter Barry Hearn forecast a six thousand crowd for Dublin favourite Steve Collins but pulled out after twenty-seven tickets were sold. Dunne changed all that with massive crowds for his big fights, exciting nights that put the paid side of the sport back into the headlines, even though Peters just about managed to break even on his first few shows.

The future world and European champion was born in Neilstown, a predominantly working class area in West Dublin on 6 February 1980 to Brendan and Angela Dunne. 'It was a harsh environment but a good one,' he would recall. 'I grew up instinctively knowing how to fight, how to look after myself. The Neilstown and neighbouring Clondalkin districts produced many notable soccer players but it seemed that nearly everybody else boxed at some stage. Almost every family on Neilstown Avenue had sons boxing so the game was all around us. It seemed only natural that I would become a boxer,' added Dunne, who first pushed his hands into boxing gloves when he was only five years of age and could barely lift his hands under their weight.

Neilstown Amateur Boxing Club was nearby, and its favourite son was the classy Ken Egan, a future ten-time Irish senior champion and winner of a silver medal at the 2008 Beijing Olympics. However, Dunne trained out of the C.I.E. Boxing Club gym, formerly the home of the British Legion, across the city in Inchicore as his father was a member there as well as his two older brothers Willie and Eddie. Indeed, boxing was steeped in the Dunne family.

Brendan Dunne was a champion boxer in his day and in 1974 at the city's National Stadium became Ireland's first ever senior champion in the newly created lightflyweight division. It was a title he would successfully defend twice. Bernard's mother, too, had a boxing connection, as her brother was Eddie Hayden, a two-time Irish amateur lightmiddleweight champion in the 1970s.

Four years before Bernard was born, Brendan would represent Ireland at the 1976 Montreal Olympics, winning his opening bout, the only member of the Irish team to leave the ring as a winner, but losing his second. 'I wouldn't even consider comparing myself with Bernard,' he says now. 'Bernard was something special.'

Bernard was taken to the CIE Boxing Club when he was about five years of age. Learning fast as he grew up, he came up through the ranks, from boys and youths level to junior and senior status. Bernard won the Irish senior bantamweight championship in 1998 and the featherweight title the following two years. Boxing internationally, at home and abroad, he collected a cabinet full of gold, silver and bronze medals and it seemed certain he would be on Ireland's Olympic team for Sydney in 2000 to achieve his ambition.

'Ever since the 1996 Olympics in Atlanta, I'd set my mind on the games,' he recalled. 'I used to wake up in the morning thinking about the Olympics and the same going to bed.' Dunne Senior used to tell his son it was the ultimate achievement. 'It really was something special,' said Brendan, who recalled with pride the occasion twenty-four years earlier walking out on the field with the rest of the Irish team for the opening ceremony. 'I had a tingling feeling all over my body.' Bernard could not get the Olympics out of his mind even if he was studying anatomy in Dublin's Trinity, Ireland's most renowned college.

Training seven days a week under his coaches, his father Brendan and Peter Perry, Bernard knew there would be a small grant available from the Irish Sports Council, though not as much as it should be. Those were the days before the High Performance Programme was introduced into Irish amateur boxing when more money and better facilities would become available to allow boxers compete at the highest level. No more training in rundown gyms in often damp conditions, worn wooden floors, poor lighting and no heating. But back then, it was still the stone age for Irish boxing.

With boxing writers and columnists confidently predicting, even a year before the Sydney Games, that Dunne seemed to be Ireland's best hope for a boxing medal, only one Irish boxer qualified, Cork lightmiddleweight Michael Roche. This would make it the smallest ever Irish side to take part in the world's most prestigious and toughest tournament. Consolation for Dunne was that he would travel as a reserve featherweight, his only hope being that one of the others at his weight would have to drop out for whatever reason. During a training session in Newcastle, about one hundred miles up the coast from Sydney, however, he injured his right hand but felt that he would get through 'and keep boxing as long as I could if I got the chance to get into the ring'.

To make matters infinitely worse, when the little team got to Sydney, Bernard picked up a bad cut near his left eye during a sparring session with the Thailand featherweight Somluck Kamsing and automatically ruled himself out of any further competition, irrespective of any featherweight pulling out. As it happened, it was a disastrous Olympics for Ireland as Roche, in his first contest, was eliminated when defeated 17–4 by Firat Kurugollu of Turkey.

Bernard has no happy memories of Sydney. 'I was treated like the H.G. Wells character The Invisible Man,' he recalled for this writer. 'The next flight home was not scheduled until the end of the Olympics so I decided to stay on in Sydney and watch the action but while I was not entitled to the benefits of team membership, I certainly did not expect to be left without accommodation. I was desperately short of money too. I was lucky that a family from Cork, the O'Driscolls who had come to visit us in training camp, were able to put me up for two and a half weeks.

'Nor could I get any tickets for any of the events, from the opening session to the closing ceremony and I wouldn't have seen any of the boxing had it not been for Jimmy Magee, the RTÉ boxing commentator, who managed to secure accreditation for me. Fair play to Jimmy. I would have been lost without him.'

When Dunne returned home, it was time to think about his future. Bitterly disappointed at missing out in Sydney, he had long talks with his family as to what was next for him in boxing. The World Championships were set for Belfast in February 2001 and there was always the Irish title and more importantly the 2004 Olympics in Athens. His record was standing up well, with something like one hundred and thirty amateur bouts all over the world and losing only eleven. He was never beaten at home, by an Irish or foreign opponent. But his mind was made up.

On a cold morning in January 2001, the day Dunne was due to weigh-in to defend his featherweight title in the Irish Senior Championships at the National Stadium in Dublin, he came to a momentous decision. He was finished with the amateurs. 'I asked myself a question,' he said, looking in the mirror in his bathroom. 'I asked myself what happens in four years if I don't qualify for the Olympics? I can't see myself sitting at home, waiting and wondering what was going to happen, if anything, and doing nothing. I'm going to turn professional.'

Dunne never made the journey across town to the weigh-in. The paid side of the sport had been on his mind since returning from Sydney and there were persistent rumours sweeping the boxing scene that his amateur days were numbered before news of his imminent departure from the amateurs became public. There were panic stations in the high ranks of the Irish Amateur Boxing Association.

Officials were dismayed that he was going to walk away from such a promising amateur career with so much to look forward to. A squad of twenty-four boxers was being announced for the World Championships and indications were that Dunne would be the team captain. But Bernard Dunne would not be in the squad. His mind was elsewhere. The Pro game.

Not surprisingly, offers from all over the world came in to manage and promote Dunne. They came from Britain, Europe, the US and of course Ireland. Frank Maloney, one of Britain's leading managers who had guided Lennox Lewis to the world heavyweight championship, wanted Dunne's signature on a contract. London-born Maloney, whose mother came from Wicklow and his father from Tipperary, worked with the established promoter Panos Eliades and forecast a very bright future for Dunne, with a world title fight along the way. But it was a twenty-nine-year-old publican and restaurant proprietor from Dunshaughlin, County Meath named Brian Peters who would eventually get Dunne's signature.

When they met over lunch in an office above his premises, the County Club in Dunshaughlin, in November 2001, Peters did not promise global domination for the promising young Dubliner but he had all the contacts to make headway in the hard, competitive world of professional fisticuffing – and who knows? A chance to progress to a world title was always possible, even very likely in Peters' estimation.

The contract was for five years, with a two-year extension if Dunne made it into the world's top ten, a further two-year extension if he won a European title and another two years if he won a world championship. The agreement was not made public at the time but it was ironclad and tied up the Dubliner pretty well. But as Gerry Callan of the Irish Daily Star recalled: 'What cannot be underestimated, or ever forgotten, in the Dunne story was the role Peters played, in particular his foresight, commitment to the cause and, not least, his abiding faith in his protégé.'

Peters was interested in the sweet science from a very young age but it was not until he travelled to Las Vegas in the summer of 1986 as a teenager to see Barry McGuigan defend his world featherweight title against the Texan, Steve

Cruz in the stifling heat that his passion was ignited. Fascinated by the razzmatazz of the whole fight scene, despite the terrible disappointment of McGuigan's defeat, Peters vowed he would get involved in the sport as a promoter and come up with a champion.

He staged his initial show in association with the American promoter Mat Tinley at the National Basketball Arena on the outskirts of Dublin in September 1993. It featured three boxers who would go on to win world titles, Belfast bantamweight Wayne McCullough, Sheffield superbantamweight Naseem Hamed and Chicago lightheavyweight Montell Griffin. Encouraged by the success of the show, he joined up again with Tinley in November 1994 and at the old Point, later the O$_2$, on Dublin's docklands, he matched McCullough once more, this time against the Frenchman Fabrice Benichou, resulting in another win for Wayne.

Four months later Peters went into the big time when joining forces with Matchroom Promotions in the UK and had Steve Collins winning the world supermiddleweight title from Chris Eubank at the Millstreet Arena in Cork in March 1995. The lad from Dunshaughlin was on the way.

By December 2001, Peters had jointly promoted ten shows, including two in the US when he signed Dunne. They set their sights on America, with the West Coast, where most of the action was taking place, as their target. The US had also been the route Dunne's fellow-Dubliner Steve Collins had started on as a professional. 'If you really want to learn about the game, the only sensible thing to do is to go west,' the two-weights world champion told Dunne and Peters. 'America is the toughest school in the business, and I've absolutely no regrets in taking that route. And if you want the best trainer in the game, then Freddie Roach is your man. He has a fully equipped gym in Hollywood and there is nobody better I can personally recommend. He was in my corner and he can be in yours.'

When the news got around boxing circles that Dunne had turned professional, promoters came out of the woodwork like wolves on the scent. They were led by Bob Arum. A former New York attorney running the hugely successful Top Rank boxing organisation based in Las Vegas, Arum was a major force on the American scene and let it be known that if Dunne went along with him that the road was wide open for a world title.

Dunne and Peters were a bit cautious, even a little dubious, with all of Arum's big promises, even though they had the greatest respect for him. They felt that Arum, with so many big names on his books, might forget about 'the little guy from Dublin, Ireland'. Instead they settled with a major promotional organisation based in Denver, Colorado and known as America Presents. It was run very successfully by Mat Tinley, who had staged three shows in Dublin with Peters, and his partner Bob Goossen. More importantly, Tinley had helped guide Wayne McCullough to the world bantamweight championship so he knew his way around the fight scene.

'I first came across Bernard in March 1996 when Wayne McCullough was staying in Luttrellstown Castle in Dublin and preparing to fight Joe Luis Bueno at the Point,' Tinley remembered. 'Bernard sparred with him for two or three days and even then, I was tremendously impressed. He was only sixteen at the time but he wasn't in the least bit intimidated by a reigning world champion. And what you have to remember is that Wayne was never noted for taking it easy on sparring partners no matter how young or inexperienced they were. It was at the moment that I felt Bernard Dunne was something special and had the makings of a champion, yes, a world champion.'

Even before Dunne took off his amateur vest for the last time, Peters and his boxer flew to Los Angeles and called in at 1123 Vine Street, which happens to be the location of the Wild Card Gym, something of a temple to boxing's gods. There they met its owner Freddie Roach. Of Irish, Canadian and French descent from South Boston and a former world lightweight championship contender, Roach was and still is arguably the world's best coach. At this writing he has been named Trainer of the Year four times by the Boxing Writers' Association of America as well as being inducted into the World Boxing Hall of Fame and the Californian Boxing Hall of Fame.

Roach is in constant demand, having to date put close to thirty world champions through their paces, including Mike Tyson, Oscar De La Hoya, Bernard Hopkins, Sugar Shane Mosley, James Toney, Steve Collins and Wayne McCullough. Not short of a dollar because of business interests in Las Vegas, Roche is one sporting magnate who seems most comfortable in a baggy t-shirt, faded tracksuit trousers and a well-worn pair of trainers. An unruly shock of hair and a pair of steel-rimmed glasses complete the identikit picture of a man who toils each day for love and not for money.

Despite his work rate, Roach suffers from Parkinson's disease but he is able to control it through medication, injections and his all-consuming work as a trainer. He just gets on with his job of working with champions, near-champions and even never-will-be champions. After watching Dunne work out, he told Peters he would train the Dubliner. Following the signing of contracts, Dunne and the manager had a good look around the gym and were fascinated by the photographs and fight posters covering the walls.

They had no trouble spotting the faces of the likes of Rocky Marciano, Joe Louis, Marvin Hagler, Floyd Patterson, Evander Holyfield and the two Sugar Rays, Robinson and Leonard, even if many of them were before their time. There too were photographs of Hollywood icons like Elizabeth Taylor and Marilyn Monroe, perhaps a nod to current movie stars including Denzel Washington, John Travolta, Christian Slater, Mickey Rourke and Cuba Gooding Junior, all regular visitors to the gym who pay their $50 a month for workouts. Hilary Swank, a two-time Oscar winner, trained there in preparation for her acclaimed role as the waitress-turned-boxer Maggie Fitzgerald in the 2004 movie *Million Dollar Baby*.

Roach is not only a superb trainer but a brilliant conditioner who understands both the physical and psychological side of boxing. His mentor was another legendary trainer Eddie Futch, who listed Wayne McCullough among his many champions so Dunne was in capable and sure hands. 'I would soon be sparring with the likes of world champions such as Manny Pacquiao and Sugar Shane Mosley, with Freddie overseeing the sessions,' recalled Dunne. 'Mind you, I was conceding weight but I didn't mind. Now where would you get those kind of workouts outside of America. It was something of a sacrifice to leave Dublin and my family and friends behind but in the end it was well worth it. I've certainly never had any regrets about starting my career in America.'

Peters rented an apartment for Dunne on Hollywood and Vine, but the area was somewhat seedy, with its parking lots, low-rent shops, cheap motels, hookers, drunks and drifters. Before returning to Ireland, the manager got Bernard a place in the more fashionable Santa Monica district, where Dunne would soon be joined by his girlfriend in Dublin, Pamela Rooney. He felt safer to run through the area's leafy streets and then down Sunset Boulevard leading to the shores of the Pacific Ocean. But he still took the ten-mile ride on the LA Metro bus to the Wild Card Gym every day for workouts with Freddie and his champs.

Bernard made his professional debut as a featherweight on an America Presents promotion six days before Christmas 2001 at the Feather Falls Casino in California against Rodrigo Ortiz. A capacity crowd of thirteen hundred cheered as they watched him punch with authority and force the Mexican to retire after two rounds. Ortiz had his nose broken shortly before the bell ended round two and he failed to come out for the third. Dunne was surrounded by well-wishers when he left the ring and many asked him for autographs. The Dublin Dynamo had made a successful entry into the tough American fight scene and local sportswriters were very complimentary to him. 'New Irish kid gets US career off to an explosive start,' said one local newspaper headline.

Dunne was to have boxed again in February 2002 but an ankle injury ended that plan. It was a blessing in disguise for Freddie Roach as the trainer wanted Dunne to do some quality work in the gym and work on a few faults like holding his hands too low, leaving himself open to counter punches. Meanwhile, problems, big problems, lay ahead. America Presents, the promotional organisation which had Dunne and others under contract, was having financial difficulties with crippling debts mounting up and Mat Tinley announced they were closing down operations, leaving their boxers high and dry.

With no immediate promoter available at short notice, Dunne's American adventure had come to a sudden halt, at least temporarily. This is when Sugar Ray Leonard came into the picture. He was a legend in the sport. Less than six months after his 1976 Olympic success as a lightwelterweight gold medal winner in Montreal, Leonard turned professional and continued his winning ways.

Many disliked the way he was able to dictate his own career by calling the shots and getting what he wanted, but the fans continued to pay good money at the box office to watch him. Leonard represented glamour but was no playboy. He had the steel, the character, the desire, the temperament and above all the supreme boxing skills to make him the outstanding boxer of the 1980s, the sport's Golden Boy. He finally retired from the ring in 1997 after several comebacks.

Leonard set up a promotional company, SRL Promotions, in the summer of 2001 and staged regular cards. He had also landed a lucrative television contract with the ESPN network, something on the lines of an American equivalent to Sky Sports. Through Brian Peters' US connections, the manager got in touch with Leonard and suggested he use Dunne on his next show. Sugar Ray was putting together a show at the Foxwoods Resort Casino in Ledyard, Connecticut scheduled for 2 August 2002 and mentioned to Peters that Dunne could go in against Christian Cabrera from the Dominican Republic who was having his first professional fight. Peters took about two seconds to agree.

With Leonard and his partner Bjorn Rebney at ringside, Dunne racked up his second win with a stoppage, again in two rounds, after the Dubliner punished his man with smashing lefts and rights. Cabrera never boxed again. Thoroughly impressed with Dunne's workmanlike display, Leonard and Rebney came in as his new promoters, signing him to a three-year deal structured for eight fights. Leonard also shortened his name to Ben Dunne and promptly put him on their next promotion, set for 19 October against Tony Espinoza of Denver, Colorado at the HBCC Arena in Buffalo, the New York State border town on the brink of Niagara Falls.

Dunne did intensive training for the fight, sparring almost on a daily basis with world champions Manny Pacquiao and Willie Jorrin as well as former champion Gerry Penalosa. The bout was scheduled for live transmission across the US and all tickets had been sold in advance, producing a record Buffalo attendance of fifteen thousand nine hundred and forty.

But there was big trouble ahead. Far greater than America Presents folding. In a routine pre-medical examination in the offices of the New York State Athletic Commission at the official weigh-in twenty-four hours before he was due to enter the ring, Dunne got the shattering news. Ray Katz, matchmaker for the card, announced to the packed media that 'a tiny shadow, possibly a cyst' had showed up on Dunne's MRI scan. He explained that he had just got the news from the eminent neurosurgeon Dr Barry Jordan who had examined Bernard and passed on the information to Dr Ralph Petrillo, Chief Medical Co-Ordinator of New York State. The result was that the fight was off.

'I understand that something showed up on the screen: white matter,' Petrillo explained to the boxing writers. 'It's not definitive, and new scans will need to be taken. Due to this, we cannot allow him to box tomorrow night. But it does not rule out his boxing career. I want to see this lad when he's eighty years old and he has children and grandchildren. When you have any potential risk with the brain, among the things that can happen are paralysis, permanent seizures and, in the worst case, you could be killed. On no account can we have that.'

Petrillo also announced that Dunne was being placed under automatic suspension. The disclosure, at the very least, put Dunne's fledging career in serious jeopardy and, at worst, could end it permanently. Ironically, he had undergone the same tests by a prominent Buffalo neurosurgeon two days earlier and was cleared. The Dubliner was gutted about having to pull out of such a high-profile promotion but the medical people on the New York Commission had the last word.

Dunne had an even further problem, though a slightly lesser one, on his hands when he realised that a party of twenty-two, consisting of his family, friends and fans had already landed in New York and were on their way to Buffalo. 'I had to hurriedly contact all of them,' he recalled. 'I knew they had come a long way to see me fight and had gone to a lot of expense in doing so. Naturally, I didn't want them turning up at the box office and no Bernard Dunne in action. Also, I didn't want them overreacting to the situation until I knew exactly what the situation really was. It could be something serious, or it could be nothing but there was no way I was going into a panic straight away.'

By a remarkable coincidence, the same drama had been played out two years earlier to the very day when Wayne McCullough suffered a similar traumatic fate when a planned bout in Belfast fell through. McCullough spent two years out of the ring while neurosurgeons differed and argued on the exact seriousness or otherwise of the matter before he eventually boxed again, with no ill effects.

On returning to Los Angeles, with Leonard and Rebney indicating that there was no change in their contract, Team Dunne contacted the UCLA Medical Centre and after long, drawn-out meetings and debates with physicians and neurosurgeons Dunne was finally given the all-clear by the Californian State Athletic Commission. It had not been as serious as first thought. Neurologists at UCLA had carefully studied charts and reports, discovering that the 'white matter' was, in essence, a normal and not dangerous occurrence. The findings were sent on to New York and they cleared Dunne too.

When Sugar Ray Leonard was given the news by Brian Peters, he said: 'I'm just thrilled for Ben on two fronts. Firstly, the tests have established that he can come back to the ring in perfect physical health and second, he can resume his career and climb towards the world featherweight title.' Leonard himself knew all about health scares in the ring. In the build-up to a world title defence in 1982, also in Buffalo, he suffered a detached retina which forced him into temporary retirement. Five years later, he scored the greatest victory of his career by taking the world middleweight title from the great Marvin Hagler over twelve rounds.

Dunne returned to the ring after an absence of four months, although it seemed like a year to him, when, at the Thunderbird Wild West Casino in Norman, Oklahoma on 3 January 2003, he knocked out Simon Ramirez in sixty-nine seconds. Referee Gary Rilter went through the formality of counting out Ramirez but he knew, everybody knew, the man from Oklahoma City had no chance of beating the 'ten and out'. Dunne was back, and Jim Brady, the American correspondent of *Boxing News*, referred to him as the Pride of the Emerald Isle and said that he could well be the 'new' Barry McGuigan.

The Dubliner would run up eleven more victories in the US, five inside two rounds, before deciding to launch himself on the Irish scene in early 2005 because of a touch of homesickness. In any event, Sugar Ray Boxing (SRB) had been disbanded because the former world champion had signed up with Hollywood star Sylvester Stallone to oversee a new reality TV show with a boxing theme called *The Contender*, with a $1 million jackpot for the winner. There were also stories circulating that Leonard and Rebney were not getting along together, with regular rumours of bitter rows.

Leonard did ask Dunne to take part in *The Contender* but Bernard had his mind made up. They were packing their bags for Dublin. There was an additional reason for leaving American shores. In January he and Pamela had also taken a quick trip home to their native city to get married and both wanted to bring up any children they might be blessed with in Dublin. Leonard and Dunne shook hands and he wished Bernard all the luck in his career. 'I'll be following your progress and rooting for you,' he told Dunne.

Dunne's first appearance in Dublin in February 2005 as a paid puncher attracted wide interest. Peters was now acting in the dual role of manager and promoter. He matched Bernard with Yorkshire's experienced Jim Betts, a former British championship contender and ranked eleventh in the world, five places above Dunne. The bout was set for the National Stadium, the scene of some of his most notable amateur fights for a decade.

The venue, with a capacity of two thousand three hundred, was completely sold out within a week of being announced, and touts did a brisk trade, with tickets going at two and three times their original value. It didn't matter. Dunne had won all his fourteen fights in the tough school of American boxing and everybody wanted to see him in his own hometown. With the national broadcaster, RTÉ, telling Peters that their tight budget would not permit them to televise the fight, the promoter told them: 'Ok, have the fight for free, and we'll talk about your budget the next time.' They agreed.

With one of Ireland's top trainers Harry Hawkins, from Belfast's Holy Trinity Boxing Club, in his corner, Dunne was a little rusty after being out of action for six months but his left jab gave him the edge in the opening round. In the second, third and fourth he brought his right hooks into play, though Betts was putting up stiff resistance, countering with good shots of his own as he tried to narrow the Dubliner's lead.

It was all over in the fifth. Dunne dropped Betts to his knees with a powerful left hook to the body. When he groggily climbed to his feet, the Dublin Dynamo moved in again and another left hook put him down, this time for good, as Belfast referee David Irving counted ten and out. The round had lasted sixty-one seconds. The big crowd gave Dunne a tumultuous reception.

Peters had his man back at the National Stadium three months later against the tough Ukrainian featherweight champion Yuri Vorinin, a southpaw, ranked seventh in Europe, before another sell-out crowd. But what a scare he had. Vorinin, well behind on points going into the tenth and final round, caught the Dubliner, his hands down, with a smashing right to the back of the head less than a minute into the session.

Dunne wobbled, with his arms dangling by his side, eyes glassy, his legs like papier mâché and his defence practically non-existent, and sank to the boards. He got up but fell down again, fortunately without a count either time. Trainer Hawkins was roaring: 'Move, move!' And move he did, to the centre of the ring, where he had dominated the action in the earlier rounds, before going on a fast retreat, with the Ukrainian in hot pursuit, until the bell. Dunne deservedly received referee Irving's 96–94 decision but he never realised how desperately close he came to defeat. 'Sure, he gave me a scare but I always knew where I was,' he said to this writer in the dressing room. 'I will put it down to a learning experience.'

It was. Five wins and eighteen months later, Dunne, now down to super-bantamweight, was nominated to box for the European Championship against Esham Pickering, a tricky and rugged fighter from Nottingham, at the Point, a concert venue on Dublin's docklands and later known as the O_2. The date set was 11 November 2006. Nicknamed Brown Sugar, Pickering was an only child whose father walked out on his mother early on. His mom never wanted her son to box, preferring him to play soccer, but when he began to have success in the amateur ring she changed her mind and encouraged him along the way. He began as a professional in 1996, five years earlier than Dunne and had lost only four of his thirty-three fights, as against Dunne's all twenty-one wins.

Coached ironically by Brendan Ingle, a member of a large and well-known boxing family from Dublin, Pickering figured to give the local hero some problems with his shifty style and hand movements. A former European and Commonwealth superbantamweight champion and a world title challenger, the Englishman told a packed media conference on arrival in Dublin: 'I'm the puncher in this fight and I'll knock your man out. I'm due to fight for a world title and when I win that one, I'll come back here and defend against Dunne. Ok, Dunne's a good box-fighter and he can fight but I don't think he can fight in the trenches, like I can. I know too the crowd is going to be against me but, hey, they can't get into the ring and help him.'

Sitting alongside Pickering, and listening intently, Dunne retorted: 'Esham is a genuine world-class fighter but then again, so am I. I'm in the ring with him on merit so let's see how he reacts when I hit him. I've prepared for a twelve-round fight but if I always look for the quick exit and if I can end this fight inside the distance, then I will. I get the same money if I do it in the first round as the last, or win on points. I'm ready for anything he brings to the table, or I should say the ring.'

The championship fight created tremendous publicity, with posters all over town and daily reports in the newspapers for what was the first major championship card in the city since world featherweight champion Naseem Hamed, the self-styled Prince from the Yorkshire steel town of Sheffield, headlined a triple-title show by stopping Mexico's Manuel Medina in 1996, also at the Point. Not surprisingly, a crowd of seven thousand filled the venue. It started fast. Pickering boxed and punched well, moving in and out, but Dunne would not be denied in what would be his moment of truth. He controlled the action with strong jabbing with the left, and hooking with both gloves.

Though cut over the right eye in the sixth round, it never bothered Dunne as he moved in and out like a revolving door as Pickering switched from orthodox to southpaw in an effort to confuse but it did not work. The Dubliner kept as close to his opponent as his own shadow, and the decision was unanimous. Two of the three judges, Denmark's Freddy Rafn Christensen and Jean-Louis Legland had it 117–111, with Germany's Kurt Stroer surprisingly calling it a tight 115–113. But no matter, there was only one winner.

When Italian referee Massimo Barrovecchio raised Dunne's right hand, it was a signal for the fans to erupt into a sea of cheering, singing and handclapping rarely experienced in an Irish ring as the belt was clasped around his slim waist by Mel Christle, president of the Boxing Union of Ireland and a former Irish amateur superheavyweight champion. Dunne had become the eighth Irishman to win a European title and the first from the capital. As he recalled recently: 'It was a good feeling to be champion of Europe. The belt was an early Christmas present.'

After two more successful title defences, both in Dublin, Dunne was ready to face the formidable Spaniard, Kiko Martinez at the Point on 25 August 2007. A menacing figure from Alicante, the swarthy Martinez, twenty-one and billed as La Sensacion, had never lost in forty amateur bouts, all but two inside the distance, and sixteen professional contests, thirteen by stoppages or countouts.

On arrival in Dublin, he told reporters: 'This is the fight I've wanted for a long time. I might be a little shorter than Dunne but I'm a five-foot four inches headache for him.' When this writer asked him if he had any fears of boxing before a partisan crowd in Dublin, he said: 'Never. I've boxed in front of big crowds before. Anyway, I like to fight under pressure and I'm fully confident of taking anything Dunne has to bring to the ring and doing it better.'

When these comments were relayed to Dunne on his arrival back from long weeks of hard training in Belfast, he replied: 'This a massive fight for me. Everybody has been talking about a Martinez fight for months and now it's happening and I can't wait. A guy can be the biggest hitter in the world but he has to land first. I've watched tapes of him in action and I'm fully confident I can take him. Besides all that, the crowd is not going to be easy for him. It has to be like walking into the Coliseum and everyone baying for blood. He can't have encountered anything like that.'

Martinez stood passively in his corner while Dunne loosened up as MC Mike Goodall made the formal introductions. There was high drama from the opening seconds. After both moved around seeking openings, the menacing Spaniard, looking like a miniature Mike Tyson in his prime, even down to the black boots with no socks, slipped inside Dunne's defence. A cracking overhand right followed by a whiplash left hook sent the Dubliner down on the seat of his trunks as the crowd gasped. Dunne climbed to his feet, as much shocked as hurt, and took the mandatory eight count from Birmingham referee Terry O'Connor. Dunne backpedalled furiously and tried to hold off his tormentor but the Spaniard would not be denied.

He drew Dunne's left jabs like a magnet attracting steel filings and put the Dubliner down on all fours with a smashing right to the head. Bernard got up, his plans for survival scattered, and was put down again, this time with a powerful right, before O'Connor bent down, helped him to his feet, cradled him in his arms and led him to his corner. It was all over, even the shouting. The shock finish stunned the fans, who had earlier cheered and chanted Dunne into the ring with *The Irish Rover* and *Ole! Ole! Ole!*, a legacy from the soccer era of Jack Charlton and his 'Irish army'. The fight, if it could be called that, had lasted precisely eighty-six seconds, making it the shortest European super-bantamweight title fight in boxing history.

'I'm disgusted with myself,' said a crestfallen Dunne at a packed post-fight conference. 'Not so much for losing, as I will get another chance hopefully, but because I let down the fans who have always supported me. But I've no excuses. He's the better man. He caught me fair and square. One punch can change a fight. It happens to the best.' Martinez, hardly breathing, said: 'I'm sorry for Bernard but there had to be a loser. That's boxing.' It was disclosed later that the Martinez camp had placed €3,000 in bets on a first round stoppage at sixty-six to one, and €9,000 to win by any means at eleven to four, raking in a tidy profit of €250,000 in the process.

Dunne, determined to put the shattering Martinez loss behind him, began a comeback, or what manager Brian Peters and trainer Harry Hawkins called 'a rehabilitation' eight months later with a convincing points win over the

Venezuelan, Felix Machado, in Castlebar, County Mayo. Two more wins followed before Dunne got news that the World Boxing Association had named him to meet the Panamanian southpaw Ricardo Cordoba for the world super-bantamweight title. The match was set for 21 March 2009 at the O$_2$ Arena.

Cordoba arrived in Dublin with an impressive record of thirty-four wins, two losses and one draw since turning to the paid ranks in 2000, a year before Dunne became a professional. Aged twenty-four and from the small village of Santa Marta in the central highlands of Panama, Ricardo Alberto Cordoba Mosque, nicknamed Mastrito, had been a boxer almost from the day he was born into a family of nine other siblings. 'I learned how to fight in the streets,' he explained to the author shortly after arriving in Dublin.

'That's how I got my start. All the kids in Panama do it all the time and loved it. When I was nine, I heard about a gym in the neighbourhood so I just walked up and joined. All the great fighters from Panama, like Roberto Duran, Ismael Laguna and Eusebio Pedroza, came from the streets. It's their breeding ground. Now I'm going to spoil your boy's world title hopes and keep on winning.'

The Panamanian entered the ring a prohibitive three to one on favourite, with Dunne a nine to four outsider, but Bernard was not going to allow the underdog tag to deter him. With the title fight beamed by the national broadcaster RTÉ to half a million TV viewers, it was all down to Dunne, with just one loss in twenty-eight fights. 'This is my big chance, to join the great Irish world champions before me and I don't intend to let anybody down,' he said, adding with a smile and a wink, 'Except the Cordoba camp, that is. I'm prepared to go to the gates of Hell if that's what it takes.'

There was a wide cross-section of Irish life among the capacity crowd of nine thousand at the cavernous venue, all caught up in the excitement of big fight night in Dublin town. The ladies were out in high fashion too. There were even a few priests, no doubt saying a silent prayer that the clean-living, tee-total Irish Catholic boy at the top of the nine-fight bill would pull off a big win, and hoping their prayers would be answered.

Straight away Dunne made up his mind to tear up the bookmakers' script and dump it in the wastebasket. What followed was one of the most sensational fights in Irish ring history. Cordoba moved around well, shooting out his long right jabs and following up with sharp hooks as Dunne countered well, awaiting his openings. With twenty-five seconds left in the third round, the Dubliner moved in fast with a swift left hook which sent Cordoba reeling across the ring for a count. In the fourth, the Panamanian had success with his pop-pop right but in the fifth it was nearly over – for Dunne.

Moving inside the local's defence, Cordoba landed a smashing right to the jaw and Dunne sank to the canvas. When he got up, the visitor dropped him for a second time, again with a right hook. On rising, Cordoba came in fast but

Dunne held on, fighting for survival until the welcome sound of the bell. One more heavy punch, one more knockdown, and the fight would have been automatically stopped in Cordoba's favour. With defeat now suddenly staring him in his blood-spattered face from a bad cut over his left eye caused by an accidental clash of heads, Dunne went to work in the sixth round and never let up. Though it was not going to be easy.

Going into the eleventh, the Dubliner was behind on points on the score-cards of all three judges, as well as with the ringside reporters. He now needed a knockout or a stoppage to save the fight. With the crowd now ecstatic and on their feet, Dunne summoned up one last, desperate effort and sent Cordoba to the canvas three times with crushing left hooks, the last time in the Panaman-ian's own corner, his head resting under the bottom rope. Canadian referee Hubert Earle had seen enough and yelled: 'That's it. It's all over.'

Cordoba had to receive bottled oxygen from the ringside medics as he lay prostrate on the canvas before being taken on a stretcher to a waiting ambu-lance and then to Beaumont Hospital across the city for observation. Happily he was released after several hours, possibly more hurt psychologically in los-ing so comprehensively than through any physical damage.

After he'd been chaired around the ring by one of his cornermen, and surrounded by his family, an exhausted Dunne, with the cheers of the crowd still ringing in his ears, returned to a dressing room packed with reporters. 'I didn't do it for myself, I did it for Dublin and Ireland,' he said. 'You get one chance at the big one, and I took it. I had a real scare in the fifth after two knock-downs but I knew I'd get him in the end. Now I'm going to take a short break and spend quality time with my family.' After Cordoba was released from hospital, he told reporters: 'It wasn't my best performance. My hands were slow and my legs were heavy. I should have coasted through the eleventh and finish strongly in the twelfth and won on points, but my corner insisted I should go in and finish him. They let me down.'

Every contender, even those outside the top ten, now wanted a crack at Dunne and his prized world title. America wanted him back too. But it was the World Boxing Association that had the final say. They ordered him to defend against the number one challenger from Thailand with the name that provided headaches for broadcasters, Poonsawat Kratingdaenggym. 'If he's the top con-tender, then bring him on,' said a confident Dunne. The match was set for 26 September 2009, again at the O_2. The Dubliner went into thirteen weeks of hard training at the Holy Trinity club in Belfast under chief coach Harry Hawkins and conditioner Mike McGurn, who had worked with Irish rugby teams and had been with Dunne for the Cordoba fight.

A year younger than the twenty-nine-year-old champion, Kratingdaeng-gym, from the province of Sakon Nakhon, was a professional with eight years, with just one loss in thirty-nine fights. A veteran of over two hundred Muay

Thai bouts, the national combat sport along the lines of kick boxing, he had been around the block more than once, indicating that he was going to be a pretty tough rival.

Poonsawat simply oozed menace from the moment he stepped off the plane at Dublin Airport, and he did not hide his intentions at the media conference. He said he wanted to emulate Thailand's greatest boxer and International Hall of Fame inductee Khaosai Galaxy, the former world superflyweight champion who had defended his title eighteen times. 'I will finish Dunne in seven rounds, maybe six,' he boldly told reporters. Sitting alongside him, Dunne conceded he had the utmost respect for his opponent and added: 'I've watched clips of Poonsawat in action. He's a pressure fighter and his big asset is that he has a huge engine on him to allow him to go the full twelve rounds. But I have a reach advantage and I will capitalise on that. All I want now is for the first bell to ring and get down to business.'

It was another steamy, raucous night at the docklands venue where you could almost cut the atmosphere with a knife, with Dunne a slight favourite. No sooner had MC Mike Goodall called the two boxers together for their pre-fight instructions and the bell sounded than Dunne went straight into action, jabbing and hooking from ring centre as the Thai waited for an opening to fire his heavy bombs. After two rounds, the Dublin Dynamo was in front on his sharper boxing but it was noticeable that Poonsawat was coming in relentlessly, hooking and jabbing and seeking the big punch to end it.

Then came the explosive third round. Early on Kratingdaenggym connected with a whiplash left hook that made a corkscrew of Dunne's neck and put him on the boards, face down. When he got up, a nick near his left eye and his head foggy, he faced an unmarked Thai who moved in fast and dropped him with another smashing left hook, this time on his back.

When the bemused Dubliner regained his feet, looking as disoriented as a rookie sailor encountering his first heavy storm, the challenger came in again. A thunderous left hook, his best punch, sent Dunne crumbling to the canvas, on his back again, as French referee Jean-Louis Legland waved his hands wide like the fisherman explaining the one that got away. It was all over, stopped on the three-knockdowns rule, with timekeeper Alex McKenzie's clock showing two minutes and fifty-seven seconds into the third round. The local hero was no longer champion of the world, and the capacity crowd was stunned into an eerie silence. The days of wine and roses were over.

A crestfallen Dunne had to miss the post-fight media conference as he was taken to hospital for observation. Poonsawat attended and said: 'Dunne was attempting to keep the action at long range at first but my aim was to draw him on and get close enough to land my heavy punches. After two rounds I got within range and just fired away. I'm delighted my plan worked.' Dunne met the media the next day and explained: 'I knew he would be aggressive from the start but I got lured into fighting him up close and that was my mistake. I'm gutted. I wanted to win this fight for myself, my team, the people of Ireland and to the late Darren Sutherland, my pal. Tell everybody I'm sorry.'

'Poonsawat's immense punching power was the rock that ultimately broke Dunne,' wrote Michael Foley in the *Sunday Times*. 'As the third round unfolded, Dunne began to look ragged. Instead of keeping his distance, Dunne was being drawn into the trenches. The road back could be steep and long.' Famed US writer and author George Kimble, writing in the *Irish Times*, observed: 'Under the pressure of Poonsawat's relentless, two-fisted attack, Dunne found himself fighting in reverse gear from the opening bell. After the first knockdown, he was a dead man walking.'

Poonsawat received a hero's welcome at Bangkok's Suwannaphum Airport and spent over two hours showing off his new world championship belt to thousands of fans who had packed the arrival lounge to greet him. He said he was anxious to give Dunne a return, but added: 'However, I don't think he might want to meet me again, but if the money is right, we are open to talks.'

As for Dunne, he took a short holiday with his family before getting down to talks with manager Peters and trainer Hawkins about his future. There were stories and rumours about him moving up to campaign in the featherweight division but in a Dublin hotel on the afternoon of 20 February 2010, he called a media conference to announce his retirement. He was departing richer in more ways than one. World and European honours had been his, with earnings at a reported €2 million, and he retired safe in the knowledge that he had become one of Ireland's most famous, and most popular, sporting figures. He had brought professional boxing back to life in Ireland.

As in his boxing days, Dunne drew a packed house to his final media conference, with standing room only, many hunched on the floor. 'It's been an incredible journey, and I had all the support I needed following me to a world title,' he said, flanked by his wife Pamela, manager Peters and trainer Hawkins, and speaking with more than a little emotion in his voice.

'I wouldn't want the fans to pay their hard-earned cash just watching me going through the motions. I'm content with my decision. I looked at all the options and it's about what I want. I don't need boxing anymore. I was thirty just two weeks ago. I've put twenty-five years into the sport and I don't want to be one of those 35 or 36-year-old boxers chasing the dream. I fulfilled my dream. I wasn't a journeyman. I won a world and a European title.'

After a round of prolonged applause, the Dublin Dynamo left the boxing stage for the last time. He wrote a best-selling autobiography and is a popular boxing analyst on RTÉ television. He has also done a TV series promoting Irish culture and the language. With his celebrity status, he turns up as a guest on TV shows and can be spotted at movie premiers and big shows, with autograph seekers never far away. The memories linger on.

5. MIKE McTIGUE

Bombs, bullets, landmines and a title fight

Only an eternal optimist or a complete fool, or most likely a combination of both, would agree to defend a hard-won championship of the world in Dublin against an Irishman on St Patrick's Day, with the echo of bombs, bullets and landmines all over the place.

Yet this is precisely what Battling Siki, a West African from Senegal, did when he risked his world lightheavyweight title against Mike McTigue, a crafty, cagey and experienced campaigner from Kilnamona, a small village just five miles outside Ennis, County Clare, at the La Scala theatre just off Sackville Street, now O'Connell Street, on 17 March 1923.

Notwithstanding all this, Ireland was in the throes of a bitter Civil War with the nation divided following the bloody War of Independence and the 1916 Rising. Executions and homes being burned down were commonplace, and the guerrilla war had, according to one commentator at the time, all the appearance of a colonial dog-fight. It was into this scenario that Siki and McTigue arrived in the early spring of 1923 to decide the best boxer in the world at the 12 st 7 lb limit.

One of thirteen children, McTigue's pet gag was: 'I just ran out of money in a thirteen-horse race. I was the youngest.' He remembered in an interview in later years: 'My father was a stonemason and the family leased and worked a bit of land. I became a blacksmith's helper when I was twelve, and lasted just long enough to learn the rudiments. I've always had the wanderlust all my life and I ran away from home at the age of eighteen after getting into scrapes with occupying British soldiers. A few of us used to harass the sentries. Anyhow, I finished up in Sheffield with relatives.'

McTigue returned briefly to his home village two years later before making his way to County Cork and setting off from Cobh on the SS *Baltic* bound for New York. That was September 1912 and McTigue was twenty-one, anxious to explore the New World. He stayed with his brother Patrick John in the Bronx and got a job lugging sides of beef around. Mike was encouraged to take up boxing when he took up for his boss who was smacked by a drunken rowdy and sent sprawling into a pile of raw steak.

McTigue recalled: 'I says to myself, "Mike, you'll be in the bad books with your boss, who became a good friend of mine, if you don't so something about this, and if you do, you're likely to get your brains knocked out by this bully." Anyhow, I decided to sail into him with both fists flying. Mind you, he was a lot bigger and stronger than I was but no matter. He hit me with heavy blows like he had two clubs in his hands but I managed to duck a lot of his punches and smashed him in the stomach. He went down and couldn't get back up again.

'Meanwhile, my boss had watched all this and he came over to me and said: "Mike, you have the makings of a champion boxer, and you're wasting your time pulling beef around here. You should be in the ring, where the big money is." My boss gave me the name of a man called George McFadden, known as "Elbows", and told me where to find him.'

McFadden was an old time lightweight who now trained boxers at his gym on New York's East 59th Street near Madison Square Garden. He got the 'Elbows' tag because if he missed an opponent with a left or a right, he would bring his elbow back and catch his rival, bloodying his face, always outside of the referee's gaze, of course.

Famed *New York Journal* columnist and cartoonist Tad A. Dorgan said George should have worn four gloves, two on his hands and two on his elbows. But when McFadden fought fair, which was more often than not, he could hold his own with the best. His record included fights with greats such as Joe Gans, Frank Erne and George 'Kid' Lavigne, who were all world lightweight champions at one time or another.

McFadden took on McTigue as one of his pupils for preliminary instructions at the standard rate of $20 for ten lessons. On completion of the short course, McFadden told Mike: 'You have good moves, kid. It's a natural style which will develop after a few bouts. I can't teach you anything else in the gym and all you need is experience. I'll be watching your progress with interest and good luck.'

Through McFadden's connections, Mike got in touch with Dan Hickey, who was boxing instructor at the New York Athletic Club. Hickey managed a stable of boxers and he agreed to put the Clareman into a four-round fight at the club, a test bout. 'Listen,' warned Hickey as he tied on McTigue's gloves, 'you had better win because I can't be wasting my time with any stooges. I've got a few good guys here and they are going to make a name for themselves. So when you go out there, do your stuff.'

McTigue did just that, winning on an impressive knockout. Hickey congratulated him. Working with Mike several times a week in the gym, Hickey showed him how to jab and hook, duck under punches and score effectively to the body. 'Very important, too, Mike, watch your defence,' Hickey told him. 'One lucky punch can finish a man. Boxing is a fickle game. I've known brilliant young prospects who faded because they didn't pay enough attention to defence. At the same time, watch for openings and punch. I have a feeling you'll go far because you seem to have natural ability, and that always helps.'

McTigue recalled in later years: 'I owed a lot to Hickey. He taught me the rudiments of the sport. George McFadden also helped me at the start. You need experienced people when you are starting out, and George and Dan were two of the best. We kind of lost touch as the years went by, as you do, but they were responsible for my start in boxing. Thanks Dan, thanks George. Dan Hickey came into my life again when he was managing Paul Berlenbach, the world lightheavyweight champion, but that's another story for another day.

'When I mentioned to several people at the start who knew me that I intended having a go at boxing, they said I was too old to begin and that the fight game was a young man's game. Ok, I was twenty-eight, which is not young for a boxer starting out I'll agree. But I told other people I was only twenty-two and the word got around so that my fake age kind of became fact.'

In another interview in which a writer doubted his alleged age, McTigue said: 'Look, here's the truth. Before I left County Clare, I was twenty-one but the people who advised me when I applied for a boxing licence forgot to say that we Irishmen live a hardy, healthy, open-air life. So at the age of twenty-one, I was a lot younger in reality.'

It was only when several suspicious American boxing writers sent messages back to their Irish connections and asked them to check McTigue's official date of birth with the authorities in Clare that they ascertained the full truth. By then, however, Mike had become established and his age did not really matter one way or the other.

McTigue began boxing professionally in the New York area in 1909, fighting regularly against all types of opponents. He was a clever boxer, using his skills to outwit opponents but taking the initiative and going for the knockout whenever the opportunity presented itself. However, his main strength lay in his ability to outwit the hard hitters. A legitimate middleweight, he often went out of his class to tangle with lightheavyweights.

'In his first ten years, McTigue crowded close to one hundred fights into his career,' Jersey Jones wrote in *Ring* magazine. 'Mike's style was not flashy or spectacular. Nor was his physical appearance particularly impressive. He was scrawny, almost frail, in build. But he was of the rangy, wiry type, and a lot stronger than he looked. A defensive boxer and sharpshooter with either hand, there were few better.

'McTigue was what would be known today as a cutey. He was not aggressive, and his tactics were along cautious, conservative lines. But he was smart, and knew how to get the maximum results from a minimum of effort. He was a master at feinting, drawing his opponents into leads, and countering with left hooks or right crosses that packed considerable authority. Many greats found McTigue a troublesome foeman, and Mike O'Dowd and Johnny Wilson, during their reigns as world middleweight champions, would have nothing to do with him.'

McTigue took a break from his ring activity in 1918 to join up with the famed Fighting 69th, an infantry division of the American Army, and saw service in the bloody Battle of the Argonne in France which lasted seven weeks and brought an end to World War I. Mike won the Distinguished Service Cross for exceptional bravery on the battlefield.

Back in New York, McTigue reflected on his career. He had been around now for over ten years and had fought most of the best middleweights in the world including the feared Harry Greb, the Pittsburgh Windmill, but a title fight was no nearer. Yes, he had won the middleweight championship of Canada during a stay over the border but it was effectively a minor title. He decided to look up Joe Jacobs.

One of boxing's most colourful characters on the New York fight beat and known as Yussel the Muscle, Jacobs was a Jew from New York's East Side. In later years he would forever be associated with his boxer Max Schmeling and memorably crying out when the German lost a disputed decision and his world heavyweight title to Jack Sharkey in June 1932: 'We wuz robbed. We shoulda stood in bed!' However, even when he met McTigue years earlier, he was a very important man around the US fight scene and one of the most influential managers in the business.

McTigue walked into Jacobs' New York office one morning in the late summer of 1921. 'What can I do for you Mike?' Jacobs asked, shifting a ten-inch cigar from one side of his mouth to the other. 'You can do my business for me, sure,' said McTigue. 'I'm looking for a manager who knows a good fighter when he sees one. What say we link up?'

Jacobs thought rapidly. He knew all about the string of managers McTigue had in his time and they had gotten nowhere with him. Andrew Gallimore, McTigue's biographer, noted in his book *Bloody Canvas* that Mike used to joke that he'd had so many managers he was figuring on getting the boys together at the dinner table some evening to talk over old times.

Finally, and somewhat reluctantly, Jacobs said he would take on Mike and promised he would do his best, and nothing more. Jacobs fixed up a match with Panama Joe Gans, a high-ranking middleweight, for Jersey City, New Jersey on 5 September 1921. Gans was born in Barbados but moved with his family to Colon, Panama where residents adopted him as a native son. Like so many great black boxers of the past, however, Gans was deprived of a rightful world title opportunity because of the colour of his skin and he fell victim to the notorious colour bar.

Panama Joe's name has sadly fallen into an abyss, lost in the obscurity of old record books and dusty magazines, buried among the mounds of forgotten boxers of the past. He was a black fighter at a time in America when they received few, if any, breaks. He had to be content with titles like the lightweight championship of Panama as well as the middleweight championships of South America and Central America. He later won the 'coloured' middleweight title but none of them advanced his rightful claims to a world championship fight.

Gans was managed by Leo P. Flynn, who had once been one of McTigue's managers. Said to be the first manager to own a Rolls-Royce, Flynn was a boxing man with many contacts, but when he had looked after Mike, he finally gave up on the Clareman's chances of getting anywhere in the fight business because big name opponents would not fight him for fear of risking their reputations.

'Flynn is taking this fight because he wants to see me licked and get me out of the way,' McTigue told Jacobs, 'But I have a surprise for him and Gans. I'll lick him, and I know it. You'll see.'

On the night of the fight McTigue handed a half bottle of brandy to Jacobs in the dressing room. 'When I ask you for this, let me take a slug of it. OK?,' he said. Jacobs nodded. At the bell, Gans glided around the ring like a panther. Beautifully muscled, he took the first two rounds on his better boxing and sharper hitting. McTigue did not seem able to hurt him. Before going out for the third, Mike took a big gulp from the bottle, and a few seconds later Gans must have thought he had been hit by a cyclone.

McTigue sailed in and slugged through the round, driving Panama Joe before him, punching furiously while the crowd roared. Rarely had they seen Mike fight like this. He was a re-born fighter. At the end of the round, he took another swig of the brandy, a larger one this time, before going out to put Gans through another hurricane. By the time the bottle was empty after the eleventh round, Panama Joe was almost out on his feet and just about survived to the bell ending the twelfth round and the fight.

Under the existing laws of the time, if a fight did not end in a knockout or stoppage it would go to what was called a 'no decision'. Ringside reporters would collectively come to their own conclusions and would award the newspaper decision to one of the boxers. *The Ring Record Book* noted that 'the majority of newspaper decisions were incontrovertible and were at least as accurate as any official decision would have been'. The most conclusive way to win was by a knockout or stoppage.

With the Gans–McTigue match going the full twelve rounds to a no decision, the press boys named McTigue the winner. The crowd thought the same way and gave Mike a rousing cheer as he climbed out of the ring. McTigue and Jacobs now felt that a world middleweight championship opportunity would come their way but the title was in dispute at the time and Mike was not even in the frame.

No matter how well the wily Jacobs used his managerial skills, a championship shot looked as far away as ever. As well as being a risky opponent, Jacobs reckoned that McTigue's style was not attractive enough to entice promoters to get him into the title picture, despite getting the better of the dangerous Panama Joe Gans.

Sure, Mike was a skilful boxer who knew all the moves and had a smart defence but Jacobs felt that the fans wanted a killer puncher, somebody like the reigning world heavyweight champion Jack Dempsey, the Manassa Mauler, to excite the crowds. McTigue was simply not that kind of contender. 'The guy is box office poison,' Jacobs was quoted as saying in an interview. 'He is very talented but promoters don't want to know him. Between you and me, a lot of the top guys don't want to fight him either. He's too risky. So between guys not wanting to fight him, and promoters shying away when his name is mentioned, a guy like me is in a no-win situation.'

Still, McTigue gave big names like future and past champions such as Harry Greb, Battling Levinsky and Tommy Loughran tough fights in no decision encounters. He outsmarted former world middleweight champion Jeff Smith over fifteen rounds and made things uncomfortable for strong contenders like Augie Ratner and Zulu Kid. True, on extended stays in Canada he won and successfully defended his Canadian middleweight championship, all by knockouts, but that title meant nothing on the world scene.

Mike and Jacobs parted company but not before McTigue said he might take a holiday in Ireland, look up his folks and first maybe get a few fights across in Britain to supplement the cost of the long journey. Jacobs wished him well and that was it. As things worked out, it was the best decision Mike ever made in his life. The journey to his native land in 1922 changed the course of his boxing career and began a new chapter in Irish ring history.

McTigue secured three fights in England, knocking out Johnny Basham in three rounds, Harry Knight in four, both in Sheffield, and finishing off Harry Reeve in three in Liverpool. He approached several promoters in England to get him some bigger fights. 'Match me with some of your top guys like Ted 'Kid' Lewis or Joe Beckett and see what I can do,' he told one promoter. 'I can beat all these guys over here because Britishers have always been cheese champions. What d'you say?' The promoter replied that he would see what he could do, but nothing came of it.

There was a glimmer of hope from an Irish racehorse owner and sometime boxing promoter Tom Singleton who was at ringside for the Reeve fight. He told McTigue he could get him a fight in Dublin, but Mike said he was already planning to return to New York 'to see what's happening over there'. Singleton gave the boxer his telephone number and address, and said: 'Look me up if you change your mind, Mike.'

Happenings in France, however, would change everything. Shortly before Mike had started his brief English tour, Georges Carpentier, the Idol of France, had sensationally lost his world lightheavyweight title in Paris in September 1922 to the underestimated Battling Siki, billed as the West African Jungle Child, on a knockout in six rounds. Alas, after his stunning victory, Siki completely lost his head. Fond of heavy drinking, flashy clothes and white women who threw themselves at his feet, he enraged Paris and the civic authorities by marching along the boulevards with a lioness on a leash, stopping at roadside cafes from time to time to buy drinks for both the lioness and himself. On other occasions he would fire pistols into the air to induce his two Great Danes to do tricks.

Still, boxing was boxing and the British promoter Major Arnold Wilson signed Siki to meet their heavyweight champion Joe Beckett in London just before Christmas, with the winner going in against Carpentier. But a series of events was beginning to unravel, like a ball of wool. Siki soon found himself barred in Parisian cafes and bars, as his non-stop drinking and volatile temper often led to unscheduled fights outside the ring.

Despite inevitable interventions by the gendarmes, Siki was incorrigible and never gave reform a second thought. 'Me Siki, me different, me the world champ,' he would say, beating his chest like King Kong. Siki's only concern was enjoying himself. After all, it was the Roaring Twenties, and Siki was the latest idol of the boulevards out for some fun.

Back in America, heads nodded knowingly. Newspaper editorials pointed out: What did France expect? Allowing another black man to fight for a world title. Were there not race riots all over America when Jack Johnson, the first and up to then only black world heavyweight champion, beat James J. Jeffries in 1910?

The Springfield Rifle wrote that victories like Siki's might make colonial subjects 'lose their attitudes of respectful admiration for white men'. Racist rhetoric was not restricted to the editorial pages. Sportswriters continually referred to him as a 'jungle beast' and crude jokes had him 'hopping from the branches of a coconut tree right into the ring' and exclaimed that he was 'only one generation removed from a prominent family of Senegalese baboons'.

It was only a matter of time before the French authorities became thoroughly sick of Siki. From the status of conquering hero, he had degenerated into a public nuisance. The new champion not only found himself suspended by the French Boxing Federation but issued with deportation papers 'to leave the country as soon as possible'. Britain also barred Siki, with the Home Office issuing a statement to the effect that if he set foot in the country, he would be placed under arrest, therefore washing out his proposed London fight with Beckett.

Back into the picture came Irish promoter Tom Singleton. He had been at ringside for the Siki–Carpentier fight and obtained the signature of Siki's new manager Charles Brouillet for a proposed title defence in Dublin, hopefully on St Patrick's Day, 1923 against McTigue. There was one small problem. Siki himself knew nothing of this little arrangement. He wanted to invade America and get into the big time and the big money.

Certainly the US offers were rolling in. Dave Driscoll, matchmaker for Ebbets Field stadium in New York, reportedly cabled a $20,000 offer to fight heavyweight contender Harry Wills, the Black Panther, but Helliers responded with a demand for $100,000. Tom O'Rourke of the New York Polo Grounds offered $45,000 for Siki to meet either Wills or Harry Greb, the American lightheavyweight champion. Greb responded that he would take on Siki 'any time, any place'. He said he'd had three offers already to fight Siki and was ready to talk business as soon as he saw a contract. Marty Killilea, manager of world middleweight champion Johnny Wilson, was also interested in a Siki fight, offering $50,000 to meet Wilson in Boston.

Siki, however, wanted to take on Jack Dempsey, the reigning world heavy-weight champion. In the dressing room after the Carpentier fight, he had told an Associated Press reporter: 'You had better cable the promoter Mr Rickard tonight and tell him I'm ready to take on Dempsey right away.'

When told of Siki's challenge, Dempsey's manager Jack 'Doc' Kearns smiled and said: 'We're always ready to accommodate any ambitious young man. If he is sincere in his statements that he wants a crack at the world heavyweight title, why, Dempsey will fight him right away, either in America or abroad.' Dempsey himself responded: 'I'm ready for them all.' But Dempsey's promoter Tex Rickard was unhappy about a white v. black heavyweight championship fight, remembering the racial trouble when Jack Johnson had reigned.

Johnson himself also wanted to get in on the act, challenging Siki to a fight 'anywhere he wants it' but it never happened, although they would box three six-round exhibition bouts in Canada in 1923.

While Siki was still insisting in Paris that he would invade the US and demand a Dempsey title fight, Singleton and Brouillet were making private plans between them to put on McTigue and Siki in Dublin. Singleton got in touch with James Harris, an English promoter who had booked Siki for a series of exhibition matches in London, Brighton and Liverpool with the possibility of a theatrical tour throughout Britain to follow.

The British Home Office ban on Siki, however, ended all that and with Singleton looking after the Irish side of things, the wheels were set in motion for the McTigue fight. The £2,000 purse money would be split seventy-five to the winner and twenty-five to the loser.

When they told McTigue, he punched the air in joy. The veteran Clareman, a reported thirty years of age at the time with some putting it at thirty-six at least, would readily have fought for nothing other than the chance of winning the title after years in the boxing wilderness. The championship fight, set for St Patrick's Day, would be a tremendous box office asset to him in the US. When they told Siki about the deal, the Senegal fighter refused to even talk about it. It was America or nothing – and Dempsey.

Singleton and Brouillet then hit on a plan. They would tell Siki they were sailing from Cherbourg to New York, but were in fact heading for Dublin, via Cobh in Cork. To make sure the plan worked, they filled Siki with wine and spirits and made him so drunk that by the time he sobered up, he was walking down the gangplank in Cobh. Furious at first that he was conned, he soon cooled down. 'You'll beat this Irishman anyhow and then we can take on Dempsey in America,' Brouillet assured the world champion on the train journey to Dublin, discreetly keeping quiet about the civil war raging and the danger that they all might be either shot dead or blown to pieces.

In a special issue of *Ring* magazine in March 1948 to mark the twenty-fifth anniversary of the fight, Jersey Jones wrote under the heading 'A Day For Dublin': 'It could not, of course, have been anyone but an eccentric, irresponsible character like Battling Siki, the Singular Senegalese, who would have the temerity to defend a world boxing championship against an Irishman in Dublin on St Patrick's Day. That weird incident of twenty-five years ago has earned prominent and distinctive recognition as one of the most fantastic chapters in the bulky, colourful annals of the Marquis of Queensberry's favourite pastime.

'Probably no championship bout ever has been staged amid more fantastic conditions. Spectators walked to the theatre between rows of armed men and were searched for firearms before being allowed in. Armoured cars loomed around corners. Machine guns poked their menacing noses from points of vantage.'

The big fight created tremendous interest worldwide, and among the press representatives were four Paris newspapers, four leading New York dailies as well as a large Irish and British press. It was rumoured that a number of the reporters had been insured for considerable sums by their newspapers. As Jack Farrell reported for the *New York Times*: 'Machine guns to the right of 'em, steel-jacketed bullets to the left of 'em. Milling mobs of belligerent Irishmen. Bombs bursting amid the ear-splitting din.'

As the crowd filed into the La Scala Theatre and an estimated twenty-five thousand people packing Sackville Street and surrounding thoroughfares, there was a deafening explosion in nearby Henry Place, next to the Pillar Picture House and about fifty yards from the La Scala. The blast blew two large exit doors into the cinema and large chunks of ceiling plaster came crashing down. Miraculously, nobody was killed or seriously injured, the only casualty being a young boy struck by flying glass while standing by his mother's fruit stall.

Meanwhile, the La Scala was filling up fast and finally, with a capacity crowd of fifteen thousand tensed up and ready for action, Jim Harris, the master of ceremonies, introduced several dignitaries to the audience including well-known boxing figures such as former world champion Georges Carpentier, who announced he was challenging the winner, American heavyweight

Frank Moran and British champion Joe Beckett. George Bernard Shaw, the Dublin playwright, also acknowledged the cheers of the crowd.

George Bernard Shaw was a keen boxing fan, one of his most famous plays being *Cashel Byron's Profession*, the story of a gentleman prizefighter who invades English high society. He knew Carpentier well, and would befriend Gene Tunney when the New Yorker of Mayo descent won the world heavyweight title in 1926.

Not surprisingly, McTigue entered the ring as favourite, with bookies naming him at six to four on, but many of the foreign journalists were not so sure. They felt that McTigue would tire after about ten or twelve rounds when the stronger, heavier Siki would then come on with his big hooks and uppercuts and wrap up the decision. There was no weigh-in but McTigue was merely a heavy middleweight against a full lightheavyweight and most likely weighed around a stone lighter. The fight was scheduled for twenty rounds.

After Manchester referee Jack Smith called the two men together under the white glare of the arc lights to give them final instructions, they went back to their corners, both looking very confident. In McTigue's corner was Ted Broadribb, the influential London manager who would, in later years, manage top British boxers such as Tommy Farr and Freddie Mills. In his boxing days, Broadribb, then known as Young Snowball, was the only Englishman to knock out Carpentier.

From the first bell, the McTigue plan of action was to stay on the move, keeping a close watch on Siki's heavy hooks from both hands. The Senegal fighter's intention was to keep the pressure on Mike, back him up as much as possible, and get him into range but the foxy Clareman was as slippery as an eel.

Siki seemed to be in front after six rounds, having landed smashing blows to McTigue's head and body, often driving him back to the ropes. There were clinches and bursts of action by both men, but the heavier blows were coming from the world champion, even though the Clareman was landing with the cleaner and more accurate punches. Both the French newspaper *La Populaire* and the Paris edition of the *New York Herald* gave Siki a commanding lead after ten rounds on his constant aggression and body shots, though several other newspapers had McTigue marginally in front.

There was big trouble for McTigue in a busy eleventh round when he emerged from a clinch with a cut on his left eyebrow. Ringsiders claimed it was caused by a short, sharp right hook but McTigue's corner said it was due to a head butt. When referee Smith intervened to inspect the injury, Broadribb said there was no problem, and took the opportunity to tell him to warn Siki about the illegal use of his head. Smith nodded, took a look at the cut and waved them on.

The injury had been cleaned up by the time McTigue came out for the twelfth but he had another problem now. His right thumb was hurting after being damaged probably in the tenth but he was able to conceal it from Siki and use it sparingly, mainly stabbing away with that fast left jab and picking up the points. The *Irish Times* had McTigue in front after twelve, 'penetrating the black's defence with punches to the head and body'.

McTigue was slipping the Senegal fighter's hooks and swings in the thirteenth and fourteenth, using that effective left jab, and encouraged by shouts from the crowd of 'Go get him, Mike' and 'Keep it up, Mike, you're doing fine'. McTigue's right hand was now hurting badly, having aggravated the thumb after landing a chopping right to the champion's head. While Mike would use it sparingly in these closing rounds, Siki was not to know about the damage, and he concealed it well.

McTigue's biographer Andrew Gallimore described the finish like this: 'The last round began amidst intense excitement. A hush of expectancy fell on the crowd with only the occasional isolated cheer to break the silence in the packed hall. The cigarette smoke drifted towards the lights that illuminated the soiled canvas as the two weary warriors fell into a clinch – needing each other to remain upright. Mike won the twentieth because he was marginally less tired than the champion.'

Referee Smith's scorecard has been lost in the mists of time, but at the final bell he had no hesitation in walking over to McTigue's corner and raising his right hand in victory. One of Mike's cornermen, overcome with emotion, fell to the floor, unconscious. McTigue's jubilant fans clambered into the ring and hoisted the new champion on their shoulders.

In a packed dressing room, with congratulations the order of the day, McTigue said: 'I thought I won comfortably, and only my right thumb went, I would have stopped him. I beat him to the punch two to one. He didn't land a clean blow in the full twenty rounds, and I had no doubt what the final verdict would be. Siki had only two punches all night, a left and right lead, and I was able to block them both. He's lucky I only had one hand most of the time.'

Siki was crestfallen. 'I protest that I won the fight but didn't get the decision,' he said. 'Of the twenty rounds, I felt I won at least seventeen and my corner thought so too, with McTigue winning the other three but they took the title off me. This the last time I'll box in Ireland.'

While some felt that Siki had a case, with the Parisian newspaper *Le Journal* calling the decision 'iniquitous' and Carpentier saying it was 'incomprehensible and indefensible', most neutral observers were of the view that McTigue's better boxing and ring generalship were the deciding factors. A victory for skill and scientific boxing over big punching and aggression.

Referee Smith could not be located in the packed theatre for immediate comment but in a statement the next day, he justified his verdict: 'I understand there is considerable controversy over my decision. Some, I believe, think that a draw should have been the verdict, but McTigue had secured a sufficient lead on points which left me in no doubt as to the winner.

'Granted that Siki was the aggressor for the greater part of the contest, yet in his retreats and evasions the Irishman was continually scoring and generally out-boxing his opponent. Siki was the better fighter, but as a boxer he was distinctly outclassed. Except when he caused McTigue's eye to bleed, Siki never had his opponent in any difficulty.'

It was some time before everybody left the La Scala, later called the Capitol, a popular venue for cinemagoers before it was pulled down. Today it is a department store. 'When the crowd left, there was great excitement in Sackville Street consequent on a number of shots being fired,' reported the *Cork Examiner*. 'From somewhere in the vicinity there was a rapid burst of revolver fire. Immediately a wild stampede for safety occurred, many people being trampled in the rush. Screaming women ran hither and thither while several more sought to cower by throwing themselves on the ground.

'Even by doing so they took the risk of being trampled on. The crowd hastily dispersed afterwards and in a few minutes the street was deserted. A man identified as James O'Shea of Harcourt Street was admitted to Jervis Street Hospital, suffering from a bullet wound in the leg. He is said to have been shot on Westmoreland Street.'

When McTigue returned to New York, who was waiting at the docks – surprise! surprise! – but his former manager Joe Jacobs, who had earlier given up on the Clareman. Now Mike, supposedly washed up as a boxer, was world champion. They teamed up again and this time Jacobs had something to sell.

He went straight to promoter Tex Rickard and proposed a match with Gene Tunney, the American lightheavyweight champion and future world heavy-weight king. Rickard agreed, and promised if McTigue put his title on the line, there would be $125,000 as his purse. Jacobs nearly swallowed his cigar in trying to hide his joy. But Mike refused to go along with the plan. He felt that Rickard was grooming Tunney for a Dempsey title fight and that he would be cheated out of the title.

'Listen, you idiot,' barked Jacobs. 'You may be the lightheavyweight cham-pion of the world but how many more good pay days have you left? Take this one. You'll easily beat this kid anyway.' But McTigue would not be moved. Jacobs said he also had an offer to meet a local hope, Young Stribling, in Colum-bus, Georgia in a no decision contest, which McTigue accepted. 'We will bring our own referee, too, Harry Ertle,' Jacobs promised.

Billed as the Georgia Peach, Stribling was a lightheavyweight in whom the state had great faith. Born William Lawrence Stribling, he grew up in a circus family before turning to boxing. The bout was scheduled for 4 October 1923. At first, everything went smoothly, with both boxers and their teams arriving in Columbus ready for action. Mike was in the best of condition, but two days before the fight he fractured the little finger of his left hand.

McTigue refused to go through with the fight and from his hotel room called the promoter, Major John Paul Jones, head of the committee of the American

Legion who were putting on the bout. When they met, Mike told him that the fight was off. Jones, his face red with rage, told Mike he would have to go through with the contest, that everything was arranged and that was all there was to it. McTigue still refused and was starting to pack when, a little later, several men entered his room claiming to be doctors. They examined the hand and said there was no break and that the champion was fit to box.

Mike still refused before he was told they were members of the dreaded Ku Klux Klan, a right-wing organisation which advocated white supremacy and white nationalism. This time, however, they were without their traditional white robes, masks and conical hats, but still the genuine article.

'We stand no nonsense in the South, McTigue,' said one, thought to be the ringleader. 'If you don't fight, you'll never leave this town alive. We'll string you all up on that tree down the road. You will be watched wherever you go. We mean business.'

With that they left, but placed two armed guards on the door outside day and night. When the time came to go to the arena, a force of men escorted Mc-Tigue, Jacobs and trainer Dai Dollings through the streets of Columbus and into the arena. Compared with this, Dublin had been a picnic.

The Klansmen had got their way but the fans did not get good value for their money. It was a dull encounter. When McTigue entered the ring he was shocked to be told by Jacobs that the commission had changed the bout to a title fight, despite its advertisement as a no decision fight.

Even with the help of their own referee, Mike wanted to pull out there and then, but noticing some familiar Ku Klux Klan faces at ringside, with one of them revealing a pistol, he thought it best to go through with it, even if his precious title was on the line. He had also been informed that referee Ertle was instructed to award the decision and the title to Stribling, 'or Ertle would not leave town alive'.

After ten fairly even rounds, with one boxer and then the other gaining an advantage, Ertle called it a draw, allowing McTigue to keep his title, and stipulating that Stribling, the Ku Klux Klan man, was not beaten. But this did not please the Klansmen who wanted an outright victory for their boxer and several of them reached for their revolvers, as threatened. Nor were Stribling's supporters happy with the draw. Suddenly, there was a riot, with the crowd storming the ring, swamping the Klansmen. Finally, the referee appealed for calm and announced that an error had been made and that Stribling was the winner and new champion.

Meanwhile Ertle, McTigue, Jacobs and trainer Dollings made their way through the crowd to the dressing room, grabbed their things and left town straight away. The next day, safe from the clutches of the Ku Klux Klan and hundreds of miles from Columbus, the referee phoned the newspapers and agencies, as well as Jacobs, and told them that the original drawn verdict was now the official result and that McTigue was still world champion.

Five months later Mike had a return with Stribling in Newark, New Jersey but it was a no decision bout with no danger to his title. He would lose the championship in a Bronx ring on 30 May 1925 when Paul Berlenbach, a New Yorker of German origin, won a fifteen round decision. A former Olympic wrestling champion, Berlenbach simply hit too hard for the veteran Clareman. McTigue would subsequently beat Berlenbach in four rounds but the New Yorker had lost his title by then.

Just before the Christmas of 1925, Mike heard the shock news that his old rival Battling Siki had been shot dead in Hell's Kitchen, an area of squalor, drunkenness and violence in New York. At around 4 a.m., patrolman James J. Meehan on his beat discovered Siki lying face downwards on the wet pavement at the corner of Ninth Avenue and West Forty-first Street. He had two bullet holes in his back. There were stories that Siki, who was twenty-eight, had been shot after staggering from a bar where he could not pay the twenty dollars for drinks but his killer was never found.

No longer with Joe Jacobs, who had given up on him, McTigue had planned to retire once January 1926 came in, and settle back in County Clare with his wife. He had a little money and they would get by. One afternoon while strolling along Broadway, he chanced to meet boxing man-about-town James J. Johnston, who also happened to be one of the most influential managers in the business. Johnston was surprised by McTigue's retirement plans and said: 'Forget it, Mike. There's a lot of fight left in you yet, I can tell you.'

McTigue had mixed luck on his comeback, losing in four rounds to the skilful Canadian contender and future world lightheavyweight champion Jack Delaney. But he got the better of the strong heavyweight Johnny Risko and had his revenge over Berlenbach. In a match in March 1927 against Jack Sharkey, the Bostonian who was heading for the world heavyweight title, McTigue, conceding almost one and a half stone, was ahead on points when he received a badly cut mouth from a left hook in the twelfth round and the fight was stopped.

Seven months later Johnston secured a match with Tommy Loughran in New York for the vacant world lightheavyweight title at Madison Square Garden. It was close, a clash between two master craftsmen with Loughran, at twenty-five, ten years the younger man. At the finish Loughran sportingly walked over to McTigue's corner and said: 'You won, Mike.' 'No, Tommy, the decision is yours,' replied McTigue. 'You deserve it.'

Joe Humphries, the celebrated master of ceremonies, went to Loughran's corner, raised Tommy's right hand and announced him as 'Winnah and new champeen'. As both boxers left the ring, there was shouting and cheering. Those in the cheaper seats upstairs cheered Mike and waved green flags.

It was McTigue's last shot at a title. In the following years he won some, lost some, drew some and fought a few no decisions before calling it a day in the summer of 1930 after a distinguished ring career lasting twenty-one years. In his retirement he was introduced at big fights and attended boxing dinners, the celebrity ex-champion. But his $500,000 fortune was whittled away by bad investments and in particular by the Wall Street Crash of October 1929.

With the help of friends, however, McTigue later got together enough money to run a bar on Long Island before succumbing to poverty and ill health. He died in Queens General Hospital, New York on 12 August 1966 at the age of seventy-four. Thousands of people turned out for his funeral, including Jack Dempsey, Gene Tunney and former opponents like Paul Berlenbach and Tommy Loughran to pay their final respects to one of Ireland's greatest warriors who always gave his best, irrespective of the result. A true fighter to the very end.

6. Tom Sharkey

The sailor and the four-masted schooner

It was big fight night in New York. As the crowd filed into the Coney Island Athletic Club in the borough of Brooklyn on the cold evening of 3 November 1899, anticipation was high that the world heavyweight championship fight between the holder James J. Jeffries, the Californian Grizzly Bear, and his challenger Tom Sharkey from Dundalk, County Louth would not be short of action.

Jeffries was big, strong and seemingly impervious to punishment, and he had the ability to intimidate opponents as well as being able to punch with power, setting them up with a stiff left jab which carried destructive force. He had won the title five months earlier by knocking out another big hitter, Bob Fitzsimmons in eleven rounds, also in Coney Island, in one of boxing's biggest upsets. But in 'Sailor Tom' Sharkey he was taking on the toughest challenger around, a man who refused to take a backward step and was brimming with confidence.

Possessing a solid square jaw that looked to be made of iron, with broad shoulders, a bull-like neck, and power in his fists, Sharkey had no intention of missing out on his big chance. Jeffries entered the ring as the seven to five on favourite because of his impressive knockout over Fitzsimmons, the conqueror of Gentleman Jim Corbett. But Sharkey was convinced, as were his supporters in the US and back in Ireland, that he had the ability to take the title off Jeffries, and made no secret of his intentions in interviews with the press in the lead up to the fight. The battle looked like being a thriller.

The Dundalk battler stood only 5 ft 8½ in, as against Jeffries at 6 ft 1½ in, and he generally weighed around 12 st 12 lb, a little over today's lightheavyweight limit. For Jeffries he came in at a heavy 13 st 5 lb, with James J. weighing 15 st 4 lb. Sharkey feared nobody, inside or outside the roped square. Indeed, at the end of his career in 1904, the prominent names on his record read like a boxing encyclopaedia – besides Jeffries, he mixed with the likes of Corbett, Fitzsimmons, Joe Choynski, Gus Ruhlin and Kid McCoy, all formidable boxers.

The first feature Sharkey's opponents always noticed was that his massive chest was decorated with tattoos of a four-masted sailing ship and a large star, a legacy of his days in the American Navy. Crowning his overall rugged appearance was a large cauliflower ear on his left side. Cauliflower ears are more associated with rugby players today but in the past, they were many boxers' trademarks. When he retired, he put a notice in a newspaper in California where he lived, as well as spreading the word himself, offering $5,000 to anybody who could restore his ear to normality, 'to make me prettier', as he joked.

A noted specialist undertook the job but there were complications and Sharkey pulled out of the operation at the last minute, deciding to keep his trademark for the rest of his days. Looking in the mirror in the surgery, he turned to the specialist and said: 'I guess you shouldn't really interfere with nature so the ear stays put!' And that was it.

Sharkey was born in Hill Street, Dundalk on 23 November 1873, the fifth of ten children, to James Sharkey, a railwayman, and the former Margaret Kelly, both local people. Tom had very limited schooling but always had a sense of adventure, yearning to see the world. He went to work on the small merchant vessels that plied their trade to Liverpool and ports in Scotland. Later he worked as a cabin boy on larger ships on the same routes before getting on vessels that took him all around the world.

'I enjoyed my time at sea,' he recalled in later years. 'The first work I ever did was on board a ship. Going over to Scotland, I used to take my turn at the wheel and often went eighteen, nineteen, twenty hours at a stretch without sleep. Later on I shipped on larger vessels and travelled the Seven Seas, from London to Cape Town, Hong Kong to Sydney, San Francisco to the coast of China and into the Arctic, to Alaska, through the Indian Ocean and ports where no white man had ever set foot.

'I had my share of dramatic moments with typhoons in the Indian Ocean and hurricanes in the Pacific and no fewer than four shipwrecks. Many a day I spent in an open boat without a drop of water passing my lips. Yes, you could say that my experiences read like something out of Sinbad the Sailor, only mine were true.'

A few weeks after sailing out of New Orleans, Sharkey found himself in New York harbour when he decided to quit his own ship, hitch his way to the Brooklyn navy yard and enlist in the US Navy. 'If I love the sea so much, why don't I do the natural thing and join the navy,' he reasoned, and joined up. It was while watching the training sessions aboard ship every evening from seven to nine, with officers acting as referees, that he got the boxing bug. Soon, Sharkey was invited to join the sessions and enjoyed them so much that he made up his mind to become a boxer and quickly established himself as a formidable problem for any of his shipmates to tackle.

His training period completed, Sharkey was assigned to the cruiser, the USS *Philadelphia*, when it was rushed to Honolulu early in 1893 to protect American interests during a revolution that had broken out against the ruling native dynasty. It was on the Hawaiian island that Sharkey began his actual ring career, and after he blasted his way through the heavyweight championship of the American fleet, rivalry developed with British sailors also stationed there. As it happened, they were no match for the squat, powerful Dundalk man with the heavy wallop in both fists.

At one stage, the British Navy imported their own champion Jim Gardner from England 'to give this little Irishman a lesson and restore pride to their fleet' but Sharkey put him down and out in four rounds. Even though neither boxer was paid and it was therefore technically an amateur contest, some claim the Gardner fight was Sharkey's first as a professional.

Indeed, there are conflicting contemporary reports as to when the Dundalk boxer actually began his professional career, with historians coming up with different versions. Record compilers also differ, and not even his recent biographers Greg Lewis and Moira Sharkey, a distant relation of Tom, are certain. *Ring* magazine was, and still is, also unclear but the influential Boxing Register, published by the International Boxing Hall of Fame in New York and regarded universally as the world's official record book, lists the Gardner fight in Honolulu as his first official professional bout, appropriately enough on St Patrick's Day 1893.

Wherever the facts lie between his amateur and professional boxing careers, Sharkey put in eighteen months in Honolulu, and in that time had fourteen bouts, all ending in knockouts, though some records show that he lost one, George Washington knocking him out in seven rounds in February 1894. During that summer, the USS *Philadelphia* left Hawaii and put in at the Mare Island naval base in San Francisco. With his naval service coming to an end, he became a civilian and continued his ring activities by taking fights in Colma and Vallejo.

One of these fights, in Colma in July 1895 was against Australian Billy Smith, a prominent professional, and Sharkey knocked him out in seven rounds. This convinced Tom that his future lay in the ring and offered a good future for him. He was recommended to meet up with Tim McGrath, a prominent boxing manager with all the right contacts and who had emigrated from County Limerick. Under McGrath's influence, Sharkey soon gained a reputation as a very promising boxer with a solid punch with either glove, and as tough as old war boots.

McGrath matched him with Alex Greggains, a fading but still crafty veteran who knew his way around the rings. Their clash, in March 1896 at the Bush Street Theatre in San Francisco, which was one of the centres of American boxing activity at the time, ended in a draw after eight rounds, though many felt that the Dundalk battler deserved the decision.

At ringside was Joe Choynski, a former local blacksmith and now one of the world's leading heavyweight contenders. Choynski stopped Sharkey on his way out of the ring and put a proposition to him. 'Fight me, Tom, and if you're still on your feet at the end of eight rounds, you'll get the decision.' It was an offer too good to refuse and they met at the People's Palace in San Francisco in April 1896.

In the opening round Sharkey rushed the American Jew and sent him head first out of the ring. When Choynski got back, Sharkey kept the pressure on him but was unable to land another solid punch on his skilful rival. The Louthman took considerable punishment from the more experienced Choynski, who had boxed a draw with Bob Fitzsimmons, the reigning world middleweight champion and future lightheavyweight and heavyweight king. But more importantly, Sharkey was still on his feet at the finish and as per agreement won the decision.

Among the crowd was the great James J. Corbett. At the final bell, Corbett climbed into the ring in full dress attire as befitting his Gentleman Jim tag and offered to take on Sharkey. Corbett had been out of the ring since relinquishing his world heavyweight title a year earlier but was embarking on a comeback aimed at re-establishing himself as champion, even though everybody, including the boxing authorities, still regarded him as the title-holder. The match was set for the Mechanics Pavilion in San Francisco in June 1896.

James John Corbett, whose father Pat was from Kilmaine, County Mayo and his mother Catherine from Dublin, is credited with becoming the first world heavyweight champion under the new Marquis of Queensberry Rules when he knocked out John L. Sullivan in twenty-one rounds in New Orleans in September 1892. A master boxer with fast footwork and a tight defence, Corbett revolutionised the sport and is often called 'the father of modern scientific boxing'.

James J. was born and reared in San Francisco. After finishing high school and getting into many street fights, he started his working life as a bank clerk, but always with a boxing career in mind. By night he was able to sharpen his skills by taking on all comers on saloon stages. However, it was not until he was taken under the care of Walter Watson, the instructor at the San Francisco Olympic Club, on the recommendation of the bank manager, that he began to make real progress in the sport.

After winning the heavyweight title in a big upset, he made just one defence, knocking out England's Charlie Mitchell in three rounds in Jacksonville, Florida in January 1894 and contented himself by mainly boxing exhibitions and personal appearances as well as touring in a play. When he got the offer to meet Sharkey, he was somewhat out of condition and insisted the fight should be over four rounds. It was a lucky move, for Corbett that is, for while he was able to outbox the unskilful, if immensely strong, Sharkey for the first two rounds, he ran out of stamina in the third and fourth rounds when the ex-sailor was able to rough him up.

A weary Corbett flopped on his stool at the finish. Referee Frank Carr called the bout a draw but the verdict met with noisy disapproval from the crowd who clearly thought that Sharkey should have won. In truth, James J. had taken the Louthman too lightly and was so exhausted he could not leave his corner for over half an hour.

'Carr told us before we started that there should be no hitting in the clinches, but in the first round Corbett ignored those instructions and landed a punch in my right eye,' recalled Sharkey in later years. 'The punch gave me the only black eye I ever had in my career. Naturally I thought that Carr would at least say something about Corbett having such disregard to the rules but when he didn't, it made me so mad that I forgot all about Corbett being the world champion. I just put my head down and sailed in.

'Had the fight lasted another few rounds I would have knocked him out. Corbett may have gone into the ring smiling and confident but he came out of it trembling and crestfallen, having narrowly escaped being a whipped man.'

In a statement after the fight, Corbett said: 'When I say that Sharkey is a good strong man, I tell the whole story. I had no difficulty hitting Sharkey but he can stand more punishment than the ordinary man. I could have blinded him by continuing to hit him in the right eye, which I nearly closed in the second round but it would have done no good to hurt the fellow that much so I refrained from hitting the eye.

'If my seconds had made the claim I would have secured the decision on fouls as he continually gave me the shoulder and cross buttock. But they had instructions to claim no fouls. I am ready for Sharkey in a longer fight. Finish fights are what I desire and not four-round contests in which a man cannot fight scientifically but must slug and wrestle.'

Corbett was prepared to come out of his 'retirement' and defend the title against Sharkey whenever the fight could be arranged but Bob Fitzsimmons, the English-born former world middleweight champion who had now moved up to heavyweight, was claiming first call. Meanwhile, Sharkey visited New York, and in Jimmy Wakely's saloon, a popular venue for sporting celebrities, he was introduced to a man he had greatly admired, the great John L. Sullivan.

The old former world heavyweight champion was down on his luck and plans were being made to stage a benefit for him in Madison Square Garden. Sharkey offered his services and it was arranged to have him and John L. box an exhibition over three rounds as the feature of the programme. The show proved a big success and took in $10,000 for Sullivan. 'Anything for one of my idols,' said Sharkey later. 'I was glad I could help him in some way.'

Sharkey and his manager Tim McGrath stayed on in New York for several weeks before heading back to San Francisco where they learned that Fitzsimmons and his people were bidding for a title match with Corbett. Fitzsimmons fancied his chances of winning a second world title. There was now only one way to settle the matter to decide the number one contender and the next challenger for Corbett. Sharkey and Fitz were matched for the Mechanics Pavilion, San Francisco in December 1896.

Nobody looked more like a boxer than Fitzsimmons, balding, freckled and with his spindly legs, but Bob's years working as a blacksmith gave him powerful well-muscled shoulders enabling him to punch with terrific strength. Born in Cornwall, Fitzsimmons, whose father came from Omagh in County Tyrone, moved to New Zealand with his family as a boy and later to Australia before sailing to the US where he would achieve his first major success, winning the middleweight championship of the world in January 1891. Now he had designs on the heavyweight title.

The Sharkey–Fitzsimmons match attracted tremendous interest. Nearly twenty thousand fans crammed into the pavilion, while thousands of others, unable to gain admittance, milled around outside, awaiting the result. The start of the fight was delayed by a wrangle over the referee, with Sharkey's manager turning down several names on the grounds that he did not trust them.

McGrath finally came up with the remarkable choice of Wyatt Earp, the notorious gunfighter who will always be remembered for his involvement in the famous Gunfight at the O.K. Corral in Tombstone, Arizona in 1881. Earp, who was in town with some horses he was running in the races, had been deputy marshal in several towns. A fearless man who stood no nonsense, he boasted that he lived by the gun and was alleged to have shot dead ten men, including his brother-in-law Ike Clanton.

Earp's qualifications as a referee would have to be questionable but Mc-Grath felt he would be fair to Sharkey, a view that did not go down very well with Fitzsimmons' manager Martin Julian, who claimed the gunfighter was a pal of Sharkey's. Finally, Fitzsimmons intervened and said: 'Look, I don't care who's the referee. I'll knock out the Irishman anyhow.' There was further delay when an official politely asked Earp to take off his black frock coat and his gunbelt, complete with the famous six-shooter which had taken care of business at the O.K. Corral and many saloons across the Old West.

Earp whipped the gun from its holster and, holding it threateningly under the official's nose, said: 'Any objections?' It was only when the police captain Charles W. Whitman climbed into the ring and demanded of Earp that he surrendered his coat and gunbelt that he reluctantly complied.

The scrawny-looking Fitzsimmons with the big shoulders dominated the action from the start, peppering Sharkey's face with long, stinging left jabs and jarring right uppercuts. The Dundalk battler seemed unable to solve the Englishman's shifting style and a solid right to the chin almost dropped Tom in the seventh round.

Midway through the eighth Fitzsimmons hurt his man with a terrific right to the chin and the Sailor reeled like a ship in a storm. He followed up with a tremendous left hook to the body which sent Sharkey down as though a trapdoor had opened beneath him. Earp started the count before beckoning the announcer Billy Jordan into the ring, asking for his frock coat and gun belt complete with his six-shooter, and declaring: 'Tell the crowd I'm disqualifying Fitzsimmons for a low blow. He hit Sharkey in the groin and if nobody else saw it, I did. And if anybody wants to argue, I'm ready.'

As Sharkey grimaced on the canvas clutching his groin, Earp bent down and stuffed his $10,000 purse into his left glove and said: 'It's all yours.' Fitzsimmons' manager Martin Julian yelled: 'Robbery, robbery' and continued his loud protest in the dressing room, but Earp insisted the final blow was definitely low. 'No man has ever questioned my honour,' he said. 'I've been in many places and in peculiar situations but nobody ever said before tonight that I was guilty of a dishonest act. I repeat that I decided it in all fairness, and with judgement as true as my eyesight that I saw a foul blow.'

Julian obtained a court order upholding Sharkey's purse pending an investigation but the court subsequently decided in the Dundalkman's favour and the result went into the record books as a win for Sharkey by disqualification. Sixty-five years later, *Ring* magazine writer Daniel M. Daniel recalled a conversation he had with Bat Masterson, another Wild West gunslinger and who was boxing writer for the *New York Morning Telegraph* at the time.

Masterson told Daniel that the fight was part of a deal, and that Earp and Fitzsimmons' manager Julian had bet heavily on Sharkey winning, cleaning up on the result. Masterson said the court case was merely a sham. All these claims were stoutly denied by Julian. Alas, the alleged plot was never substantiated as all the principals were dead at the time of the new revelations.

Despite Sharkey's official win, public sympathy was with Fitzsimmons and it was the Englishman who got the title fight with Corbett three months later. On St Patrick's Day 1897 at Carson City, a gold rush town high in the Nevada mountains, Fitzsimmons knocked out Gentleman Jim in fourteen rounds with a similar left hook to the one which put Sharkey down. Corbett's corner called 'Foul' but the pleas were ignored. By now, the blow had become a legitimate one in the rule books and would go down in boxing history as Bob Fitzsimmons' famous solar-plexus punch.

It was revealed later that Corbett had already signed for the Fitzsimmons fight three months before Fitz fought Sharkey so the Irishman was never really in the frame. It was the second time the Dundalk battler was deprived of a rightful title fight, having previously been robbed of a chance when he got the better of Corbett, who was world champion at the time, and had to be content with a draw.

It seemed that Sharkey, nevertheless, could hardly avoid controversy. He was involved in another one three months after the Corbett–Fitzsimmons title fight when he squared off against the Galway heavyweight Peter Maher at the Palace Athletic Club, New York in June 1897. After six rounds of a wild encounter, neither boxer gained an advantage, although one right to Sharkey's face in the fifth made him dizzy and groggy. When he got back to his corner, he said to McGrath: 'I saw three Maher's in that round.' 'That's ok, Tom,' replied the manager. 'Go out there and hit the one in the middle.'

In the seventh round, Maher put Sharkey down with a right to the head. As the Dundalkman was getting to his feet, Maher landed another right to the head as the bell rang, with Sharkey's manager yelling 'Foul'. Corbett, who was assigned by the *Chicago Tribune* to cover the fight, described the scene like this: 'Tom was a raving lunatic. He was still slamming away at Maher and didn't stop even when the referee tried to pull him away.

'The ring was filled by policemen and still Sharkey fought on. He hurt Joe Choynski, his cornerman, when Joe tried to soothe him. A rope was thrown around the enraged sailor but before they had him secured, he bashed one of Maher's seconds in the face and opened a deep gash in his head. The fight ended with a draw being declared.'

Sharkey packed his bags in the spring on 1897 for a short trip home, and had three fights, though none of any great significance – knocking out Jim Craig in the first in Belfast, Pat McCourt in the second in Warrenpoint and Tom Parks in the first in Dundalk. It was now back to business in the US where he continued his campaign for a world heavyweight title fight, with a return match with his old rival Joe Choynski at the Woodward's Pavilion in San Francisco two weeks before St Patrick's Day 1898.

Sharkey had won the first fight on points two years earlier and planned to repeat his win this time. Scheduled for twenty rounds, he had the Jew down three times in the fifth and once in the sixth. In between, according to the *Kansas City Star*, 'Sharkey repeatedly used his elbows and head, wrestling his opponent at every opportunity and was lucky to avoid disqualification.'

At the start of the eighth he again rushed Choynski, this time across the ring, sending him through the ropes and to the floor, four feet below the ring. The American came crashing down directly in front of the chief of police, Captain Lees. Incensed, Lees ordered Choynski back into the ring immediately and demanded the fight be stopped. Referee George Green then yelled: 'Draw.'

Sharkey, feeling cheated of victory, rushed over to the official remonstrating and, according to the *Brooklyn Eagle*, 'was threatened with arrest'. He cooled down after being hustled to his corner by the police now in the ring, though still yelling that he was robbed.

The heavyweight scene was changing by now, with the arrival of a young man born on a farm in Carroll, Ohio named James Jackson Jeffries. The newcomer's family later moved to a farmland in California when James J., as he was now called, was seven. After leaving school he had various jobs as well as doing his stint on the farm. These included working as a meat packer and in a tin mine as well as a riveter in the boiler house of the Santa Fe railroad in San Bernardino.

Jeffries learned his boxing at the East Side Athletic Club in Los Angeles before turning professional and running up an impressive record with no defeats, picking up nicknames like the Californian Grizzly Bear and the Californian Boilermaker. Spotted by Corbett's manager, the impresario William A. Brady, Jeffries was soon a sparring partner of Gentleman Jim and picked up many tips from the former champion. Now unbeaten in nine fights, he looked set for a chance at Bob Fitzsimmons' world title, but first there was the formidable challenge of Sharkey to overcome.

Sharkey and Jeffries were matched to clash at the Mechanics Pavilion, a venue he was familiar with in San Francisco, on 6 May 1898. Interest in the scheduled twenty-rounder was so keen that promoter 'Sunny Jim' Coffroth needed to find more seating urgently. He found a builder who hastily built up the bleachers on the main floor. However, on the afternoon of the bout, the stand holding the press box collapsed but it was quickly put together again. Then, during one of the preliminaries, a high section of seats holding about five hundred fans crashed to the floor.

People were screaming and struggling to get out of the wreckage as ambulances arrived. Several people were injured, though not seriously, and it was a miracle that nobody was killed. Spectators were moved to a different stand. A little later, and still during the preliminaries, a second stand on the far side of the arena collapsed, followed by a third. Several more were rushed to hospital, again with no serious injuries but by now there was panic in the hall. Fans were screaming, and dashing all over the place. What next?

It was hoped that there would be no further disasters and there was an announcement from ringside that everything was now fine and calm could be restored. Many people who had paid good money now had to stand, and the air was full of dust. Jeffries entered the ring a slight ten to nine favourite. 'Do you see that sailing ship on Sharkey's front?' he remarked to his trainer Billy Delaney. 'Well, keep your eye on it because I'm going to sink it.'

When referee Alec Greggains, who had boxed a draw with Sharkey two years earlier in his fighting days, called both men together to the centre of the ring, it was noticeable that they were in top condition, with each looking fully confident. From the bell, Jeffries was on the attack, driving Sharkey before him with pile-driving lefts and rights, and while the gritty Dundalk battler was never in any real trouble, Tom knew he would have to keep the pressure on his bigger foe all the way.

By the sixth round Sharkey had moved in front with his powerful smashes to the head and body, roared on by a group of sailors who had come along to cheer on their old mate. As the boxers slugged it out, there was a loud crash. Both men stepped back and saw that a section of the temporary seats in the gallery had caved in and hundreds of people were sliding down and being wedged against the rail, despite an assurance from ringside after the earlier crashes that everything was all right. Just as they resumed fighting, another section of seats collapsed on the main floor. Would there be anything left of the hall by the finish?

In a bruising ninth round Sharkey smashed Jeffries' nose and cut his lip. The big man seemed to be running out of energy but he stormed back in the tenth and eleventh rounds with renewed vigour as the furious fighting continued. Just then, yet another section of the seats went down in the balcony, spectators falling to the floor, with some going over the rail. Both fighters were too intensely involved in their battle to pay too much attention this time as they heard, in Jeffries' own words: 'Shrieks, groans, cries and crashes.'

Interestingly, some twenty-four years later, Jeffries asked Sharkey: 'Did you see those seats fall?' The Dundalkman replied that he didn't because: 'I was too busy with you.' Sharkey then asked Jeffries the same question, to which James J. answered: 'No, I was too busy as you were.'

From the twelfth to the fifteenth rounds, it was a slugfest with Sharkey landing some smashing body blows but Jeffries seemed that bit fresher. Jeffries' biographer Jim Carney Junior described the last two rounds like this: 'Tom, fighting with renewed frenzy, charged in and more or less held his own. As the verdict was announced, the crowd cheered when referee Greggains raised Jim's hand and three of the four newspaper reporters present agreed with the verdict.'

Sharkey claimed he should have had a win, or at least a draw but he was not too vociferous about it. On requesting a rematch, Jeffries replied: 'Tom, you've given me my toughest fight, and when I win the title, you will be my first challenger and that's a promise.'

A knockout in just over two minutes in Brooklyn, New York over one of the leading heavyweight contenders Gus Ruhlin in June 1898 put Sharkey back in the title picture and got him a return with old foe James J. Corbett. Gentleman Jim had lost his world heavyweight title to Bob Fitzsimmons a year earlier and was anxious to re-establish himself as a strong contender for his old championship. He had also kept himself in training.

Sharkey was keen to show that his loss to Jeffries was just a blip and felt confident he would take care of Corbett again, still feeling sore about being robbed in their drawn encounter two years earlier.

They were rematched for the Lenox Club in Brooklyn, New York in November, and it ended in a near riot. With his clever boxing and neat footwork, Corbett built up an early lead but seemed to tire as the bout progressed and the durable Sharkey was beginning the make things very unpleasant for him. James J. was warned in the ninth for hitting low and a few seconds later, while the boxers were in a clinch, one of Corbett's seconds Jim McVey, angered at Sharkey's wild slugging and complete disregard for the rules including hitting on the break, suddenly climbed into the ring, demanding that the Irishman be disqualified.

McVey's actions were, of course, against the rules as nobody besides the boxers and the referee are allowed inside the ring while the contest is in progress. The referee John Kelly, with the delightful nickname Honest John, had no option but to disqualify Corbett. His decision did not please the crowd, to put it mildly, and there were shouts of 'Robbery' and 'Corbett, you quitter.'

The result meant that Sharkey had been deprived of a more decisive victory as he had been in front at the time of the termination. There were allegations of a fix, with claims that referee Kelly was not to allow Corbett to be knocked out or stopped.

'Had a decision gone against Corbett on a knockout or on points, the ex-champion would have been relegated to a rear seat forever,' said the *Brooklyn Daily Eagle*. 'That Corbett's backers could not afford to lose on anything but a foul was apparent. It was the almost unanimous opinion of the crowd that saw the fight that had the affair progressed it could only have ended in a defeat for Corbett. In eight rounds of utmost exertion, Sullivan's conqueror could not shake Sharkey nor stop his rushes for an instant.'

The truth was never really established as to the fix allegations but Sharkey continued on his campaign to get a world title fight with Fitzsimmons. He accepted a challenge from Kid McCoy, the former world middleweight champion now boxing as a heavyweight. One of the best and most popular boxers of the 1890s, McCoy, from Rush County, Indiana was also one of the most controversial. He was the inventor of the 'corkscrew punch', which added a twist at the moment of impact, slashing and mauling opponents to excess.

McCoy delighted in such illegal antics, away from the referee's gaze, or on the 'blind side'. A conman in boxing gloves, he would try any tactic to win, or gain an unfair advantage. He would sometimes stop and point to the crowd and then slug his unwary opponent who was gullible enough to look away. On other occasions he would spray tacks on the canvas and as his rival looked down, the Kid would apply the finishing punch.

When he signed to fight Tommy Ryan, the world welterweight champion, in a non-title fight in 1896, he went out to Ryan's training camp with a thin layer of white power on his face and told the champion he was not feeling well, was not in good condition, and would Ryan take it easy on him. As a result Ryan, feeling sorry for his opponent, eased up on his training. However, on the day of the fight, the Kid was in superb condition and proceeded to hammer the surprised and unfit champion round after round and won by a knockout in the fifteenth round.

McCoy won the world middleweight title the following year but fancied his chances at the heavyweight title, especially after beating one of the top contenders Gus Ruhlin. Victory over Sharkey would enhance his chances but Tom had other ideas. They met at the Lenox Athletic Club in New York in January 1899, before a crowd of six thousand, with the winner collecting seventy per cent of the $20,000 purse plus a percentage of the gate.

McCoy, much the lighter man, began confidently, dancing around and jabbing with his left. He knew that Sharkey would not fall for any of his illegal tricks and he resorted to using his skill and accurate punching. The Dundalkman, however, was much the stronger hitter and while Sharkey had to climb off the floor twice, his harder blows told in the end. In the tenth round a powerful left hook to the chin sent McCoy to the canvas.

Referee Tim Hurst counted McCoy out but neither boxer heard the count amid all the noise. The Kid struggled to his feet and attempted to land a right on Sharkey but the Irishman knocked him back against the ropes with a straight right. Hurst jumped between the two men and shouted to the Dundalk battler: 'It's all over, Sharkey, I've already counted McCoy out. Go to your corner.'

Sharkey now sought a championship fight with Fitzsimmons, and kept in shape by knocking out Jack McCormack in two rounds in Philadelphia three weeks later. But the following June, the heavyweight picture changed dramatically when Fitzsimmons surprisingly lost his title to the underestimated James J. Jeffries, who was having only his thirteenth fight, on a knockout in eleven rounds in New York. Sharkey now focussed his attention on Jeffries. He was confident of getting a title chance, especially as Jeffries had told him after their earlier fight that if he ever won the title that Tom would be his first challenger.

Jeffries kept to his word, and in the fight briefly introduced at the beginning of this chapter, they met at the Coney Island Athletic Club in Brooklyn, New York on 3 November 1899. The twenty-five rounder turned out to be one of the most punishing fights in ring history. It was held beneath the glare of four hundred blazing arc lamps radiating 100 °F heat, set up so as the fight could be held in the brightest light possible.

It was the first fight for which film was shot under artificial lights, and both boxers would complain later that because the lights were so low their scalps were blistered by the half-way stage, even though a large umbrella had been placed in each corner as a shade during the intervals. The referee was George Siler, one of America's leading officials who combined his duties in the ring with the day job as chief sports correspondent of the *Chicago Tribune*.

Neither champion or challenger asked for any favours. Nor did they give or receive any. For a purse of $25,000, winner take all, this was the big one, the heavyweight championship of the world, and they would give fans who paid from $5 to $25 their money's worth. Lighter by just under two stone and shorter by five inches, Sharkey made light of his physical disadvantages by forcing the pace. Although dropped twice in the second round he hurt Jeffries in the sixth with a pile-driving left hook to the body and roughed him up to such an extent that the champion finished the round bleeding from the ear and mouth.

By the fifteenth, Sharkey was ahead on points and kept yelling: 'Fall, damn it, fall.' But the champion was as tough as the rivets he used to drive with his bare hands into the boilers where he worked in his pre-boxing days before the invention of the electric hammer. He kept punching away and gradually began to get on top. While Sharkey was still firing with strong lefts and rights, Jeffries' was landing with more effective right uppercuts by the twentieth round and Sharkey seemed glad to hear the bell.

The Dundalk battler was still flaying away, nevertheless, in the final five rounds, determined to finish on his feet. In the twenty-fifth session, he fell short with a long right to the head, allowing Jeffries to quickly land a stunning right uppercut. They were still fighting busily up to the last bell, after which referee Siler pointed to Jeffries as 'winner and still champion'.

Sharkey stamped his feet and shouted: 'I won, I won,' before being calmed down by his cornermen. On leaving the ring, Siler said to the ringside reporters that while Sharkey might have felt he should have won, Jeffries deserved to keep his title. 'It was close all the way but how can you take away a man's title when he fought like that,' he remarked. Sharkey was still complaining in the dressing room: 'I was robbed of a justly earned victory and the heavyweight championship of the world. I outpointed Jeffries in the majority of the rounds and I should have had the decision.'

The Brooklyn Daily Eagle reported: 'Jeffries leaned heavily and bore Sharkey into and once over the ropes. The extra weight was an enormous advantage. It was worth a thousand dollars a pound to Jeff and, in many minds, that was what won him the decision, for Sharkey's aggressiveness and cleverness at equal weights would, to many minds, have turned the tide of battle in another direction.'

Moira Sharkey, a distant relative of Tom and co-author of a fascinating book on the old contender, *I Fought Them All*, recalled in 2011: 'From all accounts, it was an epic fight, leaving both men badly hurt. Some thought Sharkey deserved to win but the referee favoured the champion. The pair were simply meant to trade blows and put on a show, but they went at each other like tigers. They both still had points to prove. Tom never really recovered from that bout, although he continued on with his career but he would never fight for the title again.'

Jeffries and Sharkey remained good friends. In an interview with *Ring* magazine shortly before his death in 1953, James J. told editor/publisher Nat Fleischer: 'I split his eye open and his left ear began to swell until it was almost as big as my fist. When I landed on that ear, it was like hitting a big, wet sponge. Yet he wouldn't think of quitting. I also broke two of his ribs and he still kept coming at me.'

Sharkey recovered well from the bruising encounter and continued to take on top fighters like Joe Choynski, stopping him impressively in two rounds in May 1900. A knockout defeat in two rounds by Bob Fitzsimmons three months later, however, sent him down the ratings. Another old rival, Gus Ruhlin finished him in eleven rounds in June 1902 and he finally called it quits after being outpointed by the clumsy Jack Monroe in February 1904, ending the bout by being barely able to see through swollen eyes.

'Tom had a $500,000 fortune when he stepped out of the ring, about $10 million by today's standards, but within a little over a decade it was all gone,' recalled Moira Sharkey. The old battler purchased a palatial house in Brooklyn, ran a saloon on East Fourteenth Street and bought a stable of trotting horses as well as boxing in exhibition fights with Jeffries at carnivals and fairs. Within a few years, however, he found himself down on his luck, not helped by high living, a costly divorce and investments that went disastrously wrong.

Sharkey managed to get a few character roles in several movies after moving back to California, where his boxing career began all those years ago. He died virtually penniless in San Francisco on 17 April 1953, seven months short of his eightieth birthday. Jeffries had passed away in Burbank, California just six weeks earlier. On hearing about the death of his old friend and foe, Sharkey, then in hospital and gravely ill himself, remarked: 'It took a long time, but I finally beat the bugger in the end.'

How the Irish have missed the big title

Irish professional boxers have won world titles in almost every division but never at heavyweight. No native son has ever managed to proudly call himself heavyweight champion of the world, with Tom Sharkey coming closest. That is not to say that many haven't tried, including some with high ambitions such as Galway's Peter Maher who actually claimed the championship. While his claim was a weak one, and certainly not taken seriously, he was nevertheless a leading heavyweight in his day.

Described by a contemporary boxing writer as 'a man who had everything, height, reach, punch, magnificent physique, plenty of courage and any amount of stamina', Maher, in a busy career lasting nearly twenty-five years, took on most of the leading boxers of his day. These included Bob Fitzsimmons, Peter Jackson, Jeff Clark, Frank Craig, Joe Goddard, Denver Ed Smith, Gus Ruhlin, Frank Slavin, Joe Choynski, Kid McCoy, Philadelphia Jack O'Brien, Jack Munroe and the two Irishmen, George Gardiner from Lisdoonvarna, County Clare and the aforementioned Tom Sharkey.

Maher was born in Kilbannon, a small village near Tuam in April 1866 and when he was ten the family moved to Dublin where he started in amateur boxing and won the Irish middleweight title. His father had a job as a gardener in the Phoenix Park, and when Peter left school at fourteen he joined Maher Senior. At sixteen he got a job in the Phoenix Brewery, second only in importance to the more famous Guinness Brewery.

Maher's biographer Matt Donnellan recounted that 'the work was manual and hard, and helped develop the physique that was to win him admiring glances and aid him in his chosen career as a boxer'. A little over a year later he turned professional and became middleweight champion of Ireland. Encouraged by his success in Irish and British rings, he packed his bags in 1891 and set off for America where the big money and the greater opportunities lay.

Maher's world title claims originated when James J. Corbett, Gentleman Jim, announced late in 1895 that he was relinquishing the title to devote his life to the stage. An established and popular actor, Corbett had been touring in a successful play called Gentleman Jack. He was now hanging up his gloves with the full approval of his manager, the impresario William A. Brady, who agreed that the undefeated champion would still be a great public attraction and could go on playing in Gentleman Jack until he got tired of it.

There were allegations, too, that Corbett was avoiding his most serious contender, the Englishman Bob Fitzsimmons and that his retirement was a convenient way of getting out of the match. James J. strongly denied this, and pointed out that Fitzsimmons was only a middleweight and that there were more deserving contenders around. The broad-shouldered Cornishman hit back by stating that weight had nothing to do with it. Fitz was middleweight champion of the world at the time but he was also taking on and beating lightheavyweights and even heavyweights. He is credited as being the first to coin the phrase, 'The bigger they are, the harder they fall.'

In any event, Corbett, who disliked the cheeky Fitz intensely, announced he was through with the ring. He formally declared that he would approve of a fight between contenders Peter Maher and the Australian hope Steve O'Donnell, a former sparring partner whose father was from Cork and his mother from Kilkenny, as being for the heavyweight championship of the world.

The match was signed and set for 11 November 1895 at the Empire Athletic Club on Long Island, New York, and Corbett said he would be on hand to personally proclaim the winner as the new champion. In reality, Corbett or anybody else had no right to handpick his successor but it must be remembered that there was no controlling body in those days, and champions and challengers could do what they liked. It was no coincidence that Corbett was a close friend of Maher and had Irish blood himself, his father coming from Kilmaine in County Mayo and his mother from Dublin, as previously recounted.

There were many supporters of O'Donnell in the crowd, and when Corbett came into the arena and made his way to the ringside, he received a mixed welcome of cheers and hisses, with one fan jumping up and calling for 'Three cheers for Steve', which were given wholeheartedly. Corbett grinned but it was obvious that he was annoyed. In Maher's corner, as advisor, was the great Jack McAuliffe from Bantry, County Cork who had retired as undefeated lightweight champion of the world the previous year. The fight was scheduled for twenty-five rounds, which meant a hundred minute battle if it went the full distance. All the fans got was sixty-three seconds of action.

After sparring for a moment or two, the moustachioed Galwayman landed a straight right to O'Donnell's chin and sent him flat on his back. He rolled over and struggled to his feet but his defences were down and Maher immediately struck home another big right that knocked the half-dazed Aussie to the boards again. When he got up, Maher jumped in with a hard left hook that sent him down and very much out, his head striking the canvas with a thud. He lay motionless as referee Tim Hurst counted him out.

The crowd hissed and booed at the briefness of the contest as Corbett climbed into the ring to congratulate Maher and proclaim him as the new champion. When Maher turned around and saw Corbett, he growled: 'Ok, Mr Corbett, you can save the fancy words. I now want to take you on, beat you and make my claim official. What's more, I'll finish you off as quickly as

O'Donnell.' Corbett ignored the brash Irishman's challenge and smiling, shook Maher's hand and said: 'You are the champion of the world, my official successor Peter, and I regard you as a worthy man to hold the championship.'

When the news reached Galway, there was great excitement, particularly in Kilbannon and drinks were on the house in the bars all around. The local boy was making good. However, in the US there was condemnation of Corbett's action. Leading the outcry was the Texan impresario and promoter/gambler Dan Stuart. 'Just where and by whom Mr Corbett was authorised to give away the championship I am at a loss to understand,' barked a red-faced Stuart to reporters. 'What about the other more deserving contenders? Bob Fitzsimmons for example?' Stuart was effectively a nineteenth-century version of Don King, and whose vision of professional boxing as a spectator sport was way ahead of its time.

With public demand mounting, Maher agreed to a match with Fitzsimmons to decide 'the real championship of the world'. The Englishman had beaten Maher in twelve rounds when they met four years earlier but Peter, now more confident, felt he would reverse the result this time. Mexico was originally suggested but a small shanty town called Langtry, near El Paso in Texas, was finally agreed upon, with the date set for 21 February 1896.

In the early 1890s, the Lone Star State was, in the words of a contemporary writer, 'a wild, uncivilised wilderness infested with jack rabbits, rattlesnakes, Red Indians and treacherous outlaws'. Its tiny frontier towns consisted of crude, wooden shacks spread thinly over the barren plains, and towns with despairing names like Dead Eye, Rat River, Coffee Bow, Trigger and Lightning. The two busiest men in every town were the bartender and the undertaker, with the latter generally finishing the week's business with the larger take.

So it was in the dust-clogged, free-wheeling shack town of Langtry near the Mexican border. The man who ruled the town, with the help of a few tough-looking, trigger-happy deputies, was the white-bearded Judge Roy Bean, a renegade with brains and a natural ability to control the meanest of baddies. He owned the town from the sludge slit to the graveyard and would amass a fortune in his seventy-two year lifetime.

As well as decreeing himself the town judge, tax collector, federal marshal and coroner, and making sure that not a single silver dollar would avoid his greedy clutches, Bean ran the famous Jersey Lily saloon, the only licenced establishment in town. He was also fond of the bottle, and customers would remember going into the saloon and seeing him behind the counter more than slightly intoxicated.

Bean was indeed a very colourful character, somebody straight out of a Zane Grey western novel. He was often referred to as the Law, West of the Pecos and defied anybody to dispute it, especially with his six-gun nearby. He was once on the run after shooting and killing a Mexican desperado 'who had threatened to kill a gringo'. Another of his nicknames was the Hanging Judge.

Interestingly, several movies were made about him, most notably The Life and Times of Judge Roy Bean, a heavily fictionalised biopic filmed in 1972 and starring Hollywood leading man Paul Newman. Character actor Walter Brennan won an Oscar for his portrayal of Bean in The Westerner, made in 1940, although this one too managed to twist around the facts, giving Bean an entirely fictitious death scene.

For the Maher–Fitzsimmons fight Thomas Edison, inventor of the phonograph among other things, had just perfected what he called the kinetoscope, a moving picture camera which he claimed could take forty shots a minute and was undoubtedly one of the greatest inventions in an inventive age. It had already been found that boxing was an ideal subject for the taking of moving pictures, as towards the end of 1894 Edison's invention had been used when Corbett had boxed an 'arranged' contest with Peter Courtney in a New Jersey studio.

It was so successful that those behind kinetoscope wanted to make a film of an important fight staged out of doors, and the Maher–Fitzsimmons contest seemed to be ideal. Arrangements were completed with promoter Stuart, although neither boxer knew of any plans to film the proceedings.

Four days before the scheduled fight, ten grim-faced Texas Rangers rode into El Paso, the nearest town, and declared that the State Governor had issued instructions that boxing was banned in Texas, as it was in other states, and there was no way the fight could take place on Texas soil. If it did, then everybody involved would be thrown into jail, including Judge Roy Bean. When they left, and thinking fast, promoter Stuart merely switched the site to a convenient location less than a mile away in Mexican territory.

It could be reached by travelling down a rock-strewn track for about three quarters of a mile and then crossing a rickety bridge that spanned the roaring seventy-foot wide Rio Grande river, known in Mexico as Rio Bravo del Norte, or simply Rio Bravo. This led to a sandy, hilly land known as Couhuahua, a barren spot, bare of trees and vegetation, apart from a few scrub bushes and cacti. True, it was an odd, indeed bizarre spot for a big fight, but more important it was Mexican territory, safely away from the 'meddlesome' Texan authorities. The nearest Mexican dwellings were more than five miles away.

With the purse monies safely deposited in an El Paso bank, all was set for the contest which Stuart had ambitiously billed as being for 'the undisputed heavyweight championship of the world,' with the additional line, 'and with the full approval of the retired and undefeated champion James J. Corbett'. Bean had also brought in as extra 'security' the formidable figure of Bat Masterson, a buffalo hunter and frontier lawman who made his reputation in Dodge City, Kansas.

A notorious gunman whose mother was Irish, Masterson was better known as Black Bat, and he was joined by six of his similarly-disposed colleagues, all around to help out Bean. A trigger-happy individual who would later become sports editor of the *New York Morning Telegram*, Masterson claimed he always wore his six-gun, 'the gun that tamed the West,' and wanted to make sure everything went according to plan. Particularly as a mixture of law-abiding citizens and drunken ne'er-do-wells had descended on this Texas-Mexican outpost to see a prize fight.

There were the happy-go-lucky characters who earned a living from the ranches, mines and lumber camps in the vicinity. There were those with money to burn and those to help them burn it. And there were the undesirable elements that followed the fight game in those days. Nothing or nobody was going to get by Masterson, who, it is worth mentioning, was, like Judge Roy Bean, also the subject of several movies, portrayed by stars like Randolph Scott and Joel McCrea, as well as in a TV series starring Gene Barry.

Before the fight got under way, Bean climbed into the ring, showing distinct signs of intoxication and calling for order. He held up his right hand. 'Gennel-men,' he roared, holding on to the top rope with his other hand to steady himself, 'this is a great day for lil' ol' Langtry. From now on, the whole world will have heard of it. I am proud to have brought such a big title fight here, and I plan to force James J. Corbett to meet the winner and stage the contest on this very spot.' Bean then sat on a chair just outside the ring in a neutral corner, emptied a glass of whiskey down his throat, and awaited the first bell. Five-ounce gloves were being used, and the fight was being conducted under the Marquis of Queensberry Rules.

It did not last long. Fitzsimmons, angry after learning that he was being cut out of the proceedings of the film, planned to get down to business right away. After both men exchanged heavy punches in the centre of the ring, Maher fired a long right to the temple and followed through with a left hook aimed at Fitz's chin. The quick-thinking Fitz anticipated the punch and neatly sidestepping, hooked a vicious left to the body before crossing with a tremendous right to the chin.

The blow knocked Maher flat on his back where he was counted out by referee George Siler, one of the top referees of the day. The contest had lasted exactly ninety-five seconds including the count, and with it vanished the Galwayman's tenuous world title claims. Fitzsimmons did not even bother claiming the 'championship'. He wanted the real one.

The fight ended before the operators could get the camera even started. Eight days later the contestants faced each other again, this time in New York's Madison Square Garden where they boxed a no decision bout over three rounds for the benefit of the film project. While in the city, they also talked about their Langtry fight as publicity for the film, as Edison was naturally anxious to recoup losses incurred by a speedy affair. It was a film he intended to circulate throughout the US, but this time Edison and his company had to pay Fitz for the privilege. There is no record of Maher ever having received any monetary reward for the film rights.

With Corbett subsequently back in the ring after his 'temporary retirement', Fitzsimmons got his legitimate world title opportunity thirteen months later in Carson City, Nevada when he sensationally knocked out Gentleman Jim in the fourteenth round on St Patrick's Day in 1897. Meanwhile Maher, certainly not discouraged by his devastating loss to Fitzsimmons, continued his career but he was never again an important figure on the heavyweight scene, always losing the big ones. He made his last ring appearance in April 1913 at the AC Arena in Philadelphia when he boxed Fred McKay in a three-round no decision bout. Maher died in Baltimore, Maryland in July 1940. He was seventy-four.

It would be twelve years before another Irishman was given an opportunity to call himself heavyweight champion of the world, and this time in a fight for the legitimate title recognised worldwide. The champion Tommy Burns, a Canadian of German extraction, was on a world tour at the time, taking on the best opposition each country had to offer.

When he came to Ireland for a title defence on St Patrick's Day in 1908, Wexford's Jem Roche, as Irish champion, would be in the opposite corner. The fact that the title fight was being held on the national holiday in front of a fervently passionate crowd did not bother the confident Burns in the least. The venue was the Theatre Royal in the centre of Dublin, and the announcement caused tremendous excitement, with the sporting public convinced that Roche could be the man to end Burns' reign and bring the heavyweight title to Ireland for the first time.

Granted, John L. Sullivan, the first official world heavyweight champion, was Irish, his mother coming from Athlone, County Westmeath and his father from Abbeydorney, County Kerry. His immediate successor James J. Corbett also had Irish parents as already recounted. But while both Sullivan and Corbett were born in the US, no native son had ever won the heavyweight title. Could Roche be the first?

Burns remains to this day the shortest of all the world heavyweight champions at five foot seven inches, and one of the lightest as well, generally weighing around twelve and a half stone. Additionally, he had the misfortune to succeed the hulking figure of James J. Jeffries, all of six foot two and a half inches and fifteen stone plus. Big Jeff was simply too fresh in people's minds for a comparative midget like Burns to be readily accepted. However, the cocky Canadian was a good, solid puncher with both gloves, and one of the most underrated as well, with a knockout percentage of around sixty per cent.

A strong, independent individual, Burns was born Noah Brusso in a log cabin near Hanover, about eighty miles northwest of Toronto. When he was twelve years of age his mother sent him to work in a sawmill as his father had died. He later left home and worked as a wool spinner and a baggage handler on a steamer, always wandering and going where the work was, either on land or at sea. Once, after jumping ship, he found himself in Detroit and joined the local lacrosse team where he gained a reputation as a tough, aggressive player.

A Detroit sportswriter named Joe Jackson was impressed with his strength and rugged tactics and suggested Brusso become a boxer. He agreed, but changed his name to Tommy Burns so as his mother, who did not like boxing, would not find out. He built up such an impressive record that by 1906 he got a chance at the vacant world heavyweight title on the retirement of James J. Jeffries and defeated Marvin Hart on points over twenty rounds.

Burns promised to be a fighting champion. 'I will defend my title against all comers, nobody barred,' he declared. 'By this I mean white, black, Mexican, Indian or any other nationality. I will take on anybody irrespective of race, colour or creed. I propose to be the champion of the whole world, not the white or the Canadian or the American. If I am not the best man in the heavyweight division, then I don't want the title.'

The Canadian kept to his word. During the rest of 1906 he put his title on the line twice, knocking out Jim Flynn in fifteen rounds and drawing with Philadelphia Jack O'Brien over twenty, both in Los Angeles. In May 1907 he gave O'Brien another chance and beat him over twenty rounds, again in Los Angeles and knocked out his first foreign challenger, the Australian champion Bill Squires, in precisely 129 seconds, in Colma, just outside San Francisco.

Nevertheless, even though Burns had said publicly that he would take on any contender, there were claims that he was studiously avoiding the danger-ous black heavyweight from Texas, Jack Johnson. Burns strongly denied this and insisted the offers he received were not attractive enough to persuade him to share a ring with Johnson. When it was put to him that he was drawing what became known as the 'colour bar' he pointed out that he had boxed several black boxers and had two black sparring partners. He had also been married for a short time to a black woman.

Announcing a European tour, Burns said he would take on the national champions of the various countries he visited, and if there was not a national champion available, then the next best man would do. The tour began in Lon-don just before Christmas in 1907 when he knocked out the British champion James 'Gunner' Moir in ten rounds. He continued his demolition of British heavyweights two months later by finishing off Jack Palmer in the fourth before announcing he was now heading for Dublin and a date with the Irish champion Jem Roche.

A blacksmith by trade, Roche was born in the village of Killurin near Kil-muckbridge in County Wexford in 1878. A big, strapping lad, he played Gaelic football growing up and won a Wexford championship with his hometown club St Patrick's in 1896. According to the historian and former amateur boxer Mick Sutton, Roche had no intention of becoming a boxer until a few of his friends persuaded him to take part in a contest in Wexford Town Hall. Jem was seventeen at the time and he won that first bout on a knockout. Encouraged by his success, he won the Wexford amateur title before trying his luck as a professional in 1900. Compiling an impressive record of twenty-two wins, three losses and a draw, he was heavyweight champion of Ireland by the time he fought Burns.

For the biggest fight of his career, Roche trained in the St Iberius Club in Wexford. Barrels of fresh seawater were taken up from the harbour for his shower. Money for training, even for towels, was scarce. Then, less than a week before the big fight, he caught a heavy cold. His doctor diagnosed it as bronchial trouble and prescribed a powder to be inhaled, while keeping the incident a secret lest the fight, Roche's golden opportunity, might be called off. While the powder improved his breathing, it brought on a dazed effect and in reality, the Irishman was not in a fit state to realistically take on the heavyweight champion of the world.

Nevertheless, Roche looked very impressive in training, with the *Irish Independent* reporting: 'The Wexford man's physique is magnificent. You must see Jem punch that bag. The thunder of it not only shivers the frame from which the bag is suspended but sends a tremor through the whole building. A member of the audience was so carried away that he shouted aloud: 'Heaven have mercy on poor Burns.' With head bowed, guarded by his left, Roche advances on his adversary with his right, and quickly puts him on the defensive.'

Roche's manager and trainer Nick Tennant told reporters: 'Jem is just the sort to make a world's champion – strong, fast, clever, cool and determined. He can give and take more than his share of punishment and this makes him a tall order for any living fighter. I fail to see how Jem can lose.'

When Roche arrived in Dublin, there was a massive crowd at Westland Row railway station to greet him. Roche was leaning out the window as the train pulled in, shaking scores of outstretched hands. 'I am confident but not over-confident,' he told the throng when he got out onto the platform. 'Burns is just a braggart and he is going to get his comeuppance. I'll be the new heavyweight champion of the world.' With that, he headed off to the home of a friend, led by a fife and drum band.

Roche had a reputation for being notoriously superstitious. A few days before the fight he was out walking in the Phoenix Park with Dan Kelly, a former Irish lightweight champion who would be in his corner. Jem found an old horseshoe, an item he was well used to from his days as a blacksmith. There were six nails in the shoe and he felt this would be a lucky omen. He told Kelly he would knock out Burns in six rounds. When one of the nails fell out, he changed his forecast to five rounds.

Burns arrived in Dublin the next day, having completed his training in England, and created almost as much excitement. A huge crowd gathered outside the swanky Dolphin Hotel, where he had rented a suite of rooms. When Burns appeared at the window, he tossed coins to the crowd below. Asked by a reporter later if he was afraid of losing, he replied: 'If I were, there would be no point in coming here, would there? I understand that the opinion here prevails that Roche will win. Well, if he beats me, I will be the first man to shake his hand.'

The fight was scheduled for twenty rounds, the regulation distance. Besides the £2,000 purse on offer, each boxer's sidestake would be £500. Burns put up the money but Roche could only come up with £200 and the promoters had to make up the deficit, with the money being deducted from the Irishman's purse. The contest was billed as the biggest fight in the history of Irish boxing, which indeed it was. It got massive publicity in the Irish newspapers as well as wide coverage in Britain and abroad. All the streets around the Theatre Royal in Hawkins Street were packed by fans unable to procure tickets, as all three thousand had been snapped up once the 17 March date was announced.

The crowd in the streets was estimated to run into several thousand, as they waited for the signal in lights specifically set up inside. After each round, it would be either red for Burns or green for Roche as a guide to who won the session. Roche walked to the ring to the sounds of the orchestra's The Boys of Wexford, with the packed crowd joining in the singing.

Burns, who had been watching the preliminary bouts from the back of the theatre, strolled down the aisle to the strains of Yankee Doodle Dandy. This was not a geographical insult to Burns who always insisted he was not an American or a Briton but a Canadian. Simply, the orchestra did not have the music sheets for the Canadian national anthem, and not inclined to play God Save the King, they opted for the Yankee Doodle song composed by George M. Cohan.

Roche, wearing green trunks with a green and white sash, was already in the ring and had received a resounding cheer but discovered he had left his hand wraps behind him. One of his seconds hurried back to the dressing room and came back, not with bandages but a pack of lint. Burns was wearing red trunks with stars and stripes down the side despite his aversion to anything American, and when he climbed into the ring, he glared at Roche, trying to make eye contact.

The Canadian had told a newspaper reporter earlier in the week that he could hypnotise opponents and he was going to do the same with Roche. He continued to stare at the challenger as referee Robert Watson issued the final instructions, with the Wexford man meeting him eye to eye. Both men looked the same height but in fact, Roche, at five foot eight inches, was fractionally taller. He weighed 12 st 9 lb. Burns, whose weight often fluctuated, scaled 12 st 3 lb.

Down at ringside was Bill Squires, the Australian heavyweight champion who had been knocked out by Burns in one round eight months earlier and was ready to challenge the winner. Squires had helped train Roche for the fight but declined to forecast the result. 'May the best man win,' he would say when asked. Roche and Burns tossed for corners and Roche won. 'There's one up for

Jem,' shouted one hopeful fan. There were cries of 'Go to it, Jem' and 'Give him the old one-two, Jem' from the excited audience who were to witness what was to this day the only world heavyweight championship fight to be staged on Irish soil.

At the bell Burns came out with his long left hand extended while guarding his chin with the right. Roche struck down Burns' arm and covered his face with both gloves to protect a counter blow. Suddenly, the Canadian, feinting with his left, shot across a powerful right that smacked on the Irishman's jaw. Roche slumped to the canvas, landing on his elbows and knees. Vainly he tried to push himself upright but could not make it as referee Watson counted him out as the crowd fell silent.

As Burns and Watson helped him to his feet, Roche said to the referee: 'You didn't count me out, did you?' Watson assured him that he had. Roche then appealed to the champion and said: 'Surely the referee is wrong, Mr Burns,' to which the Canadian answered: 'I'm afraid it's all over Jem. I'm sorry.'

After he recovered his senses in the dressing room, Roche made no excuses for his shattering defeat. 'He was just too quick for me,' he said. 'That's all there was to it.' Burns admitted: 'This was the easiest fight I've ever been in. Your man stepped into what I thought was one of the most perfectly timed blows of my career. I wanted to end it early, and as quickly as possible because I had too much money at stake at long odds to take any chances. Now I'm going back to my hotel, have dinner and collect my share of the £2,000 purse and that £500 sidestake.'

The fight had lasted exactly eighty-eight seconds, making it the second shortest world heavyweight title fight up to that time, bettered only by James J. Jeffries' win over Jack Finnegan in fifty-five seconds eight years earlier. Fight fans had seen precious little for their hard-earned cash. It was reported that one man who had taken off his coat, turned to drape it over his seat, and when he turned around to sit down, found to his horror that the fight was over.

Another quick-witted individual ran out of the theatre seconds after Roche had been counted out, waving a ticket over his head. 'I can't bear to look at it,' he shouted to anxious fans waiting outside for news, as the coloured lights system to indicate how the fight was going had broken down. 'Roche is murdering him. Is there anywhere here who could bear to witness the horrid spectacle? He can buy my ticket for £2.' The crafty fellow got his money and disappeared into the night before the buyer realised he had been conned.

Ireland was in a state of shock at the sudden eclipse of their hero, but accepted that Roche was simply not good enough. 'The affair, unhappily, did not last long enough to judge the winner's full capabilities,' said the *Irish Times*, 'but what we did see was sufficient to indicate that he is very fast and very clever and has plenty of dash and resource. Beyond all doubt, he is a worthy holder of the world heavyweight championship.'

Burns would make four more successful defences of his title before losing it to his nemesis Jack Johnson, who was always on his trail. After fourteen one-sided rounds in Rushcutter's Bay arena in Sydney on St Stephens' Day in 1908, the police intervened to save Burns unnecessary punishment. Meanwhile, Roche continued his career with mixed success, finally retiring from the ring in 1910 with a respectable record of thirty wins, seven losses and one draw. He went back to his first love GAA, and helped train the great Wexford team that became the first side to win four successive All-Ireland championships from 1915 to 1918.

Roche also purchased a small hotel on South Main Street, Wexford and built up a good business, 'thanks to my grandmother's business acumen and steadfastness', remembered his grandson, the Wexford playwright Billy Roche. Jem later became a bookmaker and manager of a commission agent's office in town. For over twenty years he was a familiar figure on racecourses and coursing grounds around the country, beneath a big colourful umbrella with the lettering 'Jem Roche of Wexford'.

Roche died at the age of fifty-six in November 1934. Billy Roche recalled: 'My grandfather's cortege across Wexford Bridge to the graveyard was accompanied by marching bands, the big drums muffled with black mourning drapes. Thousands of mourners lined the route, of all denominations, of all political persuasions. In a tribute to him, one of the newspapers described him as an Irishman of note.' A simple plaque by his many admirers on the wall of a bank in the Bull Ring Square honours Roche as 'a great fighter, great sportsman but greater still in his own simplicity and modesty'.

Galway's Martin Thornton was another Irish heavyweight remembered with affection, although his farce on 24 August 1945 with the talented British heavyweight champion Bruce Woodcock at Dublin's Theatre Royal, venue of the Roche–Burns fight, is clearly one that Irish boxing wants to forget. Like his predecessors, Thornton had designs on the world heavyweight title, then held by the great Joe Louis. While it is extremely doubtful that Louis had ever even heard of Thornton, it is equally certain that if he had, he would certainly not have had any sleepless nights worrying about him.

Martin was a big puncher, especially with the right hand, but like Jack Doyle before him, he lacked the dedication necessary to make real headway in the tough, competitive world of professional boxing. A former booth fighter who would travel around Britain taking on all comers in country fairs, he once reckoned he had over two hundred fights in the booths which, he claimed 'toughened me up when I made up my mind to become a professional'.

Thornton came from the picturesque village of Spiddal on the shores of Galway Bay near Connemara and was known as the Connemara Crusher. He skipped the amateurs and went straight into the paid game in December 1937, making his debut at the Holborn Stadium, London with a win by disqualification in two rounds over Billy Taylor. He followed it up with two quick knockouts and by 1943 he had run up an impressive record, including winning a heavy-weight competition in London with a victory in one round.

Making a rare appearance in Ireland in February 1944, he knocked out Corkman Paddy O'Sullivan in three rounds at the Theatre Royal in Dublin to capture the Irish heavyweight title, and followed it up a year later with a second win over O'Sullivan, again at the Theatre Royal and this time in just seventy-seven seconds of the opening round. Just to consolidate his good form, he travelled to Waterford in May and knocked out Dixie Moore of Belfast in the first round.

It looked like Ireland could have found a heavyweight capable of taking on the big guys. Jack Doyle may have let them down, but Martin Thornton would fill that much-needed gap. Thornton even fancied taking on the great Louis himself despite the fact that the Detroit legend had held an unbroken grip on the title since 1937 with a record run of twenty-one successful defences. Louis was currently serving in the army and had not been in action since March 1942 when he knocked out big Abe Simon in six rounds in New York.

It was now the summer of 1945 and over three years of ring rust does not do a champion, even a superb one like Louis, any good whatsoever. In any event, World War II looked like nearing its end, and Louis would be back as a civilian again, ready to defend his title. There were reports that the Irish-American Billy Conn, who had given Louis a real scare in 1941, might get first crack at the title but Thornton would make sure he himself was ready for the winner.

Gerald Egan, the enterprising Cork promoter, would stage the big fight. Egan spent his early childhood in the US and claimed his Uncle Tom had acted as matchmaker for the famous boxing promoter of the 1920s Tex Rickard, who staged all of Jack Dempsey's world heavyweight title fights. He boldly predicted that he would bring Louis to Dublin to fight Thornton, 'and I'll spare no expense'.

Around this time, too, a former London fishmonger named Jack Solomons was gaining a fast reputation as an enterprising promoter, and would in a few years become one of the world's best. It was Solomons who got Thornton's signature on a contract to meet the rising Yorkshire heavyweight Bruce Wood-cock by offering the Connemara Crusher a purse of £800, then a pretty good figure. The match would be over ten rounds at the Theatre Royal, Dublin on 24 August 1945.

A talented upright boxer with a heavy punch in his right hand, Woodcock from Doncaster was British and Empire heavyweight champion, and since turning professional in 1942 after a very successful amateur career, was un-beaten in twenty-one fights, twenty either by countouts or stoppages. Wood-cock was going to be a formidable opponent, especially as he had already beaten Thornton inside two rounds in Manchester nearly two years earlier. The

Galway fighter claimed he was not fully fit in that fight and promised he would do better next time.

Solomons reckoned Thornton was a good prospect but felt that he would have to prove himself first before even thinking of going after the mighty Louis. In any event, with much advance publicity in the Irish newspapers, fans flocked to the Hawkins Street theatre in their droves in anticipation of a great night, and of course an Irish victory. Tickets sold on the black market for three and four times their printed price. Arrangements were made with Radio Éireann to broadcast a live commentary of the fight for a fee of twenty-five guineas but on the day before the contest, they increased it by an extra £10. Solomons agreed to the new price but when he told them that the fight would start at ten o'clock, Radio Éireann officials objected.

They pointed out that ten o'clock was the start of the news bulletin in English and that they could not change on any account what had become a tradition and that the Irish public would tune in at ten o'clock and expect to hear the news in English. That was it. When Solomons suggested that they could change their schedule for just one night for fans to listen to what was an important sporting event, and that big fights in Britain always started on the hour, they were adamant. 'Ten o'clock is news in English time, Mr Solomons and that is the way it has to be,' said one official. With the promoter unwilling to change his time for the start, negotiations for the broadcast project simply broke down.

The fight was hailed in the Irish media as 'one of the biggest matches in recent Irish boxing history,' but turned out to be a fiasco. A smiling Thornton ducked between the ropes to a tumultuous reception while Woodcock entered the ring to the sound of mild cheers and a few scattered boos. As Belfast referee Andy Smyth called the two boxers together for final instructions, Thornton fidgeted nervously, while Woodcock looked supremely confident.

From the first round Thornton never seemed to make even an effort to win. He appeared only intent to avoid punishment, seldom lifting his left hand above waist level and making only a few half-hearted efforts to land his big right, with his chin tucked deep into his shoulder. In that opening session, he made only one real attempt to land a punch, and that was a left swing which carried little power. Woodcock was still cautious but managed to land some stiff left jabs to the face that made the Irishman wince.

In the second round Thornton left his stool with his left eye swollen and soon the right side of his face was covered in blood from the relentless tattoo of left-hand punches. The Galwayman scored with a few light blows to the body in a rally near the ropes but Woodcock slid away and continued to score freely from long range. With the crowd now hissing and booing at Thornton's lamentable performance, the Doncaster boxer opened up for the first time in the third round with a two-gloved attack, driving Thornton across the ring with heavy lefts and rights.

The Irishman was now hanging on desperately but his few attempts to counter were brushed aside with almost contemptuous ease by Woodcock who continued to jab and uppercut. Thornton put out his tongue on two occasions and the angry crowd was now yelling at the Irishman to make a fight of it. 'You're a yellow belly Thornton,' they yelled. 'Thornton, you're a quitter.' 'Disgrace, robbery.'

At the end of the third round Thornton appealed to referee Smyth to end it but he refused. 'Go out there at the bell and give the fans what they paid good money for, a decent fight,' he said. Shortly before the bell for the fourth round was due to ring, Thornton refused to listen to the pleas of his corner to continue, and insisted they throw in the towel. Referee Smyth accepted the traditional token of surrender, and the sorry debacle was finally over.

Thornton left the ring to a chorus of jeers, boos and whistles as well as some bottles and crumpled newspapers. Looking thoroughly dejected, he said in the dressing room: 'I don't care what the crowd think. I was in there fighting a guy who moved like greased lightning. They weren't. But not to worry, I'll be back and will make up for this. Mark my words.' Not surprisingly, the newspapers next day came down heavily on the Galwayman's lamentable performance.

'What was wrong with Martin Thornton last night?' asked the *Evening Herald*. 'Where was the fighting Irish blood, that dynamic energy and that 'killer' spirit that swept him from the corner like a human volcano and demolished Paddy O'Sullivan and Butcher Howell almost before they had their gloves up? Maybe he was either under-trained or over-trained against the Britisher.'

It was revealed later that Solomons had paid Thornton his full purse of £800 in advance after Martin insisted on it or else there would be no fight. This claim prompted the question: Was this because Thornton knew he was not going to win? When the Éire Boxing Board of Control, later called the Irish Boxing Board of Control and a forerunner of the current Boxing Union of Ireland, called an urgent meeting to discuss the fiasco which had brought shame on Irish boxing and put the sport here on its knees, they suspended Thornton and relieved him of his Irish heavyweight title. He also had his licence withdrawn. The board could not order that his purse be withheld as it had already been paid out to him.

In the aftermath of the fiasco, Thornton retired from the ring but four years later, and still without a licence to box in the Republic, he made a comeback at the Ulster Hall, Belfast. Sadly out of condition, and looking decidedly flabby around the middle, he was easily beaten by the young English heavyweight prospect Ray Wilding in three rounds, the fight being stopped when the Connemara Crusher was being crushed himself.

In 1951 Thornton was hired by the Hollywood director John Ford who came to the West of Ireland to film his iconic movie *The Quiet Man*. Ford had him as a stand-in for the veteran actor Victor McLaglen in the famous fight scene with

John Wayne. McLaglen, who was sixty-five at the time, had been a prominent heavyweight boxer in his younger days, having fought world heavyweight champion Jack Johnson in a six-round no decision bout in 1909.

Little was heard of Thornton until some time later when he made a sensational disclosure in an English Sunday newspaper circulated in Ireland. He claimed he had thrown the Woodcock fight following a tempting bribe of £4,000 from Solomons and that he made an extra £10,000 from the fight by betting on his opponent. He said he invested this money in a bar in Spiddal called the Droighnean Donn. He would stick to this story, regularly spinning the yarn for customers, up to the time of his death from a heart attack while thatching the roof of a cottage in 1982.

When the author was in London for a world title fight in May 1966, the bribe allegations were put to Solomons and he laughed off the yarn as pure fiction. 'While it is true that I paid Thornton his agreed £800 purse, otherwise,' he said 'he would not enter the ring, that was the end of it,' the promoter pointed out. 'Why should I shell out £4,000 to a man who had no chance of winning and had already been summarily beaten by Woodcock in a previous fight? If you believe that story, Thomas, you must believe in fairies at the bottom of your garden, or anywhere else for that matter! In any event, I'm a man of integrity, as you well know.'

There were more shocks ahead from Thornton. In November 1968, he made the sensational announcement that he was planning a dramatic comeback, and as an amateur this time, no less. He hoped to enter the Irish Seniors early in the New Year in a bold attempt to win the heavyweight title, a feat he felt he was fully capable off with his wide professional experience. He was then forty-eight years of age. 'From what I have seen of the present crop, I'm convinced I could lick any of them,' he boldly forecast to *Evening Press* reporter John O'Shea, later chief executive of the charity organisation GOAL.

It did not seem to bother the erstwhile Spiddal veteran that he had not boxed competitively for nineteen years, that he was far from physically fit, and had never fought under amateur rules at any stage in his life. He denied he was not in shape and pointed out that he played Gaelic football regularly with the Spiddal club and helped train the amateurs at the Olympic Boxing Club in Galway. He said he weighed between thirteen and a half to fourteen stone, and had official backing from the Olympic club.

Club secretary Chick Gillen set up a meeting with officers of the Irish Amateur Boxing Association to inform them that Thornton was very serious about his intentions. 'Gentlemen,' Gillen said, 'Martin and I played around with this idea some years ago but dismissed it. However, we now think the time is right. Irish boxing needs a good heavyweight, and Martin Thornton looks the man. Really, there isn't a heavyweight in the country who could stand up to the punching power and strength of this man.' Unsurprisingly, there was a total lack of interest or enthusiasm from the IABA for the somewhat ambitious plan and while they promised Gillen that they would think about it, the bizarre idea merely fizzled out like a wet firework.

As recently as 2002, news filtered out from the US that one Martin Thornton, billed as the Irish Assassin, had made his professional debut as a lightmiddleweight in Massachusetts. It turned out that Martin was a nephew of the old Connemara Crusher. He had a brief career of nine wins, one loss and a draw, all on the East Coast, before leaving the sport in 2004. Nothing has been heard of him since.

In the 1940s there was another Irish heavyweight on the scene, a Tipperary giant named Jim Cully. Billed as the Tipperary Tower, he was seven foot two inches tall and weighed eighteen and a half stone, making him the tallest Irish boxer in history. The world record, though, goes to the Romanian, Gogea Mitu, who was seven foot eleven inches and campaigned in the 1930s.

Cully had three amateur bouts before deciding to try his luck on the professional scene to supplement his earnings from the day job, managing a touring carnival. Cully had two impressive wins, over Cork's Butcher Howell and Joe O'Neill of Belfast before coming onto the radar of Gerald Egan, the leading Irish promoter of the day. The enterprising Corkman, always on the lookout for a good heavyweight prospect, matched Cully with Chris Cole, the Mullingar fighter who once knocked out a horse. They met for the vacant Irish heavyweight title at Dalymount Park soccer ground in Dublin in June 1942.

Over a foot shorter and outweighed by four stone, Cole systematically dismantled the Tipperary Tower and brought him down in two rounds. Undeterred, Cully decided to move into the American fight scene and made a successful debut in a scheduled eight-rounder at the Jamaica Arena in the Queens borough of New York when he knocked out Wally Baden in the first round. 'Two of Cully's punches nearly paralysed me,' said the crestfallen Baden in the dressing room. Alas, in his next fight in Buffalo two weeks later, also set for eight rounds, Cully was knocked out by Earl Pierce in the third, after which he faded from the scene.

Then there was Kevin McBride, who was six foot six inches and generally weighed around twenty stone. He did most of his boxing on America's East Coast, far from his native Clones in County Monaghan where he was born on 10 May 1973. Known as the Clones Colossus which recalled Barry McGuigan's sobriquet the Clones Cyclone, McBride indeed became so 'Americanised' that the US practically claimed him as one of their own.

They had good reason to feel that way, as Uncle Sam was desperately searching for a good heavyweight, were he white or black or any colour, or from any country outside of Eastern Europe, to win the most prestigious title in the whole panorama of boxing, the heavyweight championship of the world.

As the author and ring historian Bert Sugar commented: 'To be perfectly honest, we Americans felt we owned the title, having produced the likes of Ali, Foreman, Frazier, Patterson, Marciano, Louis, Dempsey and on and on. Effectively, the heavyweight championship of the world was something of an American institution. We didn't want to let it go.'

The title has been in the iron grip of heavyweights from Eastern Europe for some years now, and despite the occasional interruption, it never lasted too long, with formidable champions like the Klitschko brothers, Wladimir from Kazakhstan and Vitali from Kyrgyzstan coming to the forefront. Then there was the Russian, Nikolay Valuev, nicknamed the Beast from the East by the London-Irish manager Frank Maloney who guided him for a while. Valuev, all seven foot and twenty-three stone of him, was the tallest and heaviest world heavyweight champion of all time.

The sheer size of Valuev, an intellectual who read Agatha Christie, Arthur Conan Doyle and Tolstoy, was enough to intimidate ordinary heavyweights. One American, after meeting him at the weigh-in, said: 'Nobody told me I was fighting Big Foot,' and headed straight for the hotel bar. Another, Larry Donald, said: 'I never faced a man like him. In fact, I've never seen a man like him. He's like something from the Dark Ages.'

The American promoter Don King aimed to smash this monopoly and he saw in McBride the very man who could accomplish it. 'I'm your man, Don,' said a confident McBride when they first met. 'You bring on the opponents and I'll polish them off.' King was one of the world's leading promoters who achieved initial fame by staging the Rumble in the Jungle between Muhammad Ali and George Foreman for the world heavyweight championship in Africa in 1974. Soon, however, there were other American promoters anxious to get McBride into the big time so it was looking like Kevin might well be spoiled for choice.

As an amateur McBride boxed in the colours of the Smithboro club in County Monaghan where Barry McGuigan had learned his boxing. He won the Irish amateur superheavyweight championship in Dublin early in 1992 and represented Ireland at the summer Barcelona Olympics, losing out on a decision to Peter Hrivniak of Czechoslovakia in the first series. By Christmas he had turned professional, boxing a draw with the Leeds heavyweight Gary Charlton at the Broadway Theatre in London.

McBride was soon on a winning track, with four victories in 1993 and seven in 1994. By now most of his fights were taking place in the US, with occasional trips to London and Dublin. In June 1997 he won the vacant Irish heavyweight title in Belfast and by the millennium he was campaigning in America, picking up the International Boxing Council of America's belt along the way.

There was talk in 2004 of matching McBride with Mike Tyson, the former heavyweight champion of the world who was on a comeback at the time.

Tyson, formerly billed as the Baddest Man on the Planet, had been one of the greatest of all time in his prime and in 1986 had become the youngest world heavyweight champion by destroying Trevor Berbick in less than two rounds. He was aged twenty at the time. But then, he always had the air of a man whose built-in self-destruct mechanism was ticking away like a time bomb. In a turbulent career, he served time on a rape charge and later a road rage assault.

In the ring Tyson chewed off part of Evander Holyfield's ear; outside it, he bit Lennox Lewis' leg at a media conference. He indulged in drugs, sex and spending sprees and was declared bankrupt in 2004, owing $50 million. Mike was then on a comeback hoping to repay his mounting debts and taxes, after being knocked out by Lennox Lewis in eight rounds and in four rounds by Danny Williams. In between he put away the moderate Clifford Etienne in forty-nine seconds but nobody took that win seriously.

By now, there were several attempts to match Tyson with McBride, with the Italian promoter Salvatore Cherchi prepared to put the fight on in Italy between April and June 2004, with Palermo or Syracuse being mentioned as possible venues. Rich Capiello, the New England promoter, was also after a Tyson–McBride match and was prepared to put it on in Dublin, naming Croke Park, headquarters of the GAA, as the likely venue. Once again, talks with both parties came to nothing as the scene shifted to the US where promoter Marty Wynn announced that he had finally clinched the fight for the MCI Centre, Washington for 11 June 2005.

McBride was out of the ring for a year while anxiously awaiting news of the on-again-off-again Tyson fight. He did not wish to risk defeat as victory over Tyson could lead him to a promised world heavyweight title bout. The Clones Colossus did eight weeks intensive training at Goody Petronelli's gym in Brockton, Massachusetts where former world champions like Marvin Hagler and Steve Collins worked out. 'This will be the whole of Ireland hitting Mike Tyson on the chin,' McBride confidently told the media. 'I've trained harder than ever before in my life. I told my father before he sadly passed away that I'd love to fight Tyson and he said that if I dreamt about it enough, it would happen.'

Tyson worked out at his camp in Phoenix, Arizona, and his new trainer Jeff Fenech, the former Australian legend, reported that Mike was in the best shape of his career. 'Jeff is right,' said Tyson at a media conference. 'I feel terrific. I'm gonna gut him like a fish. His people are getting him killed. I'm an icon, an international superstar. I've seen a few tapes of this Irish kid and he didn't look impressive. It will be all over in a few rounds.'

Wearing his traditional black boots with no stockings, Tyson was welcomed into the ring by a rapturous crowd of 15,472. He acknowledged the cheers with a wave of his hand. McBride climbed between the ropes to the sound of blazing bagpipes and declined to look Tyson straight in the eye as referee Joe Cortez called them together for the pre-fight instructions. McBride towered over the former world champion like a tent. A nine to one underdog, the Irishman knew he would have to do something special to make a fool of those long odds.

It was a foul-filled fight, with both boxers guilty of misdemeanours and Cortez had to earn his fee. McBride worked behind a long left jab and clubbing rights but Tyson was able to catch him coming in with hard left hooks to the head and body. As the rounds went on, however, Tyson began to get very ragged, and was clearly showing his age, with his thirty-ninth birthday just a matter of weeks away, though he still had a points lead.

By the sixth round it was obvious that McBride had taken over. Tyson's once devastating punches, the kind that conjured up images of Jack Dempsey, Joe Louis and Rocky Marciano and of opponents being slammed to the canvas as though they had been thrown out of two-storey windows, were things of the past. Mike missed with a big swing near the ropes as McBride used his bulk again and simply pushed his opponent to the deck. Tyson stayed there, looking forlorn and bemused, as trainer Fenech called over the referee to signal his man's retirement.

There was understandably great joy in McBride's corner, with his handler Pascal Collins, Steve's younger brother, congratulating him. In sharp contrast, Tyson left the ring with his handlers, his head down, as he was pelted with paper cups, apple butts and crumpled newspapers from fans who booed him all the way to the dressing room. Iron Mike was now being referred to as Scrap-iron Mike. 'How the mighty have fallen,' mused Graham Houston reporting for *Boxing Monthly*.

McBride's new-found success brought promoters scurrying to his door. Had Ireland finally found a heavyweight capable of becoming world heavyweight champion? Unfortunately, it did not happen. In his next eight fights, McBride lost six, finally retiring from the ring after being knocked out in four rounds by Poland's Mariusz Wach, known as the Viking, in Connecticut in July 2011.

The fight was for the vacant World Boxing Council international heavy-weight title, a minor belt and not even fully recognised in America. Meanwhile, the search continues year after year for a native son capable of becoming the holder of boxing's greatest and most elusive prize, the heavyweight champi-onship of the world.

8. STEVE COLLINS

The electrician with sparks and true grit

It was a long road but Steve Collins finally made it to the top. A tough, gritty battler from Dublin's Northside with a burning desire to win, he holds several 'firsts' to make him a standout. He remains the only Irish boxer to win world titles at two different weights, middleweight and supermiddleweight, and the first from the city on the Liffey to win one. Collins is also the winner of more world championship contests than any other professional boxer from this island, nine in succession.

Known as The Celtic Warrior, with a shamrock cut into his hair above his ears, Collins began his professional career in the United States, always a stern breeding ground for aspiring champions. Collins lost two world championship fights early on and it was not until he reached his thirties that he fulfilled his true potential.

Having competed against the best on this side of the Atlantic, Collins tends to be linked more to the eighties and nineties and he met most of the big names of the period. There was an intense rivalry, for instance, between British world champions such as Chris Eubank and Nigel Benn. He took them on and beat them twice, no mean feats. After being pushed to the limit by Collins in a world middleweight title fight in 1990, Mike McCallum, the brilliant Jamaican, felt his chin and remarked: 'Collins is the toughest opponent I've ever fought. Period.'

Steve's true grit could certainly never be called into question, and it was once reported that a concrete company wanted to sponsor his chin. He was knocked off his feet just three times, once in his last fight, during an eleven-year career involving thirty-nine contests. Collins rarely stopped going forward. Interestingly, all three reverses on his record came against world champions. Because of his aggressive, hard-punching ring style, he was very much a throwback to the great middleweights of the 1940s and 1950s such as Sugar Ray Robinson, Jake LaMotta, Rocky Graziano, Tony Zale, Marcel Cerdan, Gene Fullmer and Carmen Basilio.

It is problematic to discern whether or not Collins would have won had he clashed with any of those illustrious ringmen, but he would certainly have held his own and at the finish they would have known they were in a fight, win, lose or draw.

In what has now become a classic DVD from 2004, *Steve Collins' Boxing's Hard Men*, he introduces footage from fights involving legends such as Sugar Ray Robinson, Muhammad Ali, Rocky Marciano, Joe Frazier, Mike Tyson,

Marvin Hagler, George Foreman and others. Included is footage from his own classic wars with Chris Eubank and Nigel Benn, as Collins indeed was one of boxing's hard men. They are well worth watching, even to get a flavour of his immense talent and toughness.

Collins was born into a working class family in Cabra on 21 July 1964. 'There was boxing on both sides of the family so it has always been there,' he recalled. 'My father Paschal was a former Leinster middleweight champion with the reputation of being a very composed boxer with a heavy wallop and he was the first boxer shown live on RTÉ television. His brother Terry Collins was another fine middleweight with an even greater claim to fame. As an amateur back in the 1950s, he had fought and beaten an English teenager named Reggie Kray who, along with his twin brother Ronnie, would become London's foremost crime lords.

'Because both of the Krays were highly rated boxers, it was considered quite an achievement at the time,' he recalled. 'But when they achieved notoriety for their activities outside the ring, Terry's victory became the stuff of legend in the Collins family, and as children, we were all aware that our uncle was one of the few men alive who could say that he'd had a fight with one of the Kray twins and won. Another boxing connection in my family was that my mother's brother, Jack O'Rourke, held Irish amateur titles in two divisions, middleweight and heavyweight.'

Collins got his first taste of boxing when, at the age of eight, he was taken down to Corinthians Boxing Club in the inner-city by his father and was introduced to the coach, Maxie McCullagh, who had won the European amateur lightweight championship in Oslo in 1949. 'Everything about the gym excited me,' he remembered. 'The smell of sweat and liniment. The sound of the speed ball beating out a steady rhythm on the bangboard. The sight of boxers burying punches into the heavy bag as it creaked back and forth on its swivel.'

From that moment, Collins was smitten. McCullagh got him his first fight which he won. This was what he wanted and he would do his very best to be good at it. At the age of eleven he joined Arbour Hill Boxing Club not far from his Cabra home. At the back of his mind, however, Steve wanted to be a professional like his idol Rocky Marciano, who had retired as undefeated heavyweight champion of the world in 1956 having won all his forty-nine fights, all but six either by countouts or stoppages.

'I knew I would never be six-foot four and be a really big heavyweight, even though Marciano himself was one of the shortest heavyweight champions at five-foot eleven,' he recalled. 'But as a junior and youth boxer I actually won heavyweight titles and once bashed up the Irish superheavyweight champion. Heavyweights were easy for me because many of them were so cumbersome. You know the old saying: "The bigger they are, the harder they fall." I eventually finished up as a middleweight.'

Collins won the Irish senior middleweight title at the National Stadium in 1986 in the colours of the St Saviour's Boxing Club on the city's northside, where he was trained by the former British professional lightheavyweight champion John McCormack from Dublin. He had reached the finals the previous year. But the urge to box for pay was never far from his mind and having won the Irish title and represented his country on five occasions, all wins, he decided to make the big move.

Steve, however, would take a different route and start his career in American rings. It was never an easy option but he reckoned that if he was going to make progress as a professional, then the US was the place to be. The year was 1986. Besides being a great fan of Marciano, Collins idolised Marvin Hagler, the great world middleweight champion who was coming to the end of his career at the time.

The Dubliner knew that Sean Mannion, his friend and fellow-boxer from his amateur days, had left Connemara in the West of Ireland a few years earlier, turned professional in Boston, and worked his way up the world ratings. This is the route Collins would take. After completing his apprenticeship as an electrician, he packed his bags and headed for the gym in Brockton, just outside Boston, in the autumn of 1986 to look up the Petronelli brothers, Pat and Goody, who ran the premises.

It was no coincidence that Marciano was born in Brockton. Nor was it a lucky chance that his number one active boxer, Marvin Hagler, had started his career with the Petronellis who remained his co-managers for several years.

'I always knew what I was doing,' he recalled for the author. 'For me, Marvin Hagler was the best middleweight of all time and, while I knew I would never be a skilful boxer like two of his contemporaries Sugar Ray Leonard or Tommy Hearns, I could relate to Hagler's style. I wanted to be coached by his people, learn like he did, and fight the type of opposition he fought.'

After having a cursory look at him in the gym, the Petronellis were not quite sure if the twenty-year-old Collins was the real deal or just a cheeky Irish kid chancing his luck in the tough American school of hard knocks and knockdowns. They decided to try him out in a little-known venue such as the Memorial Auditorium in Lowell, Massachusetts in October 1986 and were impressed when Collins stopped newcomer Julio Mercado after just under two minutes into the third round.

Collins made good progress, winning his first seven fights impressively before an opportunity came on 18 March 1988 to fight Belfast's unbeaten Sam Storey for the Irish middleweight championship, not in Ireland but in the Boston Garden. An enterprising promoter thought it would be a good idea to match two Irishman in Boston, with its strong Irish population. St Patrick's Day was the preferred date but the venue was unavailable so the following day was selected.

Storey, who would be defending the title he won a year earlier, was a member of a well-known Belfast boxing family and had beaten Collins as an amateur in the Irish senior finals of 1985 but this time Steve had the better of the ten rounds, winning a unanimous decision.

By the end of 1988, Collins had run up an unbeaten streak of twelve wins, mainly around the Massachusetts and New Hampshire areas but he was becoming disenchanted with his progress under the Petronellis. 'I had been with them for two and a half years but I was unhappy with the standard of my opponents, the amount of money I was getting for my fights and the pace at which things were happening,' he recalled. 'It was not until I pressurised them into getting me some meaningful fights against credible opponents for decent money that my career really took off.'

Then came the Paul McPeak fight. They clashed at Trump Castle Casino in Atlantic City in February 1989 and it turned out to be Collins' first big break. Known as the Killer and coached by ace trainer Emanuel Steward, McPeak from Kentucky was unbeaten in sixteen fights and big things were expected from him but the Dubliner was in top form.

Battling from a cut right eye from the first round, the crew-cut Collins punched his way to a totally impressive win when referee Tony Orlando intervened in the ninth round on the ringside doctor's advice. McPeak, who had been tipped as a future world champion, had even tried switching to southpaw but nothing worked. Collins won every round on the scorecards of two judges while the third gave McPeak only one. 'Collins exposed McPeak as a face-first slugger,' wrote a local ringside reporter. Collins remembered it as 'a night when I punched holes in McPeak'.

The victory earned Collins a shot at the USA middleweight title against Kevin Watts at the Resorts International Casino in Atlantic City in May 1989. Watts, from Pleasantville, New Jersey, was, like McPeak, expected to be too good for the Dubliner but it did not quite work out like that. Steve boxed a tactical fight against the taller American, and though he was dropped on his knees from a left hook to the body in a thrilling eleventh round, the only round he lost, he continually beat Watts to be punch.

All three judges marked their cards in his favour, 118–109, 118–110 and 115–112 but Collins the perfectionist was critical of his showing as though he had lost. 'I wasn't happy with my performance out there,' he told reporters in the dressing room. 'It was only sixty per cent of what Steve Collins can do. I didn't throw my combinations and I was getting caught too easily. The knockdown was a sucker punch and it took a lot of steam out of me. As to the future, I'll take on anybody who wants to meet me.'

Winning the USA title moved Collins up in the ratings, and after successfully defending the belt, he was matched with world middleweight champion Mike McCallum at the Hynes Convention Centre in Boston on the blustery, wintry night of 3 February 1990 for the title.

Billed as the Body Snatcher because of his tremendous body punching, McCallum, born in Kingston, Jamaica, also had a fine defence. He had previously won the world junior middleweight championship and would go on to capture a third world title, at lightheavyweight. Mike had been an outstanding amateur with an impressive collection of medals in his New York home, including gold from the 1978 Commonwealth Games and silver from the 1979 Pan American Games. He had reached the quarter finals of the 1976 Montreal Olympics and also won national AAU and Golden Gloves championships.

McCallum was a three to one on favourite to turn back the bold challenge of the Celtic Warrior but a war of attrition was anticipated. Collins was convinced the Jamaican would leave the arena without his title and had trained accordingly. This was certainly not going to be a Boston Tea Party.

The fight was promoted by Bob Arum of Top Rank but Arum had to bring in a local figure Al Valenti who insisted on being part of the promotion, seeing that it was taking place in his backyard. As it turned out, Valenti messed up his side of things. Known as the Phantom Promoter, he had announced around twelve fights in the previous couple of years and this was the only one that came off.

Valenti's press agent Larry Rossoff badly handled the journalists' credentials. These were previously granted by Top Rank, an experienced organisation in these matters but suddenly, and without warning, they were rescinded by Rossoff. On one occasion, he had assigned two writers to the one seat, with one writer cracking: 'Do we play musical chairs and take turns sitting on each other's laps?' Even the official supervisors of the World Boxing Association, who were sanctioning the fight, complained that they were assigned seats 'somewhere near the back of the hall' instead of their proper places at ringside.

Even though the three judges were neutral, there was an unconfirmed report that somebody from McCallum's camp at ringside was carrying a concealed weapon and had threatened the officials to make sure Mike was not robbed if the fight went to a decision after the full twelve rounds. This claim was strongly denied by McCallum's people who said they had full confidence in the judges and that their man would be treated fairly and without question.

Nevertheless, Collins was effectively the local boy and the city had a reputation for handing out 'Boston decisions' to their favourites. One writer cited the two world middleweight title fights between Sugar Ray Robinson and Paul Pender in Boston in 1960 when the split decisions in each case went to local boy Pender, many claiming that Robinson was robbed both times.

When the fight got under way, there was a capacity crowd of three thousand in the venue, with a television audience of millions. It was Boston's first championship fight since 1981 when Marvin Hagler stopped Vito Antuofermo in four rounds. From the moment referee Bernie Soto called the two boxers together for last-minute instructions and sent them back to their corners to await the first bell, McCallum as expected was a class act.

RINGSIDE WITH THE CELTIC WARRIORS

Over the first five rounds he used a slick assortment of sharp left jabs and jarring uppercuts on the inside. 'McCallum looked so superior in those early rounds that it seemed only a matter of time before it was "lights out" for the Irishman,' wrote *Boxing News* correspondent Jim Brady. 'He was storming in with wide punches like a man who has a covenant with destiny.'

Collins, nevertheless, kept the pressure on his man, cheered on by his family and supporters including Dublin's Lord Mayor Sean Haughey, a son of the Taoiseach, Charles Haughey, who were all now on their feet. As the rounds went by, Steve was never reluctant to exchange fierce punches in an attempt to bring down McCallum, or make up the points deficit. But the world champion was proving too crafty and ringworthy.

Going out for the last round, Pat Petronelli shouted in Collins' ear so as he could he heard above the din: 'You need a knockdown, Steve, to win this fight. Go for it.' But there would be no miracle on this cold February night. McCallum was expecting the Dublin boxer to go all out in the final three minutes and he was prepared, using his left jab to keep the determined Collins at bay and catching him with long rights to the head and body.

When the final bell rang and both boxers embraced each other, there could be only one verdict, a unanimous decision for McCallum. But to add to what had been a comedy of errors outside the ring in the lead-up to the fight, the scores were wrongly totalled and announced, although all were in McCallum's favour.

After checking their respective cards, the judges gave the correct tallies. Nicasio Drake made it 118–111 and Chuck Williams called it 117–113, with Lynn Carter's card reading 117–111. Mike McCallum was still middleweight champion of the world, though the decision was booed by the partisan crowd. Promoter Arum wryly observed on the scoring mix-up: 'If we keep checking these cards long enough, maybe Collins will win the fight.'

McCallum was full of praise for the Irishman's showing. 'Collins is the toughest man I've ever fought,' he said in the dressing room, wiping his face with a towel. 'He's a good puncher, a good boxer and he's got lots of heart. He is also the most awkward. You never knew what he was going to do next.' The champion's chief cornerman, the legendary Eddie Futch, commented: 'I don't think anyone in the middleweight ranks could have put up a better challenge.'

Futch, who was seventy-eight years of age at the time, was one of the world's leading trainers with an impressive CV and had coached, among others, three world heavyweight champions Joe Frazier, Ken Norton and Larry Holmes. He was also in the corner for Ireland's world bantamweight champion in the 1990s, Wayne McCullough.

Collins said he adopted the wrong tactics. 'I should have boxed him more,' he told the reporters who packed his dressing room. 'It wasn't just one punch from him but more a combination of them. He had me off balance and hit me with some body shots but I wasn't really hurt by any of them. I thought it was a little closer than the scores indicated but then, he's the champion so some of the closer rounds would go his way.'

Looking back on the fight in his retirement years, the Dubliner observed: 'It was one of the best performances of my career. I thought I had done enough to beat him but the judges thought differently. I was a little overawed by his reputation at the start. But I gave him such a hard time of it through the middle and latter rounds that he told me that no amount of money would convince him to give me a rematch.

'There was little doubt that McCallum was a master, the most gifted guy I ever fought. While I was game, I was still very raw but I was lucky that I was durable. For the first five rounds McCallum was getting his own way because I stood off and tried to box him. After that, I switched tactics, took the fight to him and I thought made it reasonably close but he won. No doubt about that. Anyway, looking back, beating McCallum at that stage was the worst thing I could have done. In the middleweight division then were the likes of Sugar Ray Leonard, Roberto Duran, Tommy Hearns and Marvin Hagler, all great fighters. I would have been destroyed, finished.'

Two years later Collins got another chance at the world middleweight championship. The titles were now becoming fragmented, with rival organisations springing up, resulting in considerable infighting and power struggles, with each hoping to get one over on the other. McCallum had been stripped of the championship, which was recognised by the World Boxing Association, for agreeing to box for the rival International Boxing Federation title.

The WBA then matched Collins with Reggie 'Sweet' Johnson, a southpaw from Texas, at the Meadowlands Arena, New Jersey on 22 April 1992. Arthur Mercante, one of America's most respected referees, was in charge so both men knew he would not stand any nonsense. Mercante had been the referee in such world title fight classics as the second Floyd Patterson–Ingemar Johansson in 1960, the first Muhammad Ali–Joe Frazier bout in 1971, Frazier's first clash with George Foreman in 1973, and would finish his career in 2001, having been the official in a record 145 world championship fights.

The Collins–Johnson fight was a gritty battle, and Mercante deducted a point from each boxer for low blows in the fifth round. The contest went to a split decision, with judge Samuel Conde Lopez making it a 114–114 draw but judge Uriel Aguilera calling it 115–113 for Johnson and judge Marcos A. Torres having it 115–114, also for Johnson.

Collins did not make any excuses for his narrow defeat but he remembered: 'I felt I was unlucky to lose the close decision but the death of my father Paschal at the time of the fight was a low point in my life and affected me very deeply. The Johnson defeat was so devastating for me. I had a lot going on at a personal level and it was hard to come to terms with it. I really had to dig deep to find the inspiration to continue my career after that.'

A third loss in his next fight six months later, again on a split decision, against the former world middleweight champion Sumbo Kalambay for the European middleweight title in the Italian town of Verbania, did not help his confidence, not to mention his world rating. Kalambay, from Zaire, held a win over Mike McCallum and was a classy and capable performer. Collins could not quite get going against him and the close decision went to the African. That fight, on 22 October 1992, would be the turning point in Steve's career. It was the last time he left the ring as a loser. He put the loss down to a learning experience.

Having parted from the Petronelli brothers and later from Barney Eastwood, who had taken Barry McGuigan to the featherweight championship of the world in 1985, Collins was now with the influential London-based Barry Hearn who ran Matchroom Promotions. Together they set about re-building the Dubliner's career, with another chance at the world middleweight title their ultimate aim.

Six impressive wins after the defeat by Kalambay, five either by countouts or stoppages, Collins got his big opportunity – against the champion, Chris Pyatt, a Londoner based in Leicester. They met under the blazing lights at the Ponds Forge Arena, Sheffield on 11 May 1994 and this time Collins was fired up for the fight of his life. Pyatt was defending his title for the third time since winning it from Steve's conqueror Sumbo Kalambay twelve months earlier and entered the ring as favourite.

Collins, attempting his third crack at the title after his two creditable failures, strode cheerfully from the dressing room into the ring to the sounds of Thin Lizzy's *Whiskey In The Jar* and seemed in a relaxed, confident mood, while Pyatt appeared quite serious, with his head down. In the first round, a left hook clipped Pyatt's chin as the Englishman came forward crouching, and Collins grinned as he tripped over his own feet and lost balance for a second. The cautious Pyatt, with his walk-in style, was generally out of range with his shots and Collins was able to catch him with his more accurate punching.

In the second round Steve continued to put pressure on the Leicester resident and landed several right-hand punches followed by a left hook, but Pyatt was still going forward, seeking those big shots that might bring about the Cabra battler's downfall. Pyatt was using his left jab a bit better now but Collins was connecting with more accurate blows. At the bell, Steve's corner told him to get in fast with his jabs and hooks and break up the champion's defence.

Collins lost his composure in the third after tripping over Pyatt's feet and Pyatt was able to land effective left jabs to the head and right hooks under the heart. A hard, straight right drove Collins into a corner and Pyatt was looking more confident now, determined to turn back the challenge of this brash, cocky Irishman. After two fairly even rounds, with some reporters giving it to Collins narrowly, Pyatt won this one.

Eusebio Pedroza ducks as Barry McGuigan sizes him up.

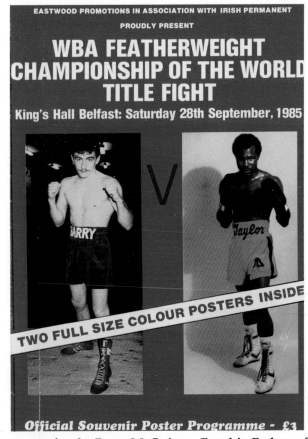

Programme for the Barry McGuigan–Eusebio Pedroza fight.

The author gloves up with Barry McGuigan.

©Matt McNamara

Above Left: **Dan Donnelly, an early nineteenth century folk hero.**

Above Right: **The monument in the Curragh in County Kildare to commemorate Dan Donnelly's fight with George Cooper.**

Jack Doyle on the offensive against King Levinsky.

'I would have beaten all these modern heavyweights,'
Jack Doyle points out to the author.

Bernard Dunne shows Thomas Myler his right fist.

©Aidan Walsh

Above: **Bernard Dunne gets through Felix Machado's defence with a long left.**

©Aidan Walsh

Middle: **Dunne wins the world superbantamweight title from Ricardo Cordoba.**

Left: **Dunne acknowledges the cheers of his fans after defeating Cordoba.**

©Aidan Walsh

Mike McTigue training in Lucan, County Dublin for his fight with Battling Siki.

McTigue on the attack against Battling Siki.

Tom Sharkey, right, and James J. Jeffries near the end of their epic title fight.

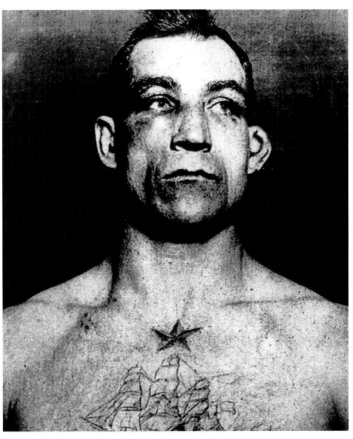

Sharkey proudly displays his tattoos, a sailing ship and a large star.

Yours Faithfully
Jem Roche

Jem Roche, who carried Ireland's world heavyweight title hopes against Tommy Burns.

Martin Thornton chats with Garda Jack Cosgrove, the former Galway full-back.

Mike Tyson sits it out against Kevin McBride in the sixth round.

Jim Cully towers over Joe Baksi in a publicity shot.

Promoter Jack Solomons and the author.

Steve Collins shakes Chris Eubank with a right cross.

Collins, Ireland's only world champion at two weights.

Muhammad Ali tells the author: 'Careful what you write about me,' as former great Billy Conn looks on.

Left: **Programme cover for the Ali–'Blue' Lewis fight.**

Right: **The author's advertisement in the Ali–'Blue' Lewis programme.**

Right: **Rinty Monaghan on all fours against Dado Marino before going on to win on points.**

Left: **A song from Monaghan alongside manager Frank McAloran.**

Above: **Michael Carruth wins an Olympic gold medal by defeating Juan Hernández.**

Left: **Carruth shows his Olympic gold medal to a young fan.**

Above: **Naseem Hamed showboating against Wayne McCullough.**

Below: **McCullough with his wife Cheryl and daughter Wynona.**

Katie Taylor in a sparring session with her dad Peter. ©Aidan Walsh

©Aidan Walsh

Katie is the poster girl for women's boxing around the world.

©Aidan Walsh

World, European and EU champion, Katie can now call herself an Olympic gold medallist.

The world champion continued his advantage in the fourth and was now grinning confidently. Could Collins wipe the smile off his face? Pyatt slammed in a hard right to the chin which jolted Collins but the resilient Dubliner fought back with a hard right uppercut, following up with a good left hook to the head. There was general agreement among the ringside press that the fight now seemed to be going Steve's way but there were still another eight rounds to go in which anything could happen.

In the fifth Pyatt took a number of rights on the chin before moving in and connecting with a left hook of his own as he continued to set the pace. Yet he often left himself open, a dangerous practice against an attacking fighter like Collins. True enough, the Dubliner saw an opening and moved in quickly with a chopping right to the chin and Pyatt crashed to the floor on his back, his legs shooting into the air. His mouth and nose bleeding, and looking the worse for wear, he got to his feet and took the mandatory count on unsteady legs.

Referee Paul Thomas looked at Pyatt closely before allowing it to go on. On the resumption he backed away, while throwing the occasional punch, but Collins was after him, pumping in the blows. Pyatt avoided most of them but had taken enough to persuade Thomas to wave it off. The time was two minutes and twenty-seven seconds. Pyatt turned to the referee in a mixture of surprise and disappointment but did not protest, although when they got to the dressing room, his corner were telling him that they were robbed.

'The referee's decision did draw criticism, in particular from ITV's Jim Watt, because Pyatt had his wits about him,' wrote Bob Mee in *Boxing News*. 'In spite of being in desperate trouble, he was defending himself well enough to make Collins miss most of the time. But the bottom line was that Pyatt was not punching back. Pyatt came forward recklessly and left himself open to counters. Collins did his share of missing as Pyatt came in, but apart from the third round, which belonged to Pyatt clearly, I felt the Irish challenger landed the cleaner punches and definitely held the edge.'

In the dressing room, a beaming Collins said: 'It's been hard getting there but I finally made it. I had my first fight twenty-one years ago. I feel like crying I'm so happy. There was a bit of talk before the fight that there was bad feeling between us but it wasn't true. Chris Pyatt's a nice guy. We are friends. He's a fighter, and with me, fighters come first, managers and promoters second.'

Pyatt commented that while he saw the finishing punch coming, he could not do anything about it. Referee Thomas and one judge John Montana had Collins ahead by two points, but Cesar Ramos and Nelson Vasquez marked Pyatt in front by two points.

Looking back on the fight, Collins recalled: 'Chris and I sparred regularly in the early nineties. Though I was the number one contender, I was never getting that fight because we were stablemates. However, when he jumped ship to Frank Warren, it was game on. You know, Chris was a blown-up welterweight and I was a boiled-down supermiddleweight. I was physically too strong for him but if Chris had known how drained I was and had jumped on me, I'd have collapsed.

'I had a very busy style but that night I waited and waited for the finishing punch because I knew I couldn't go twelve hard rounds. Though victorious, that fight convinced me I was never going to fight at middleweight again. At least it got me recognised as a world champion and gave me a springboard.'

When Collins next stripped for competitive action, he would be facing Chris Eubank for the world supermiddleweight title – and in an Irish ring. The fight was scheduled for the Green Glens Arena, an equestrian venue in Millstreet, Cork on 18 March 1995. When better, too, than on St Patrick's Weekend. Didn't Mike McTigue from Clare bring the world lightheavyweight title to Ireland on St Patrick's Day in Dublin in 1923, making up for the eighty-eight seconds loss by Wexford's Jem Roche for the world heavyweight championship on the same day in 1908, also in the capital.

Around this time Sky Sports was making inroads into the television scene with coverage of soccer and boxing. The supermiddleweight division was flourishing with boxers like Eubank, Nigel Benn and Michael Watson all setting the pace on the satellite channel and Sky bosses could not get enough of boxing. Belfast's Ray Close was originally scheduled to take on Eubank in Millstreet but a brain scan irregularity ruled him out.

Short of an opponent, Noel Duggan, the businessman involved in the promotion, turned to Collins, who had relinquished his middleweight title. Collins jumped at the chance to become Ireland's first world champion at two weights, and the nine-thousand seater arena was sold out within hours of going on sale, with Sky Sports hyping the fight at every opportunity.

Eubank, the fifth child of Jamaican parents, was born Christopher Livingstone Eubanks in Dulwich, London in August 1966 but would later drop the 's'. He spent much of his early years in Jamaica before returning to London. His young days were not without incident and in one school he was suspended no less than eighteen times for being a troublemaker, despite claiming that he was gallantly trying to protect other children from bullies. In another, he was suspended five times before being expelled.

Eubank was then put into care and spent time in various institutions under the care of local social services. At sixteen his father sent him to live with his mother in the tough South Bronx area of New York City where he was advised to keep off the mean streets. Chris joined the Jerome Boxing Club on Westchester Avenue and this turned out to be the turning point in his life. He became obsessed with training and went to the gym every day, working as a caretaker to pay his way.

Soon Eubank was taking part in amateur tournaments, graduating to Golden Gloves shows. Turning professional in Atlantic City in October 1985, shortly after his nineteenth birthday, he went on to win all his five bouts before returning to England to continue his promising career. 'My drive to succeed in boxing came from my desire to become an accepted individual,' he would later admit in his autobiography. 'I wanted to make something of myself.'

Eubank was making fast progress and by September 1991 had won two world titles, first at middleweight, which he defended three times, before moving up to supermiddleweight and putting that title on the line fourteen times. Now in Cork for his fifteenth defence, and without a loss in forty-one fights with two draws, he was going to provide a formidable challenge for Collins, whose record was twenty-eight wins in thirty-one fights. A very important factor in the challenger's favour, however, was home advantage.

A colourful character often accused of arrogance, Eubank had the reputation of making a flamboyant entry into the ring, and this time was no exception. As fireworks exploded high up at the back of the arena to spell out his name, the man billed by the Irish media as the Brighton Dandy was raised on a hoist while sitting on a glistening Harley Davidson motorcycle, revving up the engine with the lights flashing.

Then, after being lowered, he climbed into the ring to a mixture of cheers and mainly boos as the public address belted out his personal anthem *Simply The Best*, the hit song made famous by Tina Turner. This fight was the Goody v. the Baddie, and there were no prizes for naming who the baddie was. Paul Howard of the *Sunday Tribune* referred to Eubank as 'the pantomime villain'.

Meanwhile Collins sat on his stool, head down and eyes closed as though he was in a trance, oblivious to what was going on. He wore headphones under his dressing gown hood listening to tapes given to him by the sports psychologist Tony Quinn on his Walkman.

At the press conference to announce the fight, Collins had led Eubank to believe that he was having secret sessions on hypnotism with Quinn and had been 'programmed' to fire two punches for every one thrown by Eubank. The Dubliner let out the story that he would be helped by hypnotism when the fight got under way and would not feel pain.

Collins was simply playing mind games and the 'hypnotism' was nothing more than relaxation. This was his big break and he was merely concentrating on the job ahead. Eubank was even more convinced of the hypnotism theory when he saw Collins and Quinn in deep conversation at the weigh-in and threatened to pull out because Collins had an unfair advantage.

It was only when his handlers convinced him that it was a publicity trick that he consented to go ahead with the title defence. Still, he was definitely worried. It was a mental victory for the Dubliner. Collins admitted to the author in his retirement years: 'Tony was just a sports psychologist rather than a hypnotist, and was one of four I used during my career to help me blank out upsetting distractions. But Eubank was not to know that.'

The scheduled twelve-rounder began at a fast pace, so quick that the US referee Ron Lipton had to warn both men for infringements, telling them to 'keep it strictly professional, boys'. Collins' plan was to keep the pressure on the Londoner but Eubank was proving slippery, peppering the challenger with left jabs and winning the round. Eubank also did well in the second as Collins was somehow finding the canvas slippery and did not seemed to be able to get his big punches across.

The Dubliner was starting to find his range in the third and sent Eubank back with smashing rights to the head, following up with long left hooks, though he was often wild with swings. By the sixth, Collins was getting the range with left jabs and uppercuts, only for Eubank to storm back in the seventh with fast combinations.

It was anybody's fight up to then, with one and then the other gaining an advantage but Collins had much the better of the eighth when he put Eubank on the boards, with the big crowd on their feet, yelling themselves hoarse. He took an eight count but foiled the challenger's efforts to finish him off by moving and jabbing.

Eubank hauled himself back into contention by flooring Collins at the start of the tenth with perhaps the cleanest shot of the fight, a right to the jaw. Steve took full value from the count to clear his head, and boxed cleverly for the remainder of the round. Eubank tried desperately to find a similar opening in the eleventh but Collins fought off his determined advances with clever boxing. Eubank beckoned the Cabra battler on for a grandstand finish but the challenger wasn't having any and coasted his way to the final bell.

The decision was unanimous, with all three judges going for Collins, Roy Francis with 116–114, Cesar Ramos 115–111 and Ismael Fernandez 114–113. The venue erupted and Collins climbed on to the ropes to acknowledge the support of the crowd. Ireland had a world champion again.

'After twelve of the most frenetic and absorbing rounds, Collins was awarded Eubank's title,' wrote Paul Kimmage in the *Sunday Independent*. 'When it started, we were treated to a game of boxing chess. You have to admire a man who fights so often in another's back yard and Collins wisely decided he wasn't going to war and would box his way to the crown. When he came into this fight he carried the mantle of a fighter who had often over-reached but seldom achieved when the chips were down. This morning we are forced to re-valuate.'

Looking back recently on the fight, Collins recalled: 'Previous to meeting me, Eubank had always dominated the mind games but not this time. He knew I desperately wanted to fight him and I also knew he didn't want to fight me. Everything about the whole thing was magic. We got caught up in the middle of the St Patrick's Day parade the day before and if you wrote a script about it – the occasion, the opponent, the fight, it would be too corny to be true.

'Eubank wasn't the toughest I ever fought. The toughest I ever had weren't for world titles. They were fights in small venues and towns in America against guys nobody had ever heard of but were trying to make a living. They were the real test. Those were the fights where you learned about your nerves.

The Eubank fight was my chance to show my ability and prove I was the best. Getting there was the tough bit.

'After the American experience, motivating myself to take on the cocky showman Eubank was easy in comparison. That's why I remember the buzz before I left the dressing room. To me it was like a Rocky movie the whole way it happened. I was heading into the ring thinking, "This is it. It's happening. It's real." It really was like a movie. Think about it. A world title fight involving an Irishman taking place on the border of Cork and Kerry, the most beautiful part of Ireland, in an equestrian centre on St Patrick's Weekend.

'I never really enjoyed it at the time because, as in all my fights, I was focussed on the job and what I had to do. I'm actually enjoying it more now than I did then. I can appreciate it now. It was my ambition as a young boy to achieve the heights that I achieved that day.

'Eubank didn't want to fight me. He had seen me fight and knew my capabilities but I was next in line and he was told he had to take me on. He did, against his better wishes. Let me say though that he was the bravest, toughest fighter I met. I look at that wall over there and that was Eubank. He would die before he quit. He was great for boxing, the Muhammad Ali of his time. You either loved him or hated him but you knew of him. He brought a lot of attention to the sport.'

Collins returned to Dublin and was driven through the streets in an open double-decker bus as thousands cheered him on the way to a civic reception in the Mansion House. There was the inevitable return fight, six months later. The bout was set for Cork again, but this time at Páirc Uí Chaoimh. It was another grudge match, with both boldly and confidently predicting decisive victory.

A crowd of seventeen thousand six hundred and thirty-nine turned up fully expecting Collins to prove his first win was no fluke and that he was a worthy holder of the world supermiddleweight championship, the first Dubliner to rule the boxing world in any division. The small group of Eubank supporters who travelled over for the fight were confident that their man was far from finished and that he would reverse his lone loss in forty-six fights.

In what turned out to be another bruising encounter, or as the *Sunday Independent* had it in their ringside report under two by-lines Tom Cryan and Vincent Hogan, 'an absorbing battle that paid scant homage to the niceties of boxing but was absorbing in its intensity.' With the crowd roaring 'Collins, Collins, Collins', the Dubliner came out of his corner in the first round like a raging bull and nearly went through the ropes as Eubank sidestepped.

The Celtic Warrior composed himself, however, as the fight wore on, and while Eubank often caught him with hard, solid rights to the head, particularly in a torrid tenth round, Collins hit back and both men were still exchanging punches at the last bell. The Dubliner finished with his right eye bleeding from a cut sustained in the seventh round but cornerman Ernie Fossey kept it under control.

There was an eerie hush as the scores were announced. Judge Genaro Rodriguez had it 115–114 for Eubank, which brought the predictable boos from the partisan crowd, but the other two judges, Aaron Kizer and Paul Herman, both marked it 115–113 for Collins, resulting in tumultuous cheers, making the Dubliner the winner and still supermiddleweight champion of the world. A ringside poll of seven cross-channel boxing writers disclosed a wide winning margin for Collins. Ken Gorman, one of Britain's leading freelance writers and formerly with the *Daily Star* and the *Daily Express*, had Collins four points ahead. 'Collins wasn't an opponent,' he wrote. 'He was Hurricane Steve sweeping through Ireland's south coast.'

In the dressing room, the Cabra battler looked remarkably refreshed but was bewildered by the split decision. 'Without being biased, I can honestly say I won eight rounds,' he said. 'I was never worried by the cut, which came from a very bad clash of heads but there was no way it was going to stop me. The fight? I thought if anything that it was more exciting than winning the title. Right now, a fight with Nigel Benn is looking good.'

A stone-faced Eubank, his ring future now in serious doubt, left the arena in an ambulance for observation. He had rejected Collins' attempt at an embrace when the final bell sounded, and his solitary comment to waiting pressmen outside his dressing room was: 'He gave me a good fight and I have no complaints. He won the fight.'

In his autobiography, published eight years later, Eubank wrote: 'Collins' motivation was so intense I was taken aback. His resolve was maniacal, and despite my best intentions and meticulous preparations, I could not wrestle the crown away from him. This time, unlike the underhand first victory over me, Collins beat me fairly and squarely. I was not even as disappointed as after the first fight. I was understanding of the events of life. It was due to happen after so many victories, so many title defences, having been a professional boxer for eleven years. Winning and losing is just part of life. I just lost.'

Recalling the fight recently, Collins said: 'It was a real brawl. I had so much energy. I just harassed him, never let him settle and built up the points as the rounds were ticking over. There was a lot of things said about our rivalry but it was all hype.'

Two further defences against Englishmen followed, with Collins winning a unanimous decision over Cornelius Carr at the Point, now the O$_2$, in Dublin and stopping Neville Brown in eleven rounds back at Millstreet. But in the background loomed the shadow of Nigel Benn, the Dark Destroyer and former world middleweight and supermiddleweight champion. Benn had retired following his recent split-decision loss to the South African, Thulani Malinga but felt, even at the age of thirty-two and considerably past his best, he still had enough left to win back his supermiddleweight belt from Collins.

Born just outside London, the sixth of seven sons of Barbados émigrés, Benn developed into one of Britain's outstanding boxer-fighters of the 1980s and 1990s, but once admitted he was more scared of patrolling with the British Army in Northern Ireland during the Troubles than he ever was in the ring. He went in against Collins at the Nynex Arena, Manchester on 6 July 1996 in what was expected to be a war.

It was while it lasted. Collins was ahead when, in the fourth round, Benn, wearing his familiar black shorts and black boots, missed with a wild right, toppled over his right ankle and hit the canvas, grabbing the ankle. When he regained his feet, referee Gino Rodriguez asked him: 'Can you go on?' and he nodded. He hobbled back to the ropes but lacked the ability to escape, and after taking some heavy wallops from the confident Collins, waved his hands in surrender. It was all over just as the bell rang.

Benn said after the fight that he was not retiring, as had been rumoured, and that he wanted a return. 'There's no way I want my fans to see me bow out like that, turning my back on my opponent and going out a loser,' he said. 'I need to leave with a big victory, with a bang and I know I can beat him. I still have a lot of fight left in me.'

The return was arranged, again at the Nynex Arena, for 9 November and this one too ended prematurely. After being cheered into the ring by the twenty-two thousand crowd, Benn left it with a storm of boos ringing in his ears when he quit just at the end of the sixth round. Twice when he attempted to address the crowd, he was drowned out with a chorus of protests and shouts of 'quitter' and 'shame'.

It had been a bruising battle, with all three judges marking Collins ahead at the shock finish, Gordon Volkman by 58–55 with Dennis Nelson and Roy Francis each on 58–56. Paul Howard of the *Sunday Tribune*, and later a very successful novelist, noted: 'It was obvious that too many tough fights had taken their toll on the challenger.'

At the post-fight conference, Benn gave his views of why his sixteenth world title fight ended the way it did: 'I had a pretty tough time of it in the fourth round and when I went back to my corner they told me they were only going to give me one round to pull something out. They gave me two but it made no difference. I've probably been in more wars than anybody so how can anyone say I haven't got the stomach for a fight? After ten years and forty-eight fights, you find you don't have what you had a year or two before.'

Collins said he felt as disappointed as the crowd but conceded: 'Benn surprised me. He was tougher than in the first fight and he hit me with some harder shots. But I wanted to fight to the end. We should have been allowed to settle this argument once and for all.'

In an interview several months later, he admitted: 'It was an awful way to end a great career and I think Benn should have retired after the first fight. He knew the score then and, apart from the money, there was nothing to be gained by a rematch. He just didn't have the heart to battle on. Still, I wished he had hung on in there. I would have liked to have knocked him out. I'm not being callous as he would have felt the same about me. We became good mates later.'

Collins made two further defences of his title in 1997, stopping the Frenchman, Frederic Seillier, a two-time European supermiddleweight champion, in five rounds in London and extinguishing the Kansas City firefighter Craig Cummings in the third in Glasgow after climbing off the canvas in the first round. The Dubliner was set to defend his belt against newcomer Joe Calzaghe, a Londoner who grew up in Wales, in October 1997 but withdrew at a late stage through injury and was stripped of his world title.

Announcing his retirement at the end of the year, Collins said he had lost his motivation, and that his only viable option had been a match with Roy Jones Junior for the American's world lightheavyweight title. Jones would go on to win the world heavyweight championship. Collins said he would have no objections conceding weight to the Florida boxer and it would have been a good payday.

Jones, however, declined to even discuss the fight, despite repeated challenges from Collins, once face to face. The Dubliner, having been denied the fight he wanted, announced in a statement that he had no option but to hang up his gloves. 'There has been a lot of talk about me going in against Joe Calzaghe, and while Joe's a good up-and-coming kid, he wouldn't fill a parish church,' he commented.

In the following weeks Collins said in interviews that he would only return to the ring for a Jones fight but insisted that the Florida stylist was ducking him and was demanding from promoters 'exorbitant purses' for the fight. Jones denied this, and said he would welcome a Collins fight, but the ruling authorities insisted that Steve would have to take on Calzaghe first, with the winner going in against the American. Collins accepted this and agreed to come of retirement, but in May 1999 during a sparring session at the Lennox Lewis Gym in London, he sensationally collapsed.

Checking into a local hospital after experiencing headaches, he underwent a brain scan and failed it. Donal Shanahan, the consulting neurologist who carried out the test, told Collins, who was thirty-four at the time, that scar tissue from a previous injury, sandwiched between the grey matter of the brain and skull, had probably hardened. 'Impact on that part of your head could kill the cells and my advice is that you should not box again for fear of damage,' he said. Effectively, the neurologist was saying that another fight could kill him.

Collins recalled: 'He told me I could lead a normal life but because of the nature of boxing, I could not avoid receiving punches to that part of my head. The headaches I was experiencing in training were a warning, and that is why I had the brain scan. I could do anything else I wanted, apart from boxing, in complete safety so I announced my retirement.'

Promoter Frank Warren, who was behind the proposed Collins–Calzaghe fight, remembered: 'Steve made the right and sensible decision. Even if he wanted to fight on, I wouldn't have let him in the circumstances. He was financially secure and by walking away from the sport, he could get on with doing other things with his life.'

Collins was formerly based in Bangor, County Down and now lives on a fifty-five acre farm just outside the historic market town of St Albans, over twenty miles from London, with his second wife Donna. He had a cameo role in the crime movie *Lock, Stock and Two Smoking Barrels* as well as U2's video *Sweetest Thing*.

He runs a gym in Dublin with his brother Paschal, a former professional boxer and now a promoter, and makes guest appearances at boxing shows on both sides of the Irish Sea. As well as all that, Collins is also manager of the St Albans Polo Club and rides with the Pytchley Hunt. 'Life is good, Thomas,' he said. 'I enjoyed my boxing career and retired at the right time. I was lucky to work with two of my heroes, the great middleweights Marvin Hagler and Jake LaMotta. I've no regrets.'

9. The Croke Park Experience

When Ali came to town

There were no home boxers in the main event or the chief supporting bout at Croke Park on the warm evening of 19 July 1972. But when you have Muhammad Ali topping the card, you effectively don't need anybody else. Even though the man known as The Greatest was not world champion at the time, he was still a formidable figure on the heavyweight scene, and was going in against Al 'Blue' Lewis, a tough Detroit fighter of twenty-nine and ranked sixth in the world.

It could not be said that Ali was past his best and looking for easy money to feather his retirement nest. He was thirty, and two of his greatest victories had still to come, the classic wins over George Foreman in the Rumble in the Jungle in 1974 and against Joe Frazier in the Thrilla in Manila a year later. Lewis was twenty-nine.

All in all, the Croke Park experience remains a pivotal part of Irish boxing history. From the moment he touched down at Dublin Airport, the man formerly known as Cassius Clay was mobbed wherever he went. He met the Taoiseach, Jack Lynch and fellow politicians, movie people, sporting personalities and celebrities from many walks of life. Legendary Kilkenny hurler Eddie Kehir showed him the rudiments of the game and had him wield a camán for a photo opportunity.

Dubliners remember Ali joining in the craic at a few local bars, and a road sweeper recalled a lengthy chat he had with him outside Croke Park. He also took up the invitation from an old lady who invited him into her house for a cup of tea. He was interviewed in the press, radio and television, and it seemed everybody wanted to meet the man who still called himself 'The Champ'.

Then again, wasn't he a distant Irishman? Didn't his maternal great-grandfather Abe Grady emigrate from the Turnpike area of Ennis, County Clare in the 1860s, make his way on a cargo ship to New Orleans, work his way up the Mississippi river and finally settle in Kentucky?

Indeed, the occasion turned out to be a magical ten days for Irish boxing. Ali was considered the most charismatic boxer the world had ever seen. In the eyes of many too, he was the best world heavyweight champion of all time, too. He was a complete all-rounder with a sturdy chin, a heavier version of Sugar Ray Robinson. When he came to Dublin, he was on a winning six-fight streak since losing a decision to Joe Frazier sixteen months earlier so he could not afford a defeat in his campaign to recapture the title which he regarded, rightly or wrongly, as his.

This author was in the very fortunate position of being in the centre of things, as boxing correspondent for the *Evening Herald* and publicity officer for the fight. Perhaps not too surprisingly, in private Ali turned out to be very quiet and subdued, and usually liked to be alone, a sharp contrast to the lively and bombastic image he presented to the public.

An Ali fight in the capital was something that everybody said would never happen, against Lewis or anybody else. If the Kerry promoter Butty Sugrue from Killorglin thought he could entice the celebrated American to box in a city he had probably never heard of, and a graveyard for professional boxing, he was crazy. He was setting himself an impossible task. Why, it would be like asking the Pope to support birth control or agree to women priests. Sugrue, however, was convinced he could get Ali into a Dublin ring.

An enterprising man with little formal education, and one of three brothers, Sugrue was once a circus strongman and had performed incredible feats of strength such as lifting horses off the ground, pulling double-decker buses, bending horseshoes and lugging heavy furniture, including beds, up and down flights of stairs. The little matter of enticing Muhammad Ali, one of the world's best boxers, to Dublin was small fry compared to these.

Sugrue, who ran two successful pubs in London at the time, The Wellington and The Elephant's Head, had dabbled in occasional boxing and wrestling promotions in the UK and had brought the retired world heavyweight champion Joe Louis on an Irish tour in 1967 so he saw nothing to dissuade him from bringing Ali to Dublin. There was the little matter, though, of his Irish licence which had been suspended in 1962 after he left town suddenly following a promotion in Kilkenny without paying the British boxing agent Roger Coulson his agreed fee of £25.

Butty explained to Irish Boxing Board of Control officials when he met them in their offices in Talbot Street that he had since tried to contact Coulson but failed. 'I think he's gone away,' he told chairman Terry Rogers, who did not quite believe the story. Finally, before leaving the office, Sugrue wrote out a cheque and handed it to Jack Horton, IBBC secretary. He had no choice, as the British Boxing Board of Control had announced earlier that none of their boxers would appear on any card promoted by Sugrue unless he first settled his differences with Coulson, who had a London address, despite Butty's claims to the contrary.

Sugrue's first meeting with Ali was in May 1966 when the world champion was in London for a title defence against Henry Cooper at Highbury, Arsenal's football ground. Ali had been told that Sugrue was an admirer so he dropped in to see the Kerryman and had a conversation on boxing in general, though at no time was the idea of a Dublin fight brought up. Several years later, the thinking changed when Ali's agent Harold Conrad was back in London with Muhammad for an advertising promotion.

A boxing man for all seasons, the dapper Conrad was a former fight writer for the *Brooklyn Eagle* in New York and a sometime novelist, publicist and friend of literary giants like Ernest Hemingway and Damon Runyon. Along with Ali, he met Sugrue at the Wellington pub and Butty sold them the idea of a big fight in Dublin. They said they would think about it but privately Conrad was sceptical. 'We get these kind of offers all the time,' he said later. 'Most come to nothing, just hot air, but I told Sugrue we would look into it.'

Back in New York, Conrad made contact with Ali's attorney Bob Arum, who would in later years become one of the world's leading promoters, a position he still holds today. Arum told him that Ali would fight in Dublin provided a fee of £100,000 was lodged in a US bank three months beforehand. It did not matter who the opponent would be. 'My man will win anyhow,' Arum said confidently.

This information was relayed to Sugrue and he agreed straight away to set the whole thing in motion. He promptly arrived in Dublin on a cold February day in 1972 and held a press conference to announce that Ali would box in Dublin in the summer, even though he had no fixed date, no venue arranged, no closed circuit television in place and. no opponent. He did say, however, that the Californian heavyweight Jerry Quarry was available as was the European champion Jose Urtain from Spain. Sugrue would be looking at several Dublin venues such as Lansdowne Road rugby ground, Tolka Park soccer pitch, Leopardstown race track and the GAA ground, Croke Park.

'The weather prospects in say, June or July, would be good and I will be looking for financial support from the Irish government and local businesses,' he said. 'This will be the biggest fight, the biggest night, in the history of Irish boxing and we would be looking at a crowd of say, up to forty thousand. In that context, Croke Park might be the best bet but we'll source out all the venues I mentioned.'

The IBBC, nevertheless, were still not completely happy with the way Sugrue was treating them. 'We gave him back his licence and what does he do?' chairman Terry Rogers would remember later. 'Without saying anything, he goes off to New York and hands over a £25,000 deposit to Ali's people. We announced in a press statement that either he dealt with us direct, and informed us of what he was doing, or there would be no fight. We would take no nonsense from this fellow, who spent so little time in Ireland. Effectively, he was a blow-in.'

Sugrue arrived in Dublin in May in true cavalier fashion and called a media conference at Dublin Airport, again ignoring the IBBC, who only heard of it from a chance phone call to a boxing writer on an entirely different matter two hours beforehand. Rogers immediately despatched an official to the conference to remind the promoter once again not to be keeping them in the dark, or there would be no fight. 'This man is doing exactly what he likes, and it's all unofficial,' complained a red-faced Rogers. 'Does he not realise that the board has first to sanction the whole operation, and naturally has to know what's going on?'

The contest would be staged at Croke Park on 12 July 1972, said a defiant Sugrue, having reached an agreement with Sean O Síocháin, general secretary of the GAA. Ali's opponent would be neither Jerry Quarry nor Jose Urtain as originally mentioned but Al 'Blue' Lewis, a tough American heavyweight out of Detroit with a record of twenty-six wins and four losses, sixteen of his victories coming by way of countouts or stoppages. The fight would be over twelve rounds.

A good puncher with either glove and a hulk of a man, Lewis had knocked out the formidable Cleveland 'Big Cat' Williams in four rounds the previous year and had won seven of his last eight fights. He had also put away Eduardo Corletti in two rounds in July 1968 when the handsome Italian was number two in the world. So it certainly looked as though he would give Ali a tough fight, and would not be a pushover or a fall guy going in for the money and making a quick exit.

Sugrue also announced that Conrad would be his co-promoter, although Butty himself would be doing most of the work. Providing he got good financial backing from business interests, the Irish government and the Irish Tourist Board, then known as Bord Fáilte, he would also build a home for handicapped children on an island he owned two miles off Skerries along the north Dublin coast. He had a handicapped child himself.

As it happened, the fight was put back a week, to 19 July to allow final details to be worked out, not the least of which were the closed circuit television arrangements to beam the fight to the world at large, and particularly the US, to enable the whole operation to be profitable. Not surprisingly, like the IBBC, RTÉ were kept in the dark about all this. Michael O'Hehir, head of sport at the station, said: 'We haven't heard a word from Mr Sugrue about any TV plans, and obviously we want to know what is happening. July is a busy month for us, with GAA matches, major golf tournaments and the Sweeps Derby. We will need to know of his plans, and know pretty soon.'

Problems with television arrangements would soon arise, however, as they did a year earlier when a London company had unsuccessfully tried to beam Ali's world title fight with Joe Frazier from New York to Dublin on closed circuit TV. The idea was dropped. Another serious snag, this time a vital one, now arose when the anticipated financial backing failed to materialise.

Undaunted and without financial support, Sugrue typically went ahead, fully confident he would get up to forty thousand fans through the gate anyway. 'It's not every day you get a chance to see somebody like Muhammad Ali in live action,' he proudly proclaimed, although many detected more a sense of hope than reality in his gate prediction. Indeed, even though the date, venue and opponent had been finalised and tickets printed, doubts still remained among the general public and boxing writers in general whether the fight would ever take place at all, and that it wasn't all just a pipe dream. Was Butty Sugrue really living in wonderland?

Nevertheless Lewis was the first to arrive in town and told reporters: 'I'm in the best condition of my career, and I know I'll win.' When this writer asked him how he planned to counteract Ali's considerable speed, he replied: 'Well, I'll simply cut him off. True, Ali is a strong, accurate puncher as well as being fast but he's not invincible. This is my big chance and I don't intend to pass it up. Remember, I was one of Ali's sparring partners when he was preparing to fight Jimmy Ellis last year and I put him on the canvas. You ask him and he'll confirm this. I can tell you he didn't like the experience being on the floor.'

At a media conference the next day, boxing writers learned a bit more about Alvin Lewis, of his young days in Detroit, his escapades with juvenile gangs and an event when he was nineteen that changed his life. It was alleged that he had killed a man during a robbery. Lewis denied it but he was convicted and jailed. It was in prison that he decided to follow the example of the former world heavyweight champion Sonny Liston who turned to boxing when he was behind bars. He would spend time in the gym.

Lewis said he still might be in prison were it not for a dramatic incident during the sixth year of his confinement. A riot broke out in Jackson State Penitentiary in Michigan during which two doctors, two policemen and five guards were taken as hostages in an attempted break-out. Lewis decided to act on the side of the law. Single-handedly he waded in, knocked a number of convicts flat on their backs and secured the release of the hostages. His efforts brought swift reward. Released from prison, he was offered a fairly well-paid job as a rehabilitation officer among juvenile delinquents. It was a position he said he still held in Detroit, a city noted as being one of the most lawless in the US.

If Lewis came to town in somewhat low-key fashion, Ali's arrival the next day had a carnival atmosphere about it. When he alighted from the plane at Dublin Airport he was greeted by girl pipers dressed in green, presented with a shillelagh and escorted to the media reception room to meet a packed gathering of Irish and foreign reporters and cameramen.

'I'm really pleased that all you folks turned out in such big numbers to greet the prettiest and the greatest,' he beamed, running a comb through his hair. When this writer asked him to name the round when Lewis might fall, he said: 'Predicting is something I don't do any more, sir. Lewis is a good fighter and must be respected. All I want to do is whup him, beat Floyd Patterson in New York in September and then go on and take the title, my title, back from Joe Frazier.'

Crowds followed Ali everywhere he went, and he was never too busy to sign autographs. 'He was like the Pied Piper over there in Ireland,' recalled US sportswriter and author Budd Schulberg who was at ringside for the fight. 'It was really kind of magical. He had enormous influence on the people. Indeed, I would go so far as to say that with his Irish roots he was a fellow Irishman,' said Schulberg, whose most famous novel *On The Waterfront* was later made into a Hollywood movie starring Marlon Brando.

Among Ali's entourage was his bodyguard Roc Brynner, although exactly what protection he was doing was never made clear. A son of Yul Brynner, the famous bald-pated Hollywood actor well-known for movies like *The Magnificent Seven* and *The King and I*, Roc did not appear to even carry a gun. Moreover, he was slightly built, six inches shorter and nearly six stone lighter than Ali.

A graduate of the renowned Yale University in New Haven, Connecticut, Brynner was no stranger to Dublin, having studied at Trinity College at the age of sixteen and earned a master's degree in philosophy. After graduation, he stayed on in the city, and at the Dublin Theatre Festival performed his one-man adaptation of Jean Cocteau's *Opium*, which he had previously staged on Broadway. A close friend of Conrad, Brynner would often arrive ahead of an Ali entourage and ostensibly look things over in the city or town.

Among his outlandish outfits while in Dublin for the Ali fight was an ensemble consisting of a garish pink floppy hat, a long red crochet vest and white flared trousers. His long hair was set off by a gold earring and he told reporters that he had grown his fingernails unusually long to assist his playing of a twelve-string guitar, on which he tried to teach Ali some rudimentary chords.

Brynner could often be seen sitting crossed-legged playing the guitar in the lobby of the luxurious Opperman's Hotel and Country Club on the outskirts of the city, where the Ali party was based, and singing quietly, sometimes to himself. He would proudly tell guests that he composed a little ditty in which his boss regained the world heavyweight title.

Shortly after Ali's arrival, Sugrue presented the Taoiseach, Jack Lynch, with two complimentary ringside tickets at Leinster House. One English Sunday newspaper carried a story that Lynch showed his complete lack of knowledge of the situation when, on receiving the two tickets, allegedly asked Sugrue who exactly was fighting, and where would the ring be? The report said that Sugrue was tempted to answer, 'Joe Louis and Jack Dempsey, and the ring will be up in the stands' but kept his views to himself. The story was denied by the government press office which said it was 'pure poppycock and typical of the reporting in English papers' but several boxing writers who were there swore it was true.

The following day Lynch invited Ali to Dáil Éireann, which created the most spontaneous excitement since President Kennedy addressed both Houses of the Oireachtas nine years earlier. It seemed that the former world champion must have shaken the hand of every member of the cabinet as he made his way down the corridor to the Taoiseach's office.

'It's a truly great honour to meet the prime minister of your great country,' he told Lynch. 'I've been to Britain, Germany and Switzerland but they never honoured me like this. I would also like to compliment the Irish people on their proud history of struggle. I know what their struggle has meant because my people, too, have been underdogs for a long time.

'I can never forget how, when I was a little boy in Louisville, Kentucky, thinking of civil rights, the mayor of Louisville was a giant figure to me. Now here I am meeting Ireland's prime minister. I am just an athlete and a boxer. My ambition is to be a leader of people someday, helping people through their troubles. That's my goal.'

Lynch told Ali that he himself had a fight on his hands in a mid-Cork by-election, and added jocosely: 'Maybe you might come down and be a candidate for us. I'm certain you could pull in many votes for us. You know, I played many times on that field where you will be boxing Lewis.' Lynch would remember in later years that he was surprised to learn that he was the first leader of a government in the West to invite the boxer to make an official visit. 'Ali asked me all about Northern Ireland, having just read snatches of the conflict in American newspapers,' recalled the former Taoiseach. 'He was a most interesting man indeed.'

Before Ali signed the Visitor's Book and looked in for a while at the Dáil proceedings from the Distinguished Visitors' Gallery, he sat down for a meal in the restaurant with his party. He signed autographs for the restaurant staff and when one of them rang home to say he would be delayed, Ali took the phone out of the man's hand and said on the line: 'Don't worry, madam. Your husband is with the greatest boxer in the world. So don't go whippin' him tonight, because he is being delayed in the company of the real champion.'

'Muhammad Ali loves people,' said his trainer Angelo Dundee in between sips of Gaelic coffee. Dundee was with Ali since he first turned professional after winning a gold medal as a lightheavyweight in the Rome Olympics of 1960. 'Incidentally, this Irish coffee is good, very good. You definitely have something going for you in this.'

John Huston, the Hollywood director who lived in Galway at the time, had a new movie on release called *Fat City*, a boxing film. It was not about the glossy, glamorised side of the sport with its multi-million dollar purses in world title fights but the underbelly of the sport, where washed-up fighters fight for meagre purses in small, dingy arenas, hoping against hope to get that big break. It starred Stacy Keach as an old, discouraged boxer at the end of the line and Jeff Bridges as an ambitious newcomer, a dozen or so years younger. They meet in a gym in a small town in southern California and strike up a friendship.

The movie was considered Huston's best since *The African Queen* starring Humphrey Bogart and Katharine Hepburn twenty years earlier. *Fat City* had been premiered earlier in the summer at the Cannes Film Festival to critical acclaim and was due to open in New York shortly. Harold Conrad suggested to Huston that he get a print of the movie from Hollywood and show to the boxing writers and fight personalities in town. This was agreeable to Huston, a keen fight fan, who had been a lightweight boxer in Los Angeles in his early days, with twenty-three wins in twenty-five professional fights. The film was shown at the Regent Cinema in Dublin city and got a round of applause when the final credits rolled.

At one point in the film there was a scene where a brash school kid who bore more than a passing resemblance in voice and looks to the younger Ali, tells Bridges' character that he intended to be the champion of the world by the time he was eighteen. 'I'm too fast, and there's nobody who can beat me,' he boasts. Ali, impressed by the kid's eloquence and confidence, jumped up from his seat, and cheering, shouted at the screen: 'Stop the picture, that's me up there, listen to him. That's me talkin'. You all hear!' There was laughter and cheers in the audience.

In a wide-ranging and entertaining television interview on RTÉ with Cathal O'Shannon that night, Ali said he was fighting Lewis because he was helping him get a decent pay day. 'Nobody wants to take on Lewis,' he said. 'Joe Frazier won't fight him and George Foreman won't fight him and Jerry Quarry won't fight him. To most boxers and managers, this is just a business and they figure that if they are offered a top contender like Lewis, they won't take him because they don't want to take a chance and lose unless they are getting very well paid.

'Top notch fighters taking on Lewis can't receive a proper payment because he's not famous and yet he has a chance of beating them. In other words they have nothing to gain and everything to lose. I'm fighting him because everybody is ducking him but he's a good fighter. What sort of a chance does he have with me? Two – slim and none. After I fight Floyd Patterson next, I want the champ, Joe Frazier. That is, if he comes out of hiding. Frazier's a good slugger but he's not scientific. He's rough. Physically I beat him last time and won nine of the fifteen rounds but I didn't get the decision. Next time there will be no mistake.'

Both boxers did four miles of roadwork each morning. Ali ran in the Dublin mountains and Lewis stayed in the city, working out in the Phoenix Park. They trained on alternative days in the Croke Park glass-walled handball alley which had been converted into a gym. Veteran writers could not recall an occasion when there was more boxing talk in the air. Newspapers carried stories every day. At the weigh-in at the Gresham Hotel on O'Connell Street hundreds of people blocked the entrance and it was delayed for fifteen minutes. When both fighters eventually made it onto the scales Ali weighed 15 st 13½ lb and Lewis 15 st 7 lb.

After signing autographs, both boxers returned to their base. Ali was chauffeured by limo to his swanky quarters at Opperman's, opened just three weeks earlier and situated ten miles from the city centre on the slopes of the Dublin mountains with a magnificent panoramic view of the bay. Lewis travelled the five-minute journey along the quays in a dusty second-hand van to the modest and quaint Ormond Hotel, built over seventy years earlier and where James Joyce wrote a chapter of *Ulysses*. Lewis said the hotel was comfortable but complained of the continual noise of heavy city traffic, mainly trucks, always ringing in his ears and making it difficult to sleep.

The day before the fight, rumours spread in town that it might not go ahead or at least be postponed as: (*a*) Ali had a bad cold and had to miss some training sessions; and (*b*) ticket sales were very slow, with Sugrue and Conrad reported to be very concerned, and considering a smaller and cheaper venue than Croke Park.

Ali's trainer Angelo Dundee, aware of the rumours about his boxer, said it was only a slight head cold and that Muhammad had not missed any training sessions. 'He'll be fine,' he announced. When Sugrue was asked about the rumours, he said: 'Rubbish!' Agreeing that while ticket sales were slow, he felt fully confident they would pick up on the night. He said there was no question of switching the venue, and that the fight would go ahead as planned in Croke Park.

Ali was a five to one on favourite when the boxers entered the ring, with the evening sun still shining from a cloudless blue sky. It was the hottest July for seventeen years. At ringside were several movie celebrities including John Huston and Peter O'Toole. Nearby was future US president Ronald Reagan, at the time Governor of California. Ironically, Reagan had refused Ali a licence in the state when the boxer returned from a three-year exile after being banned over his refusal to be inducted into the US Army during the Vietnam War. A few seats away was Taoiseach Jack Lynch. Behind them sat civil rights campaigner Bernadette Devlin and former world middleweight champion, London's Terry Downes.

On the opposite side of the ring were two former world lightheavyweight champions Jose Torres from Puerto Rico and Billy Conn, the Pittsburgh Kid, whose grandmother was from Cork and grandfather from Derry. Irish reporters sat alongside top British and US boxing writers and columnists, all ready at their typewriters and notepads to record the action. After New Jersey referee Lew Eskin, who edited a boxing magazine and was a part-time fireman, called the contestants together for the usual pre-fight instructions, the sound of the bell sent them on their way. The fight that everybody said was an impossible dream was now a reality.

The pattern was set in the first round, with Ali circling the ring, spearing Lewis from long range with jabs that thudded into his face like darts. He also shook up the Detroit fighter with stiff left hooks in close, taking the round by a wide margin. By the third Lewis was looking decidedly tired, as though he was wearing deep-sea diver's boots and had lead weights on his arms. Ali was like the Scarlet Pimpernel: here, there and everywhere. Lewis did not seem able to pin his opponent down long enough to land any effective shots and was falling well behind on points.

Towards the end of the fifth, the fight suddenly burst into action like a hay-barn set alight by a discarded match. Ali landed a cracking left hook followed by a smashing straight right that lifted Lewis off his feet and dropped him to the canvas, both feet shooting into the evening air like an upturned turtle. It looked all over as the crowd yelled but somehow the Detroit boxer struggled to his feet at the count of nine. Another blow might have finished him but the bell rang and he walked unsteadily to his corner.

Lewis seemed to have shaken off the effects of that near disaster when he went out fresh for the sixth but effectively it was all over after that, with Ali pitching and Lewis catching. The end now seemed as inevitable as the rising of the sun. However, in the succeeding rounds Ali seemed to take it easy on the outclassed Lewis as though he wanted to give the fans good value and not end it too soon.

It was all over in the eleventh when, after Ali landed a barrage of hooks and uppercuts, referee Eskin jumped between them and called it off after seventy-five seconds of the round had elapsed. By then, as Peter Wilson wrote in the *Daily Mirror* the next day, 'the strength and the stamina, but never the spirit, had seeped out of Lewis as a tyre with a slow puncture loses its air.'

The finish triggered scenes of pandemonium. The ring was invaded as swarms of well-wishers clambered over the press benches and raised plat-forms, which creaked and finally collapsed under the great weight. Several typewriters were stamped on, including this writer's machine. Gardai waved their batons as they struggled to clear the ring as both boxers and their handlers pushed and heaved their way through the crowd and to the sanctuary of the dressing rooms.

Ali would admit that the battle to get to the dressing room was tougher than the fight in the ring, and the rest of the card was delayed for nearly half an hour as gardai grappled with the crowd to clear a way for Ali and to restore some kind of order. Lying on the rubbing table and covered in oil like some giant seal as flash bulbs exploded all around him, he told reporters: 'Lewis deserves to be rated higher than sixth in the world. He caught me with some good rights and he's a pretty tough guy. I'm real glad it's over. All you guys said this fellow was going to be a pushover, a no-hoper, but he proved you all wrong.'

When this writer asked him how the win compared to some of his other victories he said: 'I have been in better fights. I could have fought better but I was just getting over a cold and I wasn't at my best. Maybe I'm doing a little too much boxing and this was my sixth fight in the past nine months. I might be getting a bit stale, I don't know.

'I also have a fight coming up in New York in September against Floyd Pat-terson and that's an important one as I want to get by Patterson and take on Joe Frazier for the world title. That's my goal. But again, I want to take nothing away from Lewis. He fought a good fight but in the end I guess there could be only one result when you are in with the greatest – and the prettiest,' he added, rubbing his hand down the side of his unmarked face.

The other dressing room was much more subdued. 'Ali doesn't punch particularly hard,' said Lewis as his physician treated a badly bruised right eye. 'Let me say though that he's a wonderful boxer and on this showing he would regain the title from Joe Frazier. I'm certain of it. I'm quite pleased with my performance against the man I consider the best heavyweight, sorry, the best at any weight, in the world. It was the first time I went further than ten rounds. I might have done a little better if I'd had more fights recently, as this was my first in over ten months but that's boxing. Some you win and some you lose. If you see Ali again, tell him I wish him good luck for the future.'

The real losers were promoter Sugrue and his associate Conrad. The attendance of seventeen thousand eight hundred and twenty-five was a long way off the forty thousand Butty had confidently predicted. Having already paid Ali £100,000 and Lewis £15,000, plus purses for the rest of the six-fight show as well as various people who helped in one way or another, there was nothing left for the organisers except unpaid bills for the many overheads, including the costly hire of Croke Park.

'So what?' said a philosophical Sugrue to the boxing writers who joined him for breakfast of bacon, eggs and cornflakes at the Gresham Hotel the following morning. 'At least I put Dublin on the boxing map. Nobody can honestly say "Where's Dublin" again, can they now?'

Ali would regain the world title in 1974, but from George Foreman who had knocked out Joe Frazier in two rounds. Sadly now a victim of Parkinson's, he was back in Ireland in 2009 to trace his ancestral home in Ennis, County Clare where a crowd of over ten thousand greeted him, proving quite clearly that the man once known as 'The Greatest' had certainly not lost his tremendous popularity, or indeed ever will. During this trip he was also guest of honour at a charity function in Dublin.

On both occasions this writer preferred not to meet him. It had been thirty-seven years since the Croke Park occasion and as time passes it is often better to remember your heroes as they were, and not as shadows of their former selves. Lewis is a respected trainer in Detroit today. Sugrue died in 1976 following a heart attack at his Wellington pub. Conrad suffered a minor stroke while in Las Vegas in 1991 and passed away from a brain tumour shortly after.

10. JIMMY MCLARNIN

Baby Face with the killer punch

The birth certificate said James Archibald McLarnin but in the ring he was Jimmy McLarnin. American sportswriters tagged him Baby Face but there was nothing angelic about him once the bell rang. A killing puncher with skill to match, and a strong chin, the man from Hillsborough in County Down held the world welterweight title for the best part of two years when the competitive 10 st 7 lb division was packed with great boxers and heavy hitters.

One of the sport's major attractions in the 1920s and 1930s, often regarded as boxing's Golden Age, McLarnin struck fear into the best welterweights in the world and could target a punch with total accuracy. However, like many hard hitters, McLarnin suffered hand injuries throughout his career, and later on he was forced to become more of a boxer because of this, and a very successful one at that. It made him more of an all-rounder.

Of McLarnin's seventy-seven professional fights – sixty-two wins, three draws and one no decision – twelve victories were over men who had held world titles at one time or another. On five occasions, he defeated a reigning champion in a non-title bout, and to this day he remains the last Irish boxer to win a world championship in America.

Boxing historian Bert Randolph Sugar, the man widely regarded as the sport's greatest storyteller right up to his untimely death in March 2012, rated McLarnin as the eighth best welterweight in ring history in a list that included greats like Sugar Ray Robinson, Henry Armstrong and Sugar Ray Leonard, so Baby Face was in good company. *Irish Daily Star* boxing columnist Gerry Callan describes McLarnin as 'one who has a legitimate claim to the title of Ireland's greatest ever boxer'.

Another important element of McLarnin's career was his knack of being able to put away Jewish boxers. From a financial point of view, this Irish–Jewish rivalry proved very profitable. He beat such Hebrew stars as Jackie Fields, Joe Glick, Sid Terris, Louis 'Kid' Kaplan, Al Singer, Sammy Baker, Benny Leonard, Barney Ross and Ruby Goldstein, subsequently a famous referee.

McLarnin, by his own admission, owed his success to his veteran manager Pop Foster, a rugged ex-fighter who guided his boxer shrewdly and very successfully through the jungle that was the American boxing scene at the time. He was always one step ahead of mobsters like Al 'Scarface' Capone, Owney 'The Killer' Madden, Jack 'Legs' Diamond and their cohorts who infiltrated the sport and controlled many world champions and managers.

It was one of the great partnerships in boxing history, probably the best, a successful and highly profitable relationship that lasted until Foster's death at the age of eighty-three in 1956. Even then, their heart-warming story had a fairytale twist when it was disclosed that Foster had left the bulk of his money to McLarnin and his family. It came to $200,000. 'The amount was a surprise,' said Jimmy, 'but Pop always saved his money. I used to urge him to spend more, and enjoy himself, but he would say that he enjoyed saving.'

Stanley Weston, the American boxing writer and author, acknowledged that Foster got McLarnin to the top with a minimum of effort. 'Foster was the only manager Jimmy ever had,' said Weston. 'He was more of a father to him than a manager.'

The tender and careful manner in which Pop Foster selected opponents caused many promoters to blow their top. Pop was against taking any unnecessary risks for his boxer. He could never see the point of taking one-night stands against small town opposition. Foster felt that anything could happen in a fight. A lucky punch, a butt, a sprained ankle, anything.

Pop was also clever in playing up the Irish angle. He knew American promoters and fans loved to see an Irishman, especially a good-looking all-rounder, in their rings so he had McLarnin wear a bright green robe with his name in gold letters. After a fight, win, lose or draw, he would do a cartwheel across the ring.

Several record books and many magazine articles over the years wrongly list his birthplace as the Lisburn Road in Belfast. One current source has him even coming from Inchicore, a suburb of Dublin. The facts are that McLarnin was born in Hillsborough, County Down, some twelve miles from Belfast on 19 December 1907. Indeed, Ireland narrowly missed losing him as a native son. McLarnin's parents Samuel and Mary, who were living in Alberta, Canada were visiting their former hometown of Hillsborough at the time when Jimmy came into the world.

After living in Hillsborough for three years, the family returned to Canada, settling this time near the town of Mortlach in the province of Saskatchewan. Samuel became a homestead wheat farmer and they raised twelve children, six boys of which Jimmy was the eldest. In 1918, at the end of World War I, the family moved to Vancouver where Samuel bought a second-hand furniture store with the money he had made through farming.

Later on Samuel built a gym in the basement of the store and young Jimmy became fascinated with boxing, spending hours there after school, punching the bag, exercising on the floor, imagining he would be a famous boxer one day. He also read the *Ring* magazines his father bought.

Then Pop Foster came into his life. Foster was born in Liverpool and was of Irish descent. He learned how to use his fists in over two hundred fights in the booths of English fairgrounds where fighters would take on all comers. In 1895 the young Foster decided to quit fighting and manage a talented, tearaway English featherweight named Spike Robson and guided him into the world class.

On Robson's retirement, Pop returned to Canada, and in 1914 he donned a uniform and fought in World War I, having previously seen action in the Boer War. At Poperinghe in the Belgian province of Flanders, his legs were badly injured during an artillery barrage and he was sent home to Vancouver Army Hospital to undergo surgery which left him with a noticeable limp and a small pension as a wounded veteran.

On his gradual recovery, Foster began visiting the McLarnin furniture shop and became friendly with the family. One day in the gym, accompanied by Samuel McLarnin, he watched the twelve-year-old Jimmy work out and told McLarnin senior that his son had the makings of a good boxer. Samuel wanted to know what kind of boxer. 'A champion,' said Foster. 'That's the only kind worth making.' Pop told the elder McLarnin that Jimmy reminded him of the great featherweight Jim Driscoll, the Welsh Wizard.

They had a word with Jimmy and after consulting Mary, the family came to an agreement that Pop would take charge of the boy's career. 'I will make you not only a champion but a world champion,' he told Jimmy. 'But you must always behave yourself and do what I ask.' That was 1920. Sixteen years later, when McLarnin retired from the ring, they were still together as boxer and manager, and remained good friends until Pop's death.

In the gym Foster showed McLarnin how to punch, hard and accurately, how to slip punches, how to jab and hook, the art of good footwork, in short the correct way to do things. He instructed Jimmy to increase his hand speed as he glided in and out against imaginary opponents. 'Forget the bad habits you picked up in neighbourhood scraps,' he said. 'When you get into the ring for your first amateur fight, it's for real,' he said. 'No messing around.'

Foster also taught McLarnin how to skip rope although naturally he could not do it himself because of his war injuries, and he used to place a book on Jimmy's head and ask him to shadow box or punch the heavy bag to get his balance. Pop often put on the gloves with his charge, and even though he weighed over fourteen stone and had to move around slowly due to his legs, he still had sharp reflexes and could dazzle the boy with his fast hands. McLarnin weighed less than six stone and stood just four foot six inches but Pop never did anything to hurt Jimmy's confidence.

McLarnin compiled an amateur record of twenty wins and no defeats by 1923, and Foster was so impressed that he approached Jimmy's parents and proposed that the boy, who was heading for his sixteenth birthday, be permitted to box professionally. They agreed and allowed Foster to be named his official guardian. McLarnin and Pop would eventually head for California where fights were limited to four rounds, and would campaign mainly around the San Francisco area, as well as Oakland and Sacramento. But first, Jimmy had two fights in Vancouver at the end of 1923, both resulting in victories, in one and seven rounds. McLarnin and Foster were on the way.

'It must have seemed a little funny to Jimmy's mother and father with me taking over their son and moving him to the US,' Foster would recall. 'Here I was, an old guy from England spending so much time with the kid, teaching him the boxing racket. I suppose it never occurred to them, never in their wildest dreams, that he would turn into a great boxer, even a boxer, period. Anybody who looked at his baby face would never have thought so either but I thought so. I knew he would be a great boxer someday.'

McLarnin remembered Foster's great care in him: 'I always got paid, and Pop always made sure of that in dealing with promoters. I got one dollar for my first fight and $60,000 for my last one. But between one and sixty, boy, there was a lot of hard work. Boxing is a very hazardous business and anybody that goes into it for fun has to be out of their cotton picking minds because it's a rough, tough business, although Pop always took good care of me. He taught me the science of boxing, and while I had a lot of fights, I was rarely hit so it wasn't too difficult.

'As I went along, aged sixteen, seventeen, I was getting $20, $30, then I began to get $50, $75. Well, that was a lot of money when I was a youngster. I'd never been used to a lot of money. By the time I was nineteen years old, I had $100,000 in the bank so all of a sudden I realized that boxing was for me and I put my entire mind to it. I remembered what Pop had told me about making me a champion and that I would have to behave myself and do as he told me.

'Pop was from the old school. He knew boxing from A to Z. He developed speed. The important thing about boxing is speed. If they can't hit you, they can't hurt you and they can't beat you. So speed is the great science of boxing. It took me two years to develop speed and then I worked on a real fast platform bag to develop the eye to get co-ordination.

'After a couple of years I found I could move pretty good but I used to work out three or four times a week, day after day. There is no romance in boxing. In my case, it was a tough, tough ordeal, but as the years went by I got to know boxing and I got to thinking that it wasn't as tough as I had thought it might be. Although having said that, it isn't the easiest game in the world.'

In his retirement years, he reflected: 'It's not really fair to expect anyone who hasn't been through it himself to understand what you have to do to be a professional boxer. For some, the formula has come easier than it came to me, although I am sure it never came easy to anybody. Boxing was my business from the time I was twelve years of age. I had nothing to start with except a quick, wiry pair of legs and Pop Foster's promise that he would make me champion of the world if I did what he told me to.'

After the two fights in Vancouver, McLarnin and Foster set off for the West Coast on the SS *Dorothy* bound for San Francisco the first stop. Jimmy had his mother's last $20 in his pocket. Pop was told the sport was thriving in the city, with lots of boxers and plenty of cards. San Francisco was known as the Cradle of Fistic Stars because of the number of top boxers coming from the city.

The most famous one that San Francisco had produced was James J. Corbett, Gentleman Jim, the former heavyweight champion of the world and the man who revolutionised the sport around the turn of the twentieth century. A master boxer with brilliant footwork, the handsome Corbett was one of McLarnin's idols as a kid and one day he would get to meet the great man in person, which was a real thrill. 'Corbett often used to come to my camp and give me advice,' he remembered in later years. 'He used to say, "Jimmy, remember one thing. A boxer can always afford to be a gentleman." I've never forgotten that.'

Pop and Jimmy got a surprise, however, when they arrived at the Observatory Gym in the city where they had an appointment with Frank Schuler, who put on regular shows at the Dreamland Rink. Schuler said boxing in the city was under strict police supervision because of a recent death in the ring and the sport was not exactly the most popular activity in San Francisco.

Looking down at McLarnin, Schuler turned to Foster and said: 'In any event, I couldn't use your skinny kid here, even if everything was ok. He doesn't need a fight. He needs a nursemaid. He'd get killed. I'm telling you.' When Foster pulled out some press clippings and showed them to Schuler, the promoter was still unimpressed. 'Come back when he grows up,' he said.

Undeterred, Foster and McLarnin moved on to Oakland where Jimmy made a successful US debut by outpointing a young Italian prospect, Frankie Sands over four rounds on 23 February 1924. It was a very promising start for a sixteen-year-old, and the first of nine fights in Oakland, all wins, before they moved to Sacramento and then on to Vernon for six more victories and two draws.

Foster would clear all the matches in advance, making sure that his boxer was not being overmatched. At the same time, Pop did not want pushovers just to boost Jimmy's record but opponents he could learn from. Inevitably, there would be the odd defeat, and the occasional surprise, but Foster would make sure they were few.

Right now, they were going along the right path. In three bouts in Vernon against the promising Fidel LaBarba, the first two near the end of 1924 and the third early in 1925, McLarnin won two with the other drawn. These were significant results as LaBarba, born in New York and brought up in Los Angeles, had won the flyweight gold medal in the Paris Olympics of 1924. Seven months after McLarnin outpointed him over ten rounds in their final bout, LaBarba would win the world flyweight title. McLarnin would remember him as 'one of the great left hookers and when he landed, I thought all my teeth were being pulled out. He was a real puncher and I had to keep moving all the time.'

Promoter Jack Doyle handed McLarnin and Foster a cheque for $3,000 as their share of the gate receipts. It was the biggest money they had ever seen.

After the fight, they had a short break in Vancouver to allow Jimmy to see his family, and hand his parents $1,000 in cash. Back in action soon, McLarnin notched up three more wins before coming up against the experienced Bud Taylor who handed the Hillsborough boxer his first loss on a decision over ten rounds in June 1925. Taylor was considered the uncrowned world bantamweight champion and Foster put the loss down to his man's inexperience more than anything else.

An offer came to go in against the Filipino and reigning world flyweight champion Pancho Villa in Emeryville, California on 4 July 1925, American Independence Day. Foster was cautious about accepting the fight but the confident McLarnin insisted they go ahead. Villa's title would not be on the line but Jimmy reckoned a win over Villa would enhance his reputation. He would also have a weight and height advantage.

Villa, who stood only an inch over five foot, was the son of a cowhand and had never been knocked out in 103 fights. Regarded by many as the greatest Asian boxer of all time, he had risen from obscurity to the world title, which he won from the great Welsh flyweight Jimmy Wilde, the Ghost with the Hammer in His Hand, in seven rounds. Wilde had been champion for seven years and never boxed again.

A day before the McLarnin fight, Villa had an ulcerated tooth removed, but rather than disappoint the promoter, he went through with the bout. McLarnin and Foster felt the tooth incident was just 'camp talk' and Jimmy concentrated on his boxing, moving in and out, collecting the points and won the decision over ten rounds.

After the fight Villa and his entourage toured the local cafes and bars, wining the dining as though Pancho had won. However, as the days passed, he complained about not feeling well and went into hospital, where it was discovered that the infection had spread to his throat. The world champion was rushed into surgery but lapsed into a coma while on the operating table and died the following day, ten days after the fight and two weeks before he would have celebrated his twentieth-fourth birthday. His death made headlines all over the world and he was given a state funeral in Manila. Foster and McLarnin sent a large wreath of flowers, mourning the great champion along with the rest of the boxing world.

'A lot of people blamed poor Pancho's manager for not calling off the fight,' McLarnin is quoted as saying in Andrew Gallimore's book *Baby Face Goes to Hollywood*. 'But I can't help thinking then, that if his manager had been Pop Foster, Pancho wouldn't have died. With Pop, the boxer always came first and so many things could happen to hurt a fighter in the ring that the manager had to be sure that nothing was going to hurt him outside.'

Jackie Fields would be McLarnin's next opponent. Born in Chicago, Fields had won the gold medal as a featherweight in the Paris Olympics of 1924, two fights after Fidel LaBarba, a previous McLarnin rival, had taken the flyweight title. At the time of the McLarnin fight, at the Olympic Auditorium in Los Angeles in November 1925, Fields showed great promise and inside four years he would win the world welterweight title. McLarnin sensationally knocked him out in two rounds. Fields won the first round but once the Irishman got him in his sights in the following session, the end was near. He finished off the Illinois fighter with a smashing right to the jaw, setting the framework for future Irish–Jewish rivalries.

McLarnin and Foster returned to Vancouver for Christmas, with Jimmy having a family reunion and going shopping with his long-time girlfriend Lillian Cupit. But not before Jimmy defeated his lone conqueror Bud Taylor on a disqualification in two rounds for a low blow.

Taylor, a noted body puncher, went for McLarnin's midriff from the start, and while the Downman's sharper boxing won him the opening round, he admitted to Foster back in the corner that Bud was going to be a tough one. In the second, one of Taylor's shots, aimed at the body, went well below the belt and referee Benny Whitman had no option but to rule him out. They met again, in January 1926 and this time Taylor won a clear decision over ten rounds, despite two good last sessions by McLarnin, who was now a fully-fledged featherweight, having graduated from flyweight and bantamweight. It would not be too long before he would become a lightweight.

The defeat convinced Foster that McLarnin still had a lot to learn and that he was not really ready yet for ten rounders against tough battlers like Taylor. He would put down a loss as a chance to gain more experience. 'Jimmy's chance will come when he will be able to go in against these guys but there is no rush,' Pop told reporters in the dressing room. 'The kid's learning all the time.'

Through the rest of 1926 and 1927, McLarnin had thirteen fights – ten wins, two losses and a draw. His last but one appearance in 1927 was significant as he went in with Louis 'Kid' Kaplan, the former world featherweight champion, on 18 October. It was McLarnin's debut at the Chicago Stadium and a crowd of over six thousand, including many of the city's mobsters, came to see the action, with the Irish–Jewish rivalry being played up.

Kaplan was a Russian who settled in Connecticut with his family when he was five. He was neither a graceful boxer nor a powerful puncher but a relentless fighter who ploughed straight ahead, throwing a barrage of punches. His opponents had to be wary of his left hook, and he could absorb punches like a sponge holds water. Foster was cautious of accepting promoter Jim Mullen's offer of the fight as Kaplan was still a leading contender but McLarnin insisted: 'He's ok. I'll take him. We've seen him on the West Coast and his style is made to order.'

In the opening round Kaplan came out fighting and by the end of the round, he had put McLarnin on the boards for a short count from a heavy attack. The Irishman did not feel badly hurt but this was going to be one hell of a fight.

The Kid put him down in the second round too, from another barrage of blows, and when McLarnin got back to his corner, Foster admonished him: 'Look, why don't you hit him first. He won't like that.'

McLarnin did just that in the third, catching Kaplan with punches from both hands as The Kid came in and won the round. A cracking right hook dropped Kaplan for a count of three in the fourth. Enraged, the Russian charged at Jimmy but the Irishman was able to block most of the blows now. Kaplan was down again in the fifth, this time for a nine count. It was all over in the eighth. McLarnin floored him with a short, chopping right and when he got up on wobbly legs, Jimmy moved in with another big right to the jaw and Louis sank to the boards for the full count.

The Hillsborough boxer was not to know until two months later that his own jaw had been broken, after complaining that it felt sore. After a visit to the dentist, he was told the jaw could be set properly after being 'wired up' and rested for six weeks. The dentist was sworn to secrecy.

With the jaw now fully healed, Pop and McLarnin resumed their boxing plans. Jimmy was now in the forefront of contenders for the world lightweight title, held by Sammy Mandell. Eddie Kane, Mandell's manager, opened negotiations for a McLarnin defence but the canny Foster wanted too much money and talks broke down. Instead, Pop accepted an offer from promoter Tex Rickard for a date in Madison Square Garden in February 1928 against New York's latest sensation from the East Side, Sid Terris, the Galloping Ghost of the Ghetto. Once again, the Jewish–Irish rivalry would be played up.

This was a big break for McLarnin and Foster as Rickard, the Don King of his day, had ushered in a new era in boxing, the million dollar gate, with world heavyweight champion Jack Dempsey as his major drawing card. Born in Missouri, Rickard left school at the age of nine and while still a youngster, worked cattle drives from Texas to Montana and became a town marshal.

The enterprising Rickard also tried cattle ranching in Brazil and discovered gold in Alaska, later admitting that he sold his claim 'for far too low a price'. His first big promotion was the Joe Gans–Battling Nelson world lightweight title fight in Goldfield, Nevada in 1906 which took in $69,715, a record for a boxing match at the time.

Rickard planned to match the winner of the McLarnin-Terris fight with Sammy Mandell for the title. Tex knew that Foster had earlier turned down the offer of a Mandell title fight from promoter Eddie Kane but he would make Pop an offer he could hardly refuse.

McLarnin wore his usual bright green bathrobe and when he heard that Terris was an eight to five on favourite to win and take the Mandell title shot, he decided to get the New Yorker out of there as soon as possible. True to his word, it did not last long, with many late-comers missing the fight, if it could be called that. From the bell, Terris was moving and jabbing confidently when

Baby Face moved in, caught the Jew with a combination left-right followed by a terrific right to the chin that dropped Terris face down.

He seemed out to the world as referee Jack O'Sullivan's count went on: 'seven ... eight ... nine ... ten ... and out'. It had lasted a total of one minute and forty-seven seconds. Rickard was ecstatic. 'The boy's another Dempsey,' he beamed. McLarnin was now the toast of New York. The new Irish sensation. To add to his joy, he collected the biggest purse of his career, $19,645, plus $1,000 for movie rights.

The next issue of *Ring* magazine commented: 'McLarnin's successful New York debut aroused the Irish in the big city to such an extent that a two-day celebration followed. For all we know, it may still be going on. This was the first time in sixteen years that the Celts had a real, honest-to-goodness chance to root for one of their own.' Jimmy made the cover, with his image posed against a green background, with a headline above that read, 'Jimmy McLarnin Next Lightweight Champion.'

Looking back in 1953 on McLarnin's career and the Terris fight, Stanley Weston noted in *Boxing and Wrestling* magazine: 'Eighteen thousand packed Madison Square Garden and went away certain they had just seen the hardest lightweight puncher since 'Terrible' Terry McGovern fifty years ago.'

Promoter Rickard carried out his promise and matched McLarnin with world lightweight champion Sammy Mandell for New York's Polo Grounds, one of America's most celebrated outdoor stadiums. The date was Friday, 17 May 1928. Rickard predicted an attendance of sixty thousand and receipts of $300,000 but rain caused a postponement until the Saturday. That day there was more rain and the new date was Monday. On that evening the sky cleared but the gate was hit, and a little more than twenty thousand paid $137,467 through the turnstiles, still respectable figures.

Mandell was of Italian–Albanian descent and arrived in America with his father at the age of three and settled in Rockford, Illinois. He entered the ring a seven to five on favourite, and justified the odds by handing McLarnin a boxing lesson. Mandell had the edge in the first eight rounds, with the Irishman taking the next two when the world champion took a breather. Sammy regained the initiative in the eleventh, with McLarnin winning the next three but Mandell easily won the fifteenth and was awarded a popular, and unanimous, decision.

McLarnin and Foster were naturally disappointed but reckoned that their chance would come again. They put it down to the champion's greater experience and the fact that the Irishman was now a welterweight and had to sweat to get inside the lightweight limit, although they did not offer these as excuses. 'The best man won,' acknowledged Pop in the dressing room.

The next day James P. Dawson of the *New York Times* praised McLarnin's showing but said: 'Mandell put on an exhibition of ring wizardry which stamps him as a worthy successor to the great boxers of the ring who have held the lightweight title.' McLarnin would defeat Mandell in two subsequent matches but the title was not at stake.

After two more impressive wins, one in the first round and another in the fourth, Jimmy came unstuck in November against Chicago's Ray Miller in Detroit. In later years Miller became a noted referee, and is probably best remembered as coming in for the exhausted Ruby Goldstein, another McLarnin opponent, after the tenth round of the world lightheavyweight title fight between Sugar Ray Robinson and Joey Maxim during a New York heat wave in 1952. This was the only fight in ring history that had two referees.

Miller was a big hitter, always aggressive, and in one of the biggest upsets of the year, he won in the seventh round when Pop pulled McLarnin out after his injured right eye, cut as early as the first round from one of the Chicago boxer's powerful left hooks, was now bleeding profusely. Miller was always superior but it would be the only loss by McLarnin inside the distance in his career.

With the eye clearing up inside a few weeks, Jimmy was anxious to get back. Rickard was angling for a return fight for the New Year but suggested a couple of warm-ups. First up was Joe Glick, a New Yorker who was in impressive form at the time. The fight was set for Madison Square Garden for 11 January 1929. The Irish–Jewish rivalry was on again. But tragedy intervened when Rickard died suddenly of a ruptured appendix in Miami Beach, Florida five days earlier, making headlines all over the world. His body was returned to New York to lie in state at Madison Square Garden and thousands passed by the casket to say a final farewell to boxing's greatest and most colourful promoter.

Among the mourners were McLarnin and Foster. It hardly seemed possible that the man who created the million dollar gates and ruled boxing for a quarter of a century was no more. Rickard was good for both of them and he had been making big plans for the Irishman. Pop said they would reluctantly go through with the Glick fight, and a crowd of over twenty thousand showed up to pay tribute to Tex and see a good fight. McLarnin won on points after a hard, close bout but the result was greeted with scattered boos.

Glick demanded a rematch. He got it in March, again at Madison Square Garden, and this time McLarnin made no mistake. In the first round he countered the Brooklyn fighter's rushes with well-placed punches. In the second McLarnin floored his man twice with left hooks and knocked him out with a smashing right to the jaw after ninety-seven seconds of the round. In his next fight, three weeks later, the man from Hillsborough gained revenge over Ray Miller with a unanimous decision over ten rounds.

Before the year was out, the Irish–Jewish rivalry would continue when McLarnin was matched with boxing's latest sensation Ruby Goldstein, the Jewel of the Ghetto, at Madison Square Garden on 13 December. Goldstein would later become one of boxing's most famous referees, officiating at thirty-nine world title fights involving greats like Sugar Ray Robinson, Joe Louis, Floyd Patterson, Tony Zale, Rocky Graziano, Willie Pep, Sandy Saddler and Emile Griffith.

Back in December 1929, however, Ruby was a contender. At twenty years of age, he was on a comeback after two surprise defeats when he was over-matched, but had put those losses behind him. Earlier he had been considered by many as a likely successor to the great world lightweight champion Benny Leonard, now retired. Ruby was now back on track, and fully confident of 'putting this brash Irish kid in his place'. Over 20,000 people packed the Manhattan venue and expected to see a thriller. They did, while it lasted.

Goldstein came out fast in the first round and caught McLarnin with a fast, hard right to the chin, a punch Ruby said was the hardest he had ever landed. Jimmy felt it too but shook it off and pressed Goldstein into a retreat across the ring and caught his man with a barrage of hooks and uppercuts sending the Lower East Side contender to the canvas with the crowd on their feet, yelling like mad.

Goldstein climbed to his feet and survived the round but in the second, McLarnin immediately went on the attack. Ruby was in real trouble again, and slipping under Goldstein's left, the Irishman connected with a wicked right to the jaw that sent the New Yorker down to be counted out by referee Lou Magnolia. After McLarnin did a handspring in the center of the ring, he told reporters at ringside: 'They said Ruby had a glass chin but he also has a coura-geous heart.'

With McLarnin's sights set on a world welterweight title fight and possess-ing a nine-fight winning streak including three knockouts inside three rounds, he ran into trouble against the dangerous Billy Petrolle in November 1930. From Fargo, North Dakota, Petrolle was a powerful puncher, shamefully denied a world title opportunity because it was claimed champions studiously avoided him. Billy had something like two hundred and fifty-five fights in a long career and was called the Fargo Express after a cartoonist pictured him as a runaway train.

Jimmy and Pop knew a victory over Petrolle in the ten-rounder would en-hance his title claims but things worked out differently. The Fargo battler kept the pressure on McLarnin throughout with a constant barrage of hooks and upper-cuts, never giving the Irishman a chance to settle down. Both Foster and referee Patsy Haley wanted to stop it after the seventh round as McLarnin's face was cut and bruised but Jimmy insisted: 'Please don't. I want to finish on my feet.' He did, and the Madison Square Garden crowd gave them a standing ovation.

McLarnin learned well from the heavy defeat, scoring two unanimous decisions over Petrolle in return fights in 1931, again at the Garden. 'Every time I read about the glamour attached to the prize ring in general and the career of

Jimmy McLarnin in particular, I think about my fights with Billy Petrolle,' he recalled in his retirement years.

'We all know how it feels, even those of us who were lucky and handed out two or three for every one we took. That's why, when somebody asks: "Was it fun, Jimmy?" I try especially hard to give the right answer if the person wants to know what happens to a kid with stars in his eyes and a promising left-hand. For one in a thousand the money can be fast. But even for that one it never can be easy.'

McLarnin's fight with the veteran Benny Leonard in October 1932 at Madison Square Garden was one fight Jimmy hated because of his great admiration for the former world lightweight champion who was then on a comeback, having hit hard times. The handsome Leonard is considered by many as the greatest boxer at this weight of all time, a fast, clever boxer with a fine defence and tremendous punching power. He held the world title for seven years.

In a career of over two hundred bouts, Leonard was knocked out only four times. Born on New York's East Side, Leonard learned to fight in neighbourhood battles where only the toughest and best survived. He was also a Jew, nicknamed the Ghetto Wizard, so the Garden people were able to play up the Irish–Jewish angle. With McLarnin's great record against Hebrew boxers, Pop was confident the trend would continue.

The ethnic match drew nearly twenty-two thousand fans, with standing room only signs outside, and handsome receipts of $65,355 in a year when America was in the depths of the Great Depression. Leonard had a good first round when he dropped his opponent to one knee with a chopping right but after that it was all McLarnin, McLarnin, McLarnin.

Leonard went down from a solid right to the jaw in the second, and while he blocked many of the Irishman's blows in the following sessions, most of the punches got through and the old champion was a thoroughly beaten man by the fifth round. 'Every time McLarnin hit Benny a good solid punch, Ben started to come undone all over at once,' wrote Paul Gallico of the *New York Daily News* and later a successful novelist and author.

'He was just like a second-hand car that knocks up against the curbstone – all the parts start falling out at once. His legs would go wobbly, his wind would go, his eyes would glaze up and he could do nothing but stand pitifully and take it. And when he tried some of his old-time footwork he looked as silly as a grandmother attending a fancy dress ball in kiddie rompers.'

In the sixth, with McLarnin looking pleadingly at referee Arthur Donovan to intervene, the official compassionately threw his arms around Leonard and stopped it, with two minutes and fifty-five seconds on the clock. The crowd admired Leonard's brave showing and he was given a thunderous ovation as he made his way from the ring to the dressing room. Ringside writers gave McLarnin a new nickname, the Jew Killer, and Leonard never fought again.

McLarnin got his long-awaited world welterweight title opportunity on 29 May 1933 against Young Corbett III, so called because there was already a Young Corbett and a Young Corbett II. Born Raffaele Capabianca Giordano in Italy, his family moved to Pittsburgh when he was a baby before settling in California. A hard-hitting southpaw, he was making the first defence of the title he had won three months earlier and the venue was Wrigley Field, Los Angeles. It would be McLarnin's first appearance in the Golden State in six years, and he was looking forward to it.

It turned out to be a brief visit, at least in the ring. Corbett, a southpaw, tore from his corner and almost buried McLarnin in a shower of punches, determined to end it all in the first round. Jimmy managed to bob and weave but the champion was resilient and continued to fire jabs, hooks, uppercuts and everything in the Queensberry Rules. Then, as Corbett took a breather momentarily to plan his next move, or moves, and started a right hook, the Irishman got there quicker with his own lightning left hook and short right to the chin that dropped the transplanted Italian as though he had been shot. It was the first time he had ever been on the floor.

Corbett struggled to one knee and managed to get to his feet at the count of nine, standing on sheer courage. McLarnin sent him down again with three powerful left hooks, and as he climbed groggily to his feet, Jimmy said to referee Patsy Haley that he should stop it. But he waved them on. The challenger moved in fast and a terrific right to the jaw sent Corbett sprawling through the ropes, halfway out of the ring.

There was no reason to count. It was all over in exactly two minutes and thirty-seven seconds. Corbett was carried to his corner as McLarnin let out a shout of glee and did a handspring. There were tears of joy running down the face of the tough Pop Foster as he embraced his new champion.

'Corbett was unlucky, I was fortunate,' McLarnin recalled in later years. 'You try for years and years. You struggle and you get to the top of your profession. I imagine it's the same in any kind of endeavour and I was thrilled, no kidding about it. It was probably the happiest night of my fight career. Finally, after a long struggle, getting to the top, being the champion.'

McLarnin took a break for a year, dividing his time between dining and golfing with movie stars in Hollywood, seeing the sights in Los Angeles and surrounding areas and spending time with his folks and girlfriend Lillian in Vancouver. Meanwhile, there was criticism that he and Foster were wrapping the title in cotton wool. Eddie Borden in *Ring* magazine said that McLarnin should either put the title on the line or retire, as there were several legitimate contenders around. Foster's answer was that if some promoter came up with his asking price, a $40,000 guarantee, they would sign on the dotted line straight away.

RINGSIDE WITH THE CELTIC WARRIORS

One fight Pop was interested in was against Barney Ross, the lightweight champion of the world who he understood was anxious to move up into the welterweight division. Being the son of a Rabbi, Ross going in against McLarnin appealed to Foster as they would be able to play up the Jew Killer angle once again. They did not personally like the tag but it always guaranteed healthy box office takings.

In any event, the New York State Athletic Commission were demanding a McLarnin title fight, not necessarily against Ross but any other leading contender. Finally, a date and venue were named for a Ross challenge – Madison Square Garden's outdoor arena, the Long Island Bowl on 28 May 1934. Foster was offered, not the $40,000 asking price for his boxer's services, but an option of $50,000, or forty per cent of the gate, whichever was larger, so great was the demand to see the clash of the two world champions. As it happened, they finished up with $58,936 from the gate receipts.

Ross was born Barnet David Rasofsky, the third son of Russian parents who were forced to flee to America when the pogroms made life a living hell for Jews throughout Czarist Russia. They settled in New York's Lower East Side, where Barnet, later changed to Barney, was born. They subsequently moved to Chicago where Papa Rasofsky bought a small grocery store. Both wanted the future world boxing champion to be a teacher but all that changed dramatically when, one day in December 1924, two gunmen demanded the contents of the till and as Barney's father reached for a long knife, he was shot dead.

The eldest in the family, Barney became the principle breadwinner and having been a successful amateur boxer for about a year, persuaded his mother to let him try professional boxing, at which he could earn much more than at an ordinary job. Now Barney Ross, he made fast progress and won the world lightweight title in 1933. Also on the line was the world junior welterweight championship, though this title was not taken very seriously at the time. Now Ross was aiming to become the first boxer to win both the world lightweight and welterweight championships. Jimmy McLarnin stood in his way.

The New York fight turned out to be a classic, with the crowd of forty-five thousand on the edge of their seats for the full fifteen rounds. McLarnin had the edge in the opening round on his sharper hitting but Ross won the middle sessions. Both went down briefly in a thrilling ninth round and were bloodied by the final bell in a close fight.

There was a split decision. Announcer Joe Humphries reached for the overhanging microphone. 'The judges have disagreed,' he declared as a hush came over the whole arena. 'Judge Harold Barnes makes it twelve rounds for Ross, two for McLarnin and one even. Judge Tom O'Rourke has it nine rounds for McLarnin, one to Ross, and five even. Referee Eddie Forbes calls it thirteen for Ross, one to McLarnin and one even. The new welterweight champion of the world … Barney Ross.' Pop visited the dressing room to congratulate the new champion and his mother Sarah. 'You've got a fine boy there,' he said, 'but he

162

took an honest licking tonight, and no technical judges or rules can tell me any different.'

There was an immediate demand for a rematch, and it was held at the Polo Grounds, New York four months later before a crowd of 23,777, with the referee being Arthur Donovan, one of America's best. It turned to be another close one, with one then the other gaining the advantage. McLarnin had the best of the first five rounds but then Ross began to drive the challenger back with powerful rights, one starting a swelling under McLarnin's right eye which by the closing rounds was completely shut.

Hampered by only one good eye, the Down battler fought on, hurting Ross, who now had a cut right eye, in the eleventh. Ross fought back in the twelfth and the final three rounds could have gone either way before the bell rang to end another classic. As Paul Gallico of the *New York Daily News* wrote from ringside: 'The Jews said it was Ross, the Irish said it was McLarnin and the Italians said they didn't know. There was dead silence in the park when announcer Joe Humphries said the judges had disagreed but also a great cheer when he announced that McLarnin had re-won the title.'

The decision was roundly booed, and a ringside poll of boxing writers showed that twenty-two of twenty-eight favoured Ross. But Jimmy McLarnin was once again welterweight champion of the world. 'I knew I'd do it, Pops, I knew I'd do it,' said a jubilant McLarnin. In the dressing room, he told reporters: 'Whew, but that Ross was tough tonight but I never doubted I'd win back the title.'

Ring magazine editor Nat Fleischer, who had predicted that the Irishman would win, said he had scored it seven rounds to six for Ross, with two even. He felt that Ross would win a third fight, 'but this was a thriller with plenty of action, and good for the sport.' Shortly after the fight Foster and McLarnin had a short holiday, visiting Dublin, Belfast and his old hometown of Hillsborough before going on to London and some sightseeing.

When they returned to New York, Pop was brought into talks for a rubber meeting with Ross but he really wanted McLarnin to hang up his gloves. 'You've nothing to prove,' he would tell Jimmy. 'You're the world champion. You've made your money. Retire and go off and marry Lillian.' McLarnin would nod his head, but never committed himself, merely saying, 'Yes, Yes', partly to keep Pop quiet.

With two close fights, there had to be a third. It was set for the Polo Grounds, New York for 28 May 1935, exactly a year to the day since the second fight. It would be refereed by Jack Dempsey, the former world heavyweight champion who, in the same ring twelve years earlier, knocked out the big Argentinian, Luis Firpo in their million-dollar clash in two sensational rounds. Over thirty-one thousand fans were now on hand to see what turned out to be another McLarnin–Ross classic.

RINGSIDE WITH THE CELTIC WARRIORS

As in the two previous fights, this one was also keenly contested. Ross won the first three rounds by comfortable margins but McLarnin began to get into his familiar pattern of hit and move as the rounds went by as both boxers suffered cuts. By the eleventh, with the crowd cheering them on, it was still fairly even, though a great left hook rocked Ross just before the bell. Ross marginally won the final round but it still was anybody's fight, and the ringside press seemed equally divided on the result.

Then came the dramatic announcements. Judge George Lecron scored it for Ross nine rounds to four with two even. Judge Abe Goldberg also had it for Barney, eight to six with one even. Finally referee Dempsey, and he had it five to Ross, three to McLarnin and seven even. The decision was unanimous and Barney Ross was the new welterweight champion of the world. In the dressing room, Pop announced that Jimmy would now retire but McLarnin told reporters: 'Why should I? This is only a little upset. Pop will get around to my way of thinking.'

McLarnin married Lillian Cupit, a schoolteacher, in July 1935 after a ten-year courtship. He then had three more fights, all in Madison Square Garden in 1936. The reigning world lightweight champion Tony Canzoneri, a transplanted Italian–American from Louisiana and based in New York, outpointed him on a unanimous decision over ten rounds in May. When Pop said to him: 'Ok, that's it', Jimmy said: 'No, not until I beat Canzoneri.'

Canzoneri lost his title in his next fight and agreed to meet McLarnin in a return in October. This time the man from County Down showed he had profited from the defeat and easily won the verdict over ten rounds. Five weeks later, in what turned out to be his last ring appearance, McLarnin outsmarted Lou Ambers, the New Yorker who had taken the lightweight title from Canzoneri two months earlier, in a one-sided, non-title ten-rounder. It was then all over. Baby Face went out a winner, like he always wanted to.

Unlike so many boxers, McLarnin invested his money wisely and was a wealthy man. He opened an electrical goods store in Glendale, California and did some acting, appearing in several movies, as well as playing golf in Hollywood, about a twenty-minute drive away, with buddies like Fred Astaire, Bing Crosby, Bob Hope and Humphrey Bogart. He never returned to the ring despite large incentives for him to do so.

Jimmy McLarnin died peacefully on 28 October 2004, just fifty-two days short of his ninety-seventh birthday. One of the all-time greats, the man from Hillsborough had been world welterweight champion on two occasions in the days when competition was intense. He was also a fine ambassador for the sport, and his lasting partnership with Pop Foster would be hard to match in the annals of boxing history.

11. RINTY MONAGHAN

When Irish eyes are smiling

With a song in his heart and fire in his fists, Rinty Monaghan brought a ray of sunshine into the lives of not only Irish boxing fans but the public in general during the dark days of World War II and its immediate aftermath. Rinty won every professional honour open to him – World, European, Commonwealth, British and Northern Ireland titles and retired as unbeaten champion at the dawn of a new era in 1950. From the date of his first paid fight in Belfast in 1934 to his final ring appearance, also in his native city, fifteen years later almost to the very day, Rinty always gave his best, win, lose or draw. London promoter Jack Solomons described him as 'a leprechaun with fists of steel'.

When Monaghan won the world flyweight championship in 1947, there were just eight divisions and consequently eight world champions unlike today where there are seventeen divisions and sixty-eight boxers claiming titles. Then, if you add in the 'super' and 'interim' champions you are left, in theory, with a staggering seventy-seven world title claimants. It does not require much imagination to work out that it is relatively easier to win a title now than in Monaghan's day when the choice was limited. Consequently, a better per-former emerged in those days.

In 1947, the US dominated the world championship scene, holding six of the eight titles with a claim on a seventh, bantamweight Manuel Ortiz being born to a Mexican family living in California. The lone 'outsider' and conse-quently the only European on the list was Monaghan. He was also the first Irish boxer living at home to win a world championship.

No matter how tired he might be too, the little Belfast warrior would grab the microphone at the end of a fight and endear himself to his supporters with a song, usually a full-voiced rendition of *When Irish Eyes Are Smiling*, or often an equally heartfelt encore of *Hello Patsy Fagan*, with the fans joining in. Some-times, too, it would be *I'm Always Chasing Rainbows*. All this prompted visiting boxing writers to christen him the Warbling Warrior. The most important thing as far as Rinty was concerned was that he always made sure he sent the fans home happy.

A natural entertainer, during World War II his career was interrupted by service in the navy but his superiors chose not to exploit his boxing instincts but sent him on tours throughout western Europe entertaining the troops alongside other big stars at the time like George Formby, Gracie Fields and Vera Lynn, who was billed as Sweetheart of the Forces. Rinty would often recall those days in later years as being among the happiest of his life. After the war he would form his own band, and tour as a cabaret act.

One of nine children, with five sisters and three brothers, John Joseph Monaghan was born in Lancaster Street on the Northside of Belfast on 21 August 1920. He got his nickname from his grandmother because of his admiration for the Hollywood dog, Rin Tin Tin. The popular canine, a German Shepherd, was found as a pup by an American soldier Lee Duncan in a bombed-out building in war-torn France in 1918 and later taken home to Los Angeles where he taught the dog all sorts of tricks.

Soon the dog, which Duncan christened Rin Tin Tin, started a very successful Hollywood career and would appear in twenty-three films in the 1920s and 1930s. Rin Tin Tin became one of the major players on the silver screen, rivalling and often surpassing the popularity of Hollywood's biggest names of the period. The canine would join the movie greats with a star on the Hollywood Walk of Fame.

'I must have been one of Rin Tin Tin's most ardent admirers,' Rinty recalled in later years. 'I loved dogs and I would bring injured dogs home and have them looked after. But Rin Tin Tin was my number one. Whenever his movies were on the local picture house I would make sure to go along and see them. Rin Tin Tin could jump from wall to wall, rooftop to rooftop, out of a car or a van, anything. You name it, he could do it. He indeed was a wonder dog and I wasn't surprised he was so popular. Nor was I surprised when Granny Margaret gave me a nickname that stuck, Rin Tin Tin.

'One day she was calling me to come for my dinner and I was nowhere in sight. She roamed all the neighbourhood streets shouting the three syllables 'Rin Tin Tin' but still no luck. She got tired of calling Rin Tin Tin and shortened it to Rinty. Eventually she located me and she said that from then on she would call me Rinty. The rest of the family did the same and I wasn't John Joseph anymore. Incidentally, I heard later that Lee Duncan also had a pet name for the dog. It was Rinty. So there you are. There were two Rintys. There's a little nugget of information for you.'

Monaghan got his first taste of scrapping when he was around eleven years of age while a pupil in St Patrick's Christian Brothers School in Donegall Street. He would get into regular fights in the yard, and whenever any heated argument developed into a scrap, the finger of suspicion usually pointed in his direction. Much to the delight of one of his teachers who wanted 'the troublesome boy' transferred elsewhere as soon as possible, Monaghan's schooldays ended somewhat abruptly. Recession hit worldwide in the 1930s, and Belfast did not escape it; Rinty, being the eldest boy, was taken out of school in his early teens and sent out to work to bring in much-needed finances for the struggling family.

The main jobs in the city could usually be found in the shipyard of Harland and Wolff, the company that put Belfast onto the global stage in the early years of the twentieth century as the biggest and most productive shipbuilders in the world. Generations there had toiled to construct ocean-going vessels including the ill-fated Titanic. Through the influence of his father, Monaghan got a job in the shipyard to supplement the small wages brought home by the family. His bigger sister Sarah worked in one of the flax mills that employed women and young girls to produce linen.

The manual work was hard but Rinty stuck it out, building up his arm and back muscles to produce the fine physique he was to display later in the boxing ring. Inside a year, however, the shipyard closed due to falling orders and Monaghan was forced to take any job he could get. Once, while working on the roof of a house, the ladder came away from its holdings and crashed to the ground, bringing Rinty with it. He was very fortunate to receive nothing more than a broken ankle but it meant he had to be out of work for some considerable time.

Monaghan, meanwhile, had developed an interest in boxing and used to read all about the famous fighters of the day, like Joe Louis, Max Baer, James J. Braddock and the lad from Hillsborough in County Down who conquered America and became welterweight champion of the world, Jimmy McLarnin. 'Someday I, too, would like to bring a world title home,' he often told his parents, and they would agree that if he worked hard enough, he would realise his dream some day. Rinty was now convinced that his future lay in the boxing ring, but first, there was that not inconsequential matter of the broken ankle.

Happily it healed sooner than expected, and Monaghan began taking part in street boxing contests organised by his pals. Passers-by would throw coins on the pavement and the winner, usually Rinty, would collect all the takings and have a fish and chip supper with the proceeds. A local boxing matchmaker named Harry Hanley, who organised professional shows for promoters and managers, happened to see one of these scraps and suggested Rinty might like to drop along to the Labour Hall on nearby York Street, around the corner from the Monaghan home, where he put on shows.

The hall was run by the Independent Labour Party, known as the ILP, and as well as professional boxing bouts, Hanley put on novelty exhibitions involving characters in large boxing gloves who would just clown around, much to the amusement of the audiences. The shows also included cabaret acts such as singers and musicians and were held on alternative Saturday afternoons.

'Why not come along, have a look around, and maybe give it a go in the ring,' Hanley told the youngster. 'If you don't like it, that's fine, but I have a feeling you will. You have natural boxing ability. I'll put you in with another kid and we'll see how it goes. Ok?'

The following Saturday afternoon, Rinty turned up at the Labour Hall, out of a sense of adventure more than anything else. A large pair of bloomers was found in a locker, and a piece of twine put around his waist to keep them up. As Monaghan remembered in later years: 'I was matched with a kid called

Pimple McKee, and much to the amusement of the crowd, it was announced as 'a special heavyweight contest'. It was a draw because if I remember, we never really hit each other, just messed around a bit.

'When it was all over, Harry asked me if I could sing. I told him I could and I sang a few bars of *Sally*, a song made famous by Gracie Fields, one of the most popular singers at the time. The audience reaction was so good that Harry asked me to sing another one, and I sang *When Irish Eyes Are Smiling*, which also went down well. The few extra shillings were very welcome in the Monaghan household, as like everybody else, we were struggling to make ends meet. After that, Pimple and I would appear together quite often on the shows, with the result always a draw. The fans would throw money in to the ring, known as 'nobbins', and this would be shared between the two boxers.'

The combination of Rinty's boxing and singing would invariably be part of his appearances, a practice he would continue throughout his ring career when no big Monaghan fight would be complete without the inevitable song or two. Some local boxing writers in those early days started calling him the Singing Puncher and the Warbling Warrior but to everybody else he was simply Rinty.

As all his contests in the Labour Hall were technically professional ones, Monaghan never had an amateur bout. On his own reckoning, he had over one hundred of these bouts. One day, after pleas from Rinty to become an official professional, his father Thomas, who had boxed as a lightweight in the Royal Marines, decided that if his son, who was now a mere thirteen years of age, really wanted to box for pay, then he would be put in the right hands. Thomas selected Frank McAloran to be that individual.

McAloran was an active boxer at the time, and he would later go on to become Irish featherweight champion. He also ran a popular gym with his two brothers, Pat and James, in Hardinge Street, although to describe it as a gym might be a blatant misuse of the word. At best it was a tumbledown place but it had a ring and a few punchbags and speedballs. Monaghan's biographer Eamonn O'Hara said that locals nicknamed the gym 'the hut' and commented that it was not much more than that.

'There were absolutely no frills, not even running water,' said O'Hara. 'James, Frank's brother, was the chief coach and he also doubled as the resident carpenter when the rickety floorboards looked to be in danger of giving way. His kitbag contained a hammer, some nails and a few strips of wood. It was not uncommon for a boxer to suffer injury after a foot disappeared through the splinters.'

Rarely, if ever, in boxing history had a potential world champion trained in such frugal conditions but it was a gym as such, and that was all that mattered. McAloran did not promise his new arrival fame and fortune but told the Monaghan family that if their young son worked hard and kept fit, he would have a future in the fight game. He pointed out that Rinty had natural ability, with his fine physique having been developed doing hard labouring jobs in the shipyard. The partnership of Monaghan and McAloran would last throughout the boxer's career and Frank was always a familiar sight in Rinty's corner and alongside the boxer after the bout as he burst into song.

Monaghan made his official professional debut as a flyweight at Belfast's new boxing arena, the Ring Stadium, previously a bus depot, on 28 September 1934 and boxed a draw with another local, Sam 'Boy' Ramsey over four rounds. Rinty was sixteen and Ramsey nineteen. They would box each other five more times over the next eighteen months, with Monaghan winning two and drawing two.

Rinty ran up an impressive record in his first three years, boxing mainly in the Belfast area, improving all the time with nineteen wins, five draws and just one defeat. This lone loss was against Lisburn's experienced Jim Keery over six rounds in April 1937. Keery would go on to have a distinguished career in Irish boxing but they never boxed each other again. Rinty was anxious to face the Lisburn boxer again but McAloran had bigger names in mind, namely a shot at either the Irish or the British flyweight championships.

By September 1939 and the outbreak of World War II, Monaghan had a record of thirty-three wins, three losses and five draws. One of his defeats was in five rounds against the hard-hitting Scottish southpaw Jackie Paterson, who would play a significant role in Rinty's career in the post war years. The shock defeat was at the Oval, the home of Glentoran Football Club, in Belfast on 23 July 1938 before a crowd of over five thousand.

'I jumped into the ring as cocky as you like,' remembered Monaghan. 'I was clad in a jazzy dressing gown, a gladiator waiting for the kill. This was going to be a pushover, as Paterson was a newcomer to the pro game. I said to Frank: "This won't take long." But he warned me to be careful, though he was still confident I would win as he left the corner early on to do some business with a friend at ringside. It was the only time in my career I did not have him in the corner.

'As the rounds went by I was sticking my chin out, inviting him to come and get me. He did. As I dashed out at the bell for the fifth round, Jackie met me with a series of lefts and rights and I was suddenly on my back, looking up at the lights. I got up at eight but I was groggy.

'Frank was now up on his feet at ringside, telling me to "Keep down, keep down." But Paterson charged in immediately and knocked me against the ropes and I rebounded to the other side of the ring, falling down for a count of nine. I rose by instinct before a left hook sent me down again as the referee counted to ten. I was knocked out for the first time in my career. The point is that I was beating him for four rounds then wham! It was all over.'

As if to prove the Paterson defeat was a mistake, or more likely part of a learning process, Monaghan was back in action inside three weeks with a points win over Joe Curran at Liverpool Stadium. It was his second appearance at the famous venue. Curran, a local favourite and future world and European title challenger, was much more experienced than the Irishman but Rinty handled him well, connecting with long lefts and rights to the head and body. After being declared winner, Monaghan entertained the crowd with a song, this time with *The Umbrella Man*. Looking very pleased, Liverpool promoter Johnny Best said: 'You always get value with Rinty. A fight and a song.'

Despite being clearly outpointed, Curran and his team sought a return match. They got it, six months later at the New St James's Hall in Newcastle. As it happened, Rinty almost missed the fight. With a lot of time on his hands after the weigh-in around two o'clock in the afternoon for the night's fight, Monaghan, an avid film fan, particularly of Hollywood musicals, took himself off to a local cinema to see *Paris Honeymoon*. This was one he couldn't miss, with his favourite singer Bing Crosby in the lead.

In those days, movie programmes were continuous and Rinty enjoyed the film so much that he decided to stay on in the darkened cinema and see it again, completely forgetting the time. McAloran knew he had gone to a cinema but did not know which one, and he searched all over town for his boxer. Meanwhile, with Rinty in another world, halfway through Bing crooning *Sing a Song of Sunbeams*, a public announcement appeared on the screen: 'If Rinty Monaghan is in the audience, would he report to the New St James's Hall immediately.'

The boxer rushed out of the cinema and darted into the hall, to be greeted by a furious McAloran. 'Sorry Frank,' he spluttered. 'I got carried away with the picture.' The angry fans, now restless and impatient at the long delay, gave him the slow-handclap as he made his way to the ring. There had been no time for even a light tea. Happily for Rinty he left the ring an impressive winner. The bout was scheduled for ten rounds but it only made it halfway. The cagey Liverpool battler, with sixty-nine fights behind him, did well for four rounds but Monaghan found the openings in the fifth with two smashing lefts and rights to the jaw for a clean knockout.

Not even Adolf Hitler could put a stop to Rinty's career. He only interrupted it. With World War II raging, Monaghan had seven fights between September 1939, when hostilities broke out, until war's end in Europe in May 1945, with three wins, three losses and a draw. But if his fistic activity was restricted, his value as an entertainer was not.

After a spell in the Merchant Navy, which ended when his ship was torpedoed, Rinty joined the Civil Defence as an ambulance driver during the Belfast Blitz. Soon he would form a group called The Three Hillbillies before coming to the attention of a talent scout for the Entertainments National Service Association, known as ENSA, an organisation set up in 1939 to provide entertainment for the troops.

Monaghan travelled with ENSA across Europe, including a visit to Normandy less than forty-eight hours after the D-Day landings and where he entertained the troops of the Expeditionary Forces. He did four shows a day and would remember it as 'a joyous experience'.

In July 1945, with the war in Europe already at an end, Rinty boxed in Dublin for the first and only time in his career. At the old Theatre Royal in Hawkins Street, he outpointed Joe 'Boy' Collins over ten rounds. Collins had a big following in the city's historic Liberties area but Rinty had to disappoint them, and Joe 'Boy', by proving too strong. The sporting Collins congratulated Monaghan after the fight and wished him luck in all his future endeavours, inside and outside the squared circle.

Monaghan's old rival, Liverpool's Joe Curran, won a points decision over him in October but less than three weeks later Rinty got an opportunity to achieve one of his early ambitions, to win a title. At the Ulster Hall, Belfast on 6 November 1945 he was matched with the formidable Eddie 'Bunty' Doran for the Northern Ireland flyweight championship. Doran, who was a cousin of Rinty's, was an experienced campaigner who had no intention of losing his title. There was too much at stake.

Already in line for a European title fight, with a world championship challenge to Rinty's old foe, Scotland's Jackie Paterson, to follow, Doran had to win this one, and he climbed into the ring as a four to six on favourite. Boxing historian and writer Brian Madden described Doran in his book *Yesterday's Glovemen* as 'a class act'. That he was.

It was a great chance for Monaghan, too, and he would later claim that he trained like never before for the fight. In the mornings he could be seen pounding the hills around Belfast in his heavy boots and in the evenings it would be tough, fast sparring sessions in the gym, giving his sparring partners Eddie McCullough, Peter Robinson and Jim Campbell no rest.

No sooner had Belfast's Andy Smyth, one of the world's leading referees, called the two together than Doran was on the attack, determined to finish off this cocky challenger. 'Bunty' was ahead after three rounds, with another nine to go, when Monaghan caught him with a cracking right hook and he took a count of eight. On rising, he was caught with another powerful right hook which put him down and out. *The Irish News* summed up the dramatic events the following morning with two big headlines: 'Belfast boxing sensation'; and 'Monaghan knocks out Doran in the fourth round.'

World flyweight champion Jackie Paterson was now Monaghan's prime target. The Scot, who had knocked out Rinty before the war, was one of the best eight stone boxers of his era. Born in Ayrshire in September 1920, when he was eight years of age his family emigrated to Scranton, Pennsylvania. When Jackie was in his early teens he returned to Scotland and worked in the John Browne shipbuilders yard on the Clyde, later becoming a butcher.

Keen on soccer, Paterson had early ambitions to become a professional player but when he was introduced to boxing by a friend, he became hooked on the noble art. He joined the Anderson Amateur Boxing Club in Glasgow and encouraged by his success with the gloves, turned professional in 1937 when he was seventeen and began his meteoric rise to the top.

Although a natural southpaw, Paterson could hit forcibly with either hand, though his most lethal punch was a left hook which could be delivered fast, hard and accurately. While serving in the RAF during the war, he also managed to continue his ring career, having won the British flyweight title in 1939 and the Commonwealth championship the following year. In 1943 he caused a sensation by flattening Lancaster's Peter Kane in sixty-one seconds, a fight that remains one of the shortest world flyweight title bouts in history. Boxing people were calling him the best Scottish eight-stoner since the great Benny Lynch in the 1930s.

A champion with a large following, Paterson flirted with the bantamweights during his reign. However, he preferred the flyweight division and agreed to defend his world title against Monaghan's old foe Joe Curran in Glasgow on 26 June 1946. The Scot's British and Commonwealth titles, as well as the European championship, would be on the line but canny Belfast promoter Bob Gardiner persuaded him to take a non-title fight over ten rounds with Rinty less than three weeks earlier at the King's Hall. 'You've nothing to lose,' Gardiner told him. 'Even if you are beaten, you still have your titles, and there is a good purse for you.'

Paterson accepted the fight – and lost. After strong starts by both men, the Scot scored two knockdowns but after six rounds Monaghan was gradually getting on top. By the seventh Paterson had sustained bad cuts over both eyes and the fight was stopped. Rinty had gained revenge and there was great jubilation in the hall. Because of the injuries, Paterson's title fight with Curran was postponed.

When it eventually took place, at Glasgow's Hampden Park on 10 July 1946, the Scot won on points over fifteen rounds but it had not been easy. There were persistent rumours that he had struggled to make the weight and that he would compete fully as a bantamweight in future. He was at the time, in fact, the European and Commonwealth champion at the higher weight.

Monaghan was now Ireland's Golden Boy, and being touted as the uncrowned world flyweight champion as well as the top man among Commonwealth and British boxers at that poundage. Negotiations opened for an important match with Emile Famechon, one of three boxing brothers and the new sensation of French boxing. The fight, which would mark Monaghan's London debut, would be held at the Seymour Hall, a popular boxing venue, in March 1947, with the winner going in against Paterson for the world title. But as so often happens in boxing, talks broke down. Famechon was out but his brother Andre agreed to come in.

Rinty's manager then got the news that the second Famechon was out, and with time running out, a promising London flyweight named Terry Allen was brought in. Fans in the British capital had heard a lot about 'the Irish boy with the big punch' and while they knew he had boxed in other British cities, they wanted a close look at him in 'The Big Smoke'.

London's first view of Monaghan, nevertheless, was a brief one. With many fans hardly settled in their seats, Rinty came out of his corner fast and rocked Allen with stiff lefts and rights. Terry backed away but the Irishman was after him and caught Allen with a long left hook which put him down. The Londoner was up at the count of six but Monaghan would not be denied and after flooring his opponent for further counts of eight, seven and nine, the fight was stopped with just a minute to go in round one. British writers heaped praise on Monaghan the next day, calling him 'the uncrowned flyweight champion of the world'.

Four months later Emile Famechon, who had previously withdrawn from a clash with Monaghan, felt he had enough ability to check the rise of the Irishman and so secure a world title fight with Paterson. They met at Olympia in London but Rinty proved too strong. The Frenchman was always dangerous with his swings and hooks but Monaghan was faster to the punch and won a clear points decision over ten rounds. He also consolidated his position as the number one world flyweight title contender in the monthly ratings by the influential *Ring* magazine. 'This Irish boy can be champion of the world,' forecast Nat Fleischer, editor and publisher.

As so often happens in boxing, however, the most deserving contender does not necessarily get the title fight, at least not straight away. Instead of nominating Monaghan as the rightful challenger for Paterson's world title, America's National Boxing Association, one of the two major controlling bodies at the time, selected the relatively unknown Dado Marino of Hawaii as the top man.

Marino was managed by Sam Ichinose, nicknamed Sad Sam by the press because he always looked forlorn even when one of his boxers won. Nevertheless, he was a shrewd businessman and dealmaker. Sam had discovered Dado in island plantation tournaments. Marino's father had been an accomplished boxer and always encouraged his son to pull on the gloves. Soon the young Hawaiian was competing in amateur tournaments on the island and in June 1941 turned professional at the relatively late age of twenty-five. Marino seemed to have the natural ability for the paid ranks and made fast progress.

With America's entry into the war on 8 December 1941 following the surprise attack on Pearl Harbour by the Japanese, Marino's career was temporarily interrupted when he enlisted with the US Seventh Air Force and served in Pacific danger spots. But he continued his boxing in between assignments and won the USA Hawaiian flyweight title in Honolulu in April 1944. He had now an impressive record of twenty-four fights, with just one defeat. All his fights had taken place in Honolulu.

With Dado's reputation growing rapidly, Ichinose began sending out feelers to the US. Soon he began pestering the National Boxing Association and the New York State Athletic Commission, the two leading American organisations who effectively controlled the destiny of the world championships, to get Marino a chance at Jackie Paterson's world flyweight title.

The New York authorities supported Monaghan but the NBA felt that Marino had the better credentials and should get an early shot at Paterson's title. Encouraged by the NBA's stance, Ichinose took Marino and the rest of the stable to New York to train at the famous Stillman's Gym and convinced the US boxing writers that Marino was the man they should support.

'Anyway,' said Ichinose, 'why should we let the British and the Europeans call the shots? Are we going to stand aside and let this happen? Let's try and get the title back to this part of the world. Remember, it is sixteen years since an American last held the world flyweight championship. Remember Frankie Genaro? Marino is the best we have so let's get him his chance.' Several New York newspapers gave prominence to the manager's case, and indeed supported him. Ichinose had won the first round.

The New York Commission, however, still stood by Monaghan, supported by *Ring* magazine. 'Rinty Monaghan is the leading contender, and any fight that does not include the Irishman cannot justifiably be called a world title bout,' said editor and publisher Nat Fleischer. 'Let us see justice done here.'

With a Paterson title defence long overdue, the NBA moved in fast and ordered the Scot to defend against Marino and the fight was scheduled for Hampden Park, Glasgow in July 1947. They also stipulated that the winner would have to defend against Monaghan. While Dado was relatively unknown outside his native island, Hawaiian and mainland America boxing writers felt he could provide a few problems for Paterson. The New York State Athletic Commission and *Ring* magazine would still recognise Monaghan as champion.

The Monaghan camp was outraged at being overlooked, not to mention Irish fans, but what could be done? Meanwhile, there had been unconfirmed stories coming from Scotland that Paterson was not well and that he had 'a mysterious illness' which was reportedly baffling doctors. Eventually it came out that Paterson was having extreme trouble in getting down to flyweight. In reality, he had been a bantamweight for several years now.

Paterson and his camp insisted that Jackie could come in at or under eight stone, and his trainer John Rafferty told British Board officials in Scotland that he would be fine, a fact relayed to the NBA across the Atlantic. However, as the days ticked by, there was concern when it was reported from Glasgow that Paterson was in fact in a sickbed, having broken out in boils and sores due to crash diets and struggles to sweat off the pounds. Quite clearly he was in no condition to train, let alone go into the ring against a hungry challenger in a world title fight. Again, there were denials.

With Monaghan already in Glasgow and standing by in case Paterson failed to show, officials told him that the Scot had apparently made a good recovery, had resumed training, and would duly turn up for the weigh-in at the appointed time on the day of the fight, 16 July 1947. A crowd of over twenty-five thousand had purchased tickets, many at high prices, for the world title bout and it received wide coverage in all the newspapers. With a week to go, Monaghan was told he would not be needed after all and that the Paterson–Marino fight was definitely going ahead. However, he decided to stay around in Glasgow and see the fight anyhow.

In a sensational development, Paterson failed to show for the weigh-in. It appeared that he was two pounds over the limit that morning on his home scales and had suddenly collapsed in the bathroom. He was clearly a sick man and certainly in no condition to step into a ring for a world title defence. The NBA promptly stripped him of the title, and the British Board, an affiliated member, followed suit. New York still supported Monaghan as the number one contender. The show would still go ahead, with Marino going in against Monaghan in what was called 'an international flyweight contest'. But where was Rinty? Yes, in Glasgow, but could he be located in time?

Search parties went out, and Rinty was eventually discovered enjoying a hearty meal in a restaurant. Told what had happened and that he was needed straight away for the weigh-in, he gulped down the rest of his food, rushed across town and stepped on the scales. He was several pounds overweight but it did not matter as there was no title on the line. The contest would be over ten rounds. Rinty knew that his big chance was not too far away, whatever happened.

What Monaghan did not take into consideration was that he was not mentally or physically prepared for the fight. It had come too suddenly. With the rain beating down making it difficult for both boxers moving around on the soaked canvas, Monaghan had Marino down in the opening round from a heavy right hook to the body.

The Hawaiian jumped up, had his gloves wiped by London referee Moses Deyong, known as Moss, but Rinty could not get another clean shot and Marino boxed his way out of trouble. By the third round, sawdust had to be sprinkled over the canvas to help the boxers keep their footing but it was getting wetter by the minute. This slowed the fight down considerably.

With both men just managing to stay balanced, Marino sustained cuts over both eyes in the fourth round but Monaghan was warned by Deyong to stop holding. The fight opened up a little in the eighth when a left-right combination had Marino on the saturated canvas but the Hawaiian boxed his way out of trouble and dropped Monaghan with a fast right hook. He was up at eight shortly before the bell rang. In the ninth, Deyong suddenly moved in and disqualified Monaghan for holding, even though both boxers were guilty of the infringement.

Deyong would later explain that the Irishman was the main culprit and that he had warned him several times. There were boos from the big crowd who felt cheated at the sudden termination of the bout, even though it was not the most exciting they had ever seen. Rinty said in the dressing room: 'Ok, I'm disappointed I lost but I've no excuses to make. I lost to a better man. It must be remembered too that I took this fight at a few hours notice whereas Marino had been preparing for it for months. But I got a good insight into Marino's style. I will be more prepared if we fight next time, with a world title hopefully at stake.'

Marino and his manager were now insisting that Dado was the world's best flyweight and would have to be involved in any discussions or plans about a world title fight. The NBA announced they would recognise a Marino–Monaghan contest as being for the world title on the basis that Paterson was now an ex-champion, was no longer fit and was consequently out of the picture. The British Board went along with the NBA ruling until Paterson sensationally came back into the scene. The Scot announced that he would sue the British Board if they sanctioned any world title fight not involving himself. So Britain, somewhat reluctantly, 'restored' the title to Paterson.

The Éire Boxing Board of Control, now the Boxing Union of Ireland, added their support to the NBA. The French Boxing Federation also agreed to recognise the fight, providing the winner would agree to meet Maurice Sandeyron, the Parisian who held the European and French flyweight titles, within three months. In default, they would consider the championship vacant. This was agreed by the principals.

Enter promoter Jack Solomons. A former London fishmonger, Solomons had become Europe's leading boxing promoter, bringing top Americans to Britain to defend their world titles and creating major transatlantic matches. Rarely seen without a long cigar clenched between his teeth, the stylish so-called Sultan of Sock had the knack for creating an air of excitement in the sport. A boxer in his teenage years who fought under the name of Kid Mears, Solomons originally became involved in the business side of the sport in the 1930s when he developed a rundown old church in north London into the Devonshire Club, which became a popular boxing venue.

Also known as Jolly Jack because of his happy disposition and optimism, Solomons had worked as a matchmaker for other promoters before venturing out on his own. He became not only Britain's foremost boxing promoter in the 1940s and 1950s but the number one in Europe as well, and one who was very highly respected on the far side of the Atlantic. He collaborated with US promoters on several big fights involving Britons, including the second match between Sugar Ray Robinson and Randolph Turpin in New York in September 1951.

Solomons matched Marino with Monaghan, the bout to be staged at Harringay Arena, the London venue where he regularly put on promotions, on 20

October 1947. Rinty would be the first Irishman to contest the world flyweight championship since the division came into being nearly forty years earlier. Boxing people wondered could he win it and make history. Having signed contracts for the Monaghan fight, Marino's manager Sam Ichinose agreed for his man to have a warm-up to get him in shape for the title fight, which would be only his third bout outside Honolulu.

Marino was matched with Lancashire's former world flyweight champion Peter Kane in a tune-up fight for Manchester on 8 August, just ten weeks before the Monaghan bout. It turned out to be bad planning, and a huge embarrassment for them as Marino was beaten on points, with the Englishman constantly putting him under intense pressure and repeatedly catching the Hawaiian with long jabs and strong hooks.

The Marino camp put the loss down to 'a lack of proper training', with Ichinose telling reporters in the dressing room: 'You will see a different Dado Marino at Harringay.' Solomons, doing his best to hide his shock, wiped his brow and said: 'This was just a blip in a fight with nothing at stake. Everything will be fine for October. You'll see.'

With no further scares, the weigh-in for the title fight was held at Solomons' gym in Windmill Street. After the boxers had stepped on the scales, it was announced that both had come in one pound inside the eight stone limit. Asked how he felt, Monaghan smiled and said: 'Fine. I'm determined to bring the world title home to Ireland and I promise not to let anybody down. This is my big chance and I'm going to take it with both hands.' Looking slightly solemn, Marino commented: 'I didn't come all the way, across two oceans, to lose this fight, the most important of my life. I'm in the best shape of my career.'

Just before the bell rang for round one, Marino walked across to Monaghan's corner and placed a traditional Hawaiian garland of white and orange flowers around his opponent's neck. 'Thanks,' said a smiling Rinty. That was the end of the formalities. Now for the real action, although it did not come too often for the packed crowd of ten thousand. Monaghan had planned a cautious fight, with a world title in the balance. Marino was on the attack early, aiming for the body but the Irishman skipped away, keeping on the retreat while using his left jab.

By the fifth round Teddy Waltham, one of Britain's leading referees, had to call both boxers together for 'a bit more action, boys'. They livened up but only in spasms, with Marino going for the body in a bid to bring his man down, while Monaghan concentrated on his boxing. Rinty would reveal later that he damaged his right hand on Marino's head in the sixth. 'From that point onwards I had to bluff Marino,' he confessed. 'I mainly used my left and threw the right sparingly, and just coasted my way through the rest of the fight.'

As Arthur P. McWeeney wrote in the *Irish Independent* the following morning: 'I imagine that to one who had not a personal or patriotic interest in the result, it must have been a disappointing affair. Indeed, there were periods when a section of the spectators displayed disapproval by stamping and slow clapping at what they regarded as lack of action. But in view of Monaghan's injured right hand, which he later showed me and which was badly swollen and obviously painful, his success becomes a very much more credible performance.'

After Monaghan's right hand was raised by Waltham as new world flyweight champion, he went to the centre of the ring and entertained the fans, who did not have much to shout about during the fight, with rousing versions of when *Irish Eyes Are Smiling* and *Hello Patsy Fagan*. Back in Belfast, the streets were soon aglow with the light of blazing bonfires and cheering, singing crowds. The local boy had made good.

Monaghan, however, did not consider himself the 'real' champion until he met Paterson, who was still claiming he was the legitimate king of the flyweights. Belfast promoter Bob Gardiner signed both men to contest what would now be a universally recognised world title fight at the King's Hall on 23 March 1948. But boxing promotions would not be boxing promotions without big problems, with rumours swirling around like confetti that Paterson was way above the flyweight limit and that there was no way he would make eight stone.

It should not have come as any great surprise as the Scot was campaigning as a bantamweight at the time and held the British and Commonwealth titles in that division. He had not defended his world, British and Commonwealth flyweight titles since winning them almost two years earlier.

Paterson was due at the weigh-in at the Grand Central Hotel in Belfast on the early afternoon of the fight but failed to show. The promoter had the Frenchman, Maurice Sandeyron standing by as a possible late substitute. When Paterson's manager Pat Collins and his trainer Johnny Rafferty were contacted in Glasgow, they said they had no idea where their boxer was. Efforts to reach the Paterson household by phone proved futile. Finally came news that Paterson was on a plane from his home and would arrive 'as soon as possible'. The Scot duly arrived, four minutes before the deadline, and stepped on the scales. He made the weight by four ounces, with Monaghan scaling seven stone twelve pounds. The big fight was on.

Inside the opening minute Monaghan almost ended it all when he rocked Paterson with a tremendous right-hand punch which sent him staggering drunkenly across the ring. The Scot managed to stay on his feet and hold on until the end of the round. Rinty was soon on the attack in the second but in his anxiety for a quick finish he was wild with some swings. By the sixth, Monaghan had a clear points lead but could not find the right shot to end it all.

Paterson went all out with lefts and rights at the start of the seventh in a last, desperate effort to pull off a dramatic victory but left himself open. Monaghan crashed across a smashing right that sent the Scot sinking to the floor, flat on his back like a starfish.

178

He scrambled to his feet just in time before Monaghan moved in for the kill, driving his opponent into the Irish corner and firing a barrage of hooks and uppercuts. Paterson took all the blows to his head and body but the end was painfully near. A powerful final right cross crashed against the Scot's jaw and he slumped to the canvas, his head on his chest, in a sitting position to be counted out.

After the official announcement Rinty grabbed the microphone and sang a rousing version of *When Irish Eyes Are Smiling*, followed by *I'm Always Chasing Rainbows*. The ecstatic crowd joined in. More than ever on this night, there was every conceivable reason to sing out. Rinty Monaghan was now recognised universally and officially as flyweight champion of the world, the undisputed number one at eight stone.

One who disagreed, however, was Maurice Sandeyron, the French flyweight who had been on standby in Belfast. The Parisian felt he had the tools to dethrone Rinty. He also held the prestigious European title. There was also that stipulation to the French Boxing Federation that Sandeyron would get first crack at the new champion. They met at the King's Hall on 5 April 1949 and Monaghan entered the ring as the underdog.

A former amateur star, Sandeyron had twenty-seven wins, nine losses and five draws since turning to the paid ranks in October 1942. Could the Irishman turn back the challenge of this formidable continental rival? This time he would be up against an opponent with no weight problems, unlike Paterson, who never boxed at flyweight again.

In what turned out to be Monaghan's finest performance, Sandeyron was well beaten over fifteen rounds before a yelling crowd of over ten thousand. The Frenchman had no real answer to Rinty's powerful jab, and while it took the Irishman a few rounds to get started, Monaghan was never in any real trouble. The durable Sandeyron used powerful uppercuts to break through Monaghan's defence and he constantly kept up the pressure but the Irishman took his best shots and always came back with his own blows. This was Ireland's big night, and Rinty's.

Monaghan's better boxing, sharper punching and ring generalship kept him in front. When Welsh referee C.B. Thomas unhesitatingly raised the Irishman's right hand at the finish, not even Sandeyron himself had any complaints about not only losing the fight but dropping his European title and forfeiting his high world ranking as well.

Meanwhile there were rumblings from London about a promising flyweight from Islington who fancied his chances of toppling Monaghan and taking over the World, European and Commonwealth titles. Terry Allen had already surprisingly outpointed Monaghan in an overweight bout in London two months before the Sandeyron match and was naturally confident of winning again, this time with three titles on the line. Of course, with the titles at stake, Monaghan would be a much different fighter.

Allen divided his time between the boxing ring and his barrow, where he sold fruit and flowers on the street, helping to serve the needs of the local community. The sellers were known as barrow boys, an old London tradition which has been around for over five hundred years. Allen's father was a professional boxer and as well as showing his young son how to use his fists, he told him about all the great champions, past and present.

Allen's mother died when he was two and he was raised by his grandmother. He started boxing as an amateur at the age of nine and won a schoolboy championship, finishing up with a busy record of one hundred and seven contests, losing only five. With six of his cousins already professional boxers, Allen made his debut in the paid ranks and was an instant success. He loved the cut and thrust of the professional game, and even when he joined the navy and served in the Egyptian port of Alexandria, he continued his boxing. By the end of 1948, the Londoner was at the forefront of the flyweight division. A title match with Monaghan now seemed a natural progression.

Belfast promoter Bob Gardiner sealed the fight for 30 September 1949 at the King's Hall, with Monaghan's World, European and Commonwealth titles to be defended. It would turn out to be Rinty's final fight. For the past few years he had been suffering from a chest ailment that affected his breathing and was always threatening his career. Allen was a resourceful boxer and had Monaghan on the canvas in the second round from a fast, hard right to the head. Rinty took the count from London referee Sam Russell on one knee and was up at eight. The knockdown made Monaghan wary, and he took few chances, preferring to use his skill to outmanoeuvre the challenger and collect the points.

Allen came on in the closing rounds but Monaghan's better ring generalship made an Irish victory seem secure. At the finish Russell surprisingly raised both boxers' hands to declare a draw, and while the result enabled Monaghan to hold on to his championships, the verdict was soundly booed by the big crowd who felt the home boxer was entitled to the decision. There were several brawls involving rival supporters but Rinty helped defuse the situation with a rousing version of *How Can You Buy Killarney?* Monaghan had boxed the full fifteen rounds with serious breathing difficulties, and clips and photographs of the fight clearly show him with his mouth open.

Monaghan clearly seemed hard done by with the draw and even cross-channel writers felt he should have won. Laison Wood in the *Daily Telegraph* said he was bewildered by the referee's scoring. 'Even if the fight was a poor one, all flurry and fret, I definitely felt that Allen never did enough to deserve a share of the verdict,' he wrote. *Boxing News*, in an uncredited report, said: 'We thought Monaghan a shade unlucky not to secure an outright victory, as did the majority of the onlookers. Allen allowed the Irishman to do nearly all the attacking and never once got his nose in front. Monaghan ended up remarkably strong.'

American promoters sent out feelers for Monaghan to make his US debut, and the EBU were calling for him to defend his European title, with presumably the world championship on the line as well, against the Frenchman, Honore Pratesi. Rinty ended all speculation in March 1950 by announcing his retirement for health reasons. He had been suffering from regular bouts of chronic bronchitis for a long time. Two years later there was talk of a comeback but nothing came of it. In his retirement years he was a regular on big fight nights in Belfast, perpetually cheerful and always prepared to sign autographs.

When Monaghan died on 3 March 1984, thousands lined the streets of Belfast to pay their last respects to the great old battler. He was sixty-four. Newspapers north and south carried full, generous tributes, outlining his life both inside and outside the ring. *The Belfast Telegraph* devoted an editorial to him. Father Myles Murray told the overflow congregation in St Patrick's Catholic Church on Donegall Street: 'Rinty was one who brought good news to us all. He was a gentleman, loved by many. This is what life is all about, touching people, bringing joy and happiness, making friends.'

12. MICHAEL CARRUTH

Gold strike in Barcelona

It was the day that time stood still in Ireland, when the streets were virtually deserted. On the hot afternoon of 8 August 1992, televisions and radios were switched on and all eyes and ears were on the fate of Dublin soldier Michael Carruth as he faced the mighty Cuban welterweight, Juan Hernández in the brightly-lit ring at the Joventut Pavilion in Barcelona. The prize was an Olympic gold medal.

It was a huge task on the broad shoulders of Carruth. The moment of truth had arrived in the world's most prestigious sporting tournament. The southpaw Liffeysider was fully aware that boxing was Ireland's most successful Olympic sport, with a total haul of eight medals. There was no doubting that the noble art had brought the most prestige to Ireland on an international scale.

After making its Olympic debut in Paris in 1924, Irish boxing's first medal success was in 1952 with silver for Belfast bantamweight John McNally in Helsinki. Four years later in Melbourne, in the same Olympics where the Arklow athlete Ronnie Delany won the fifteen hundred metres, four Irish boxers brought home medals.

Three bronze medals came from Belfast flyweight John Caldwell, bantamweight Freddie Gilroy, also from the northern capital, and Drogheda lightweight Tony 'Socks' Byrne. In the welterweight division, Dubliner Fred Tiedt achieved his greatest success, either as an amateur or professional, when he won a silver medal. By right, though, it should have been gold after he lost an atrociously bad decision in the final to the Romanian, Nicolae Linca. Tiedt swore all his life that the gold medal his opponent brought back to his home country rightfully should have been his.

Tiedt was far from alone in his belief that the judges got it terribly wrong. The crowd booed the decision and showed their anger by sitting throughout the Romanian national anthem. The referee, who had a vote, gave it to Linca while two judges marked it for Tiedt. The two remaining judges, under the old scoring system, had it as a draw but the rules meant that they had to come down on the side of either boxer by marking them under other criteria such as style, aggression and defensive work. Both marked it for Linca.

Nat Fleischer, editor of *Ring* magazine and considered the world's foremost authority on the sport, wrote from ringside: 'The verdict in the welterweight final was the most disgraceful I have ever seen, not only in these Olympics but anywhere else. The manner in which the verdict was given against the Irishman was a travesty of justice and bordered on the lunatic fringe.' Clips of the fight

182

today clearly show Linca alternating between indiscriminate swinging and holding on, while the Dubliner picks him off judiciously and does all the points-collecting with clever, skilful boxing.

There was a gap of eight years before another medal came Ireland's way when Belfast lightweight Jim McCourt brought home a bronze from Tokyo in 1964. There was an even longer space before the next medal success, with Belfast flyweight Hughie Russell winning bronze in the Moscow Games in 1980. That gold medal was proving to be as elusive as quicksilver. Now, in the 1992 Barcelona games, Michael Carruth hoped to change all that, and make up for all the disappointments. Earlier in the day, he had watched from ringside as the Belfast bantamweight Wayne McCullough won silver, and soon his own crucial Olympic test would come.

Carruth was eighteen years in the game and probably learned all there was to know. Michael was the seventh of ten children born to Austin and Joan Carruth who lived near Dublin city centre before moving to the suburbs as the city began to expand and new housing developments were springing up. They settled down in the Greenhills area of Drimnagh. Growing up, Michael played soccer and Gaelic football. He got into many scrapes with bullies at school yet more than held his own.

'It was always written on the wind that the Carruth boys, all six of us, would box,' Carruth wrote in his 1992 autobiography *Ring of Gold*. 'My father Austin was a carpenter by trade and he built an enormous playpen for us as kids and always believed that was where we cultivated our liking for boxing. Coming from a family like ours, with roots firmly embedded in the sport, I don't think we would have got a hearing if we said we weren't interested in putting on the gloves.'

Michael's father, who was later an Irish Amateur Boxing Association coach and trained his son for Olympic competition, was involved in the sport as early as the 1940s when one of the major boxing clubs was St Francis Boxing Club in the city.

The amateur club also attracted professionals at the time, big names such as Paddy Dowdall and Jimmy Ingle, who had been the first Irish boxers to win European amateur titles when the championships were held at the newly-opened National Stadium in 1939, Ingle winning at flyweight and Dowdall at featherweight. They and other professionals would use the club premises to train for their contests held in the Ulster Hall in Belfast, as professional shows were few and far between on the southern side of the border.

'There was the occasion when the American heavyweight Lee Savold came to Dublin en route to an appointment with the British champion Bruce Wood-cock in London for a version of the world heavyweight championship in 1950,' remembered Carruth. 'Savold trained for a while in the club so you can imagine the interest generated by his stay in Dublin. My dad sparred with him and he used to say until the day he died that sparring with Savold was one of his biggest claims to boxing fame.'

There was also a history of boxing on Michael's mother's side. Her brother Martin Humpston from St Francis Boxing Club was Ireland's first Irish light-middleweight champion when the eight weight divisions were revised in 1951 and two new divisions were introduced, lightwelterweight and lightmiddleweight. Joan was always one of Michael's most fervent supporters and was at ringside whenever possible when her son boxed.

The Carruth family was immersed in boxing. Austin used to bring his sons to the National Stadium to see the juvenile boxers in action in the County Dublin Leagues on Tuesday nights and the boys would get in free on Friday nights to watch the seniors, in return for selling programmes. They trained with Austin in the newly-opened Greenhills Boxing Club in the community centre, but when they had to vacate the centre, they moved and merged with the nearby Drimnagh Boxing Club, one of the leading clubs in Ireland and where one of boxing's greats, bantamweight Mick Dowling had been a member.

Carruth learned his boxing through tough competitions like inter-club tournaments, and particularly in competitions such as the National Juvenile Championships, the County Dublins, the National Youths and the Irish Juniors. 'There was a standing joke in our house that the Carruths needed to win a national senior title before they could be mentioned in the same breath as the in-laws,' he recalled. 'This was a reference to mam's brother Martin Humpston, and she would rib dad endlessly about the fact that for all the dedication and devotion to training, the Carruth triplets hadn't yet duplicated Martin's achievement.'

Carruth put the record straight in the National Senior Championships of 1987 when he won the lightweight title, repeating his success the following year. He would recall that the 'Seniors' always held a fascination for the family. 'They were the Oscars of Irish boxing, and without them, the gateway to international championships was barred,' he said. 'If you lost the National Championships, you almost certainly lost your chance of getting to box in the Olympics. I could now claim equality with Uncle Martin. More than that, I had won the lightweight championship, the one that many people would see as the most prized title of all.'

On his way into the National Stadium on the South Circular Road not far from his home, Carruth would glance at the large plaque on the wall at the entrance and read the names of some of the great lightweight champions on the list. They included Ernie Smith, Dave Connell, Tony 'Socks' Byrne, Harry Perry, Charlie Nash and Maxie McCullagh, the Mullingar boxer who brought home a gold medal as a lightweight from the 1949 European Championship in Oslo.

The immediate reward for winning the Irish title was a place in the six-man squad for the European championships in Turin in May 1987. Carruth, now in the Irish Army, reached the quarter-finals before being eliminated by Orzhbek Nazarov from the old Soviet Union, who was rated the world's number two at the time.

Nazarov got the unanimous decision, with three judges making it 59–58, two calling it 60–57, markings which the Irish camp claimed were wide off the mark. The only consolation for Carruth was that Nazarov went on to win the gold medal, one of five of his countrymen to win out. It made the Dubliner realise that to push a boxer of the Soviet's qualities so close in a major competition far from home was not a bad performance and gave him confidence for the future. There would be another day.

That came sooner than expected when he was informed by the IABA in July, just a week before his twenty-first birthday, that he had been selected for the 1988 Seoul Olympics. 'The Olympics are a real eye-opener for the first-time competitor,' he would tell Peter Byrne of the *Irish Times*. 'Like every other youngster who has ever dreamed of making it big in sport, I always wanted to take part in the Games and before arriving in Seoul, I figured I had a reasonable idea of the scene that awaited me. But no amount of reading or listening can prepare you for the shock. For one thing, it is bigger than you could ever imagine, and all those foreign languages and different races make the young competitor yearn for the security of home.'

The first series saw him paired with Japan's Satoro Higashi, a bout he won convincingly. Carruth then went in against George Gramme, a Swede he had beaten the previous year in Copenhagen. Towards the end of the first round, which the Dubliner was winning, Gramme caught him with a fast, hard left hook to the chin that put Carruth on the canvas for the first time in his life.

He rose quickly but the referee looked into his eyes, waved his hands wide and showed him back to the corner. With just five seconds of the round remaining, the Drimnagh boxer and his corner protested, claiming that after the minute's interval everything would be fine but it was all over. Carruth's Olympic dream had ended, at least for the present.

There was consolation in 1989 when he returned home from Moscow after winning a bronze medal at lightwelterweight in the World Championships, losing out in the semi-finals to Andreas Otto, a tough rival from what was then East Germany, or the German Democratic Republic to give it the official title. 'Otto was simply one of the best operators around,' Carruth would remember. 'He was a man who could fight or box as he chose. No matter what strategy I would adopt, it was certain to be a hard, unrelenting scrap. In that expectation I was not disappointed.'

Whenever Carruth tried to box, Otto would fight, and when the Dubliner went aggressive, his opponent would use long-range punching. Carruth did connect with some damaging shots to the head in the early part of the bout but the East German was always coming forward, pressing Carruth all the time.

No matter what the Irishman tried, there was no keeping Otto at bay, although Carruth landed some good long-range shots in the final round. The judges made Otto the winner by 18–1, and while there was no doubt that the East German was a convincing winner, even neutral ringsiders agreed that the scoring was much closer than what was announced.

Carruth was not to know it at the time but he would get a chance for revenge over Otto three years later. Fast forward to the 1992 Barcelona Olympics when computerised scoring would be used for the first time. Both had moved up to welterweight by now. They clashed in the quarter-finals and Michael knew what to expect, even though by now the East German was a much improved boxer, having won a silver medal in the World Championships and the Europeans.

With so much at stake, both boxers rarely made a mistake, and while Otto was constantly on the attack, Carruth used his better skills to outmanoeuvre his opponent. Michael forced a count in the first round from a good right to the body but Otto had made a strong recovery and was always in there fighting.

It was still close, with the judges awarding the East German the last round by 3-1, but the Irish corner felt their man had done enough to win. It went to a countback when the points were adjudged even, but Carruth's better work early on gained him the decision by 35–22. The Dubliner had avenged his previous loss to Otto, guaranteeing himself at least a bronze medal in the process. Overjoyed, he performed a few cartwheels. The East German sportingly came around to Carruth's dressing room later, and through an interpreter, said: 'Good show Michael. Naturally I'm sorry I lost but you deserved it and it was a good fight. Good luck on the remainder of your journey.'

Carruth's opponent in the semi-final would be the formidable Thai puncher Arkhom Chenglai, who had been marked down as a likely gold medallist not only by his countrymen but by visiting observers. There was a sensation twenty-four hours before the fight when it was thought that Carruth could get a bye into the final as Chenglai was allegedly seen around the Olympic village with a plaster over one of his eyes from an earlier bout.

That would have meant an easy route into the final but the Irish camp, including Carruth and his father, had their suspicions. As far as they were aware, the Thai had suffered no serious damage in his previous bout and while it was possible that he could have been cut in training, they planned that Chenglai would present himself in the ring for the semi-final.

In one of the best fights of his career, and fired up with the knowledge that he was closer now than ever before to that elusive gold medal, the Drimnagh boxer had the Irish supporters around the ring jumping to their feet as he outboxed and outfought his man. The Thai landed some good shots but Carruth was always faster, scoring with a cracking right to the jaw in the third round which staggered Chenglai and necessitated a count but the referee ignored the incident. Carruth won on an 11–4 margin.

'The fight was a bit of a let-down,' Carruth recalled in later years. 'Looking back now, I feel that Chenglai had been content to get his bronze medal, and a clash in the final with the Cuban, Juan Hernández, who was favourite to win the gold medal, did not appeal to him. I could sense that he wasn't up for the fight but I was really physically and mentally on fire by that stage.'

Now for the final, which was not going to be easy. An even tougher test than he had experienced against the Thai. The Dubliner would be up against one of the best welterweights on the planet in Juan Hernández of Cuba, who was being freely tipped as an outright winner of the competition. A skilful boxer who could place his punches with the precision of a Swiss watch, Hernández had won gold in the World Championships a year earlier, an achievement he would repeat in 1993 and 1995 as well as getting a bronze in 1997.

In Barcelona, an Olympic medal was his target, and he was going well to reach that target. Hernández had overwhelmed his four rivals on the way to the final, stopping two in the second round and outpointing the others 6–0 and 11–2. Cuba, now a major force on the world amateur boxing scene, had an incredible nine boxers in the finals and their camp had no intention of losing any of them. They would eventually come out with seven gold medals.

At 6 ft 3 in, unusual for a welterweight, Hernández was eight inches taller than the Dubliner, as well as having a correspondingly longer reach. Because of a previous gymnastics injury, Carruth's right arm was more than two inches shorter than his left. Although he was naturally right-handed, he was forced from early on to fight as a southpaw, making him strong with both hands.

There was nevertheless a serious problem. Carruth had come out of his opening bout against Maselino Tuifo of Western Samoa, which he won 11–2, with an injured right hand. While the X-rays proved inconclusive and the doctor had given him the all clear, it later transpired that he had broken a small bone in the hand. Luckily it did not bother him in his subsequent two bouts, but there was no guarantee that it would hold up against the formidable Hernández.

Carruth, nevertheless, had some important things going for him – supreme self-confidence, and one of the world's best coaches, Nicholas Cruz, ironically a Cuban, in his corner, as well as his father Austin, a former boxer himself. Cruz was the Irish national coach at the time and, disregarding any loyalties he may have had to his native land, he was now up for Ireland and he knew what the Dubliner was capable of. They had also watched videos of Hernández in his earlier bouts in the competition and knew a lot about his style. He was a classy long-range boxer, and the Irish camp felt that some of his punching was as good as you would see from a professional. But Carruth was ready.

'All I knew is that in a sudden moment of inspiration, I knew deep down I was going to win,' he remembered. 'I don't want to sound corny but something came over me in the dressing room. I'm not a strong believer in faith, to be honest, but I think that somebody up there had a look, maybe someone close to my late nephew Gary, who drowned in tragic circumstances three years earlier.

'But to be truthful, if you had seen me sitting in the dressing room, I was beginning to lose heart. I was a bag of nerves. I wasn't scared of getting hurt. No boxer has that fear. I was scared of losing. You can break us boxers in two and we don't care. But losing, that's another matter.'

To add to Carruth's insecurities, his Belfast teammate Wayne McCullough had been beaten an hour earlier in the bantamweight final by another Cuban, Joel Casamayor. Austin Carruth noticed his son's concerns and guessed what was going on. He pointed to Michael's legs. 'There's your ticket to the gold medal,' he said. 'That's the way you're going to win this fight – by using them.'

Michael remembered: 'I closed my eyes, concentrated and miraculously the self-doubts began to recede. I grabbed hold of dad and the man nearly passed out on the spot with fright. 'Dad,' I told him. 'I'm going to bring the gold medal back with me to Dublin. I'm sure of it now.'

When the Indian referee Kishen Narsi called the two boxers to the centre of the ring to touch gloves, the big moment had arrived. Irish team manager Sean Horkan at ringside was looking tense. He knew Carruth would do his very best and not let down his country, his club, his family. Hernández started fast, using his longer reach to jab but Carruth was able to get under the jab and punch to the body and head. At the bell, the electric scoreboard showed that Carruth had won the round with a 4–3 advantage, bringing a roar of approval from the Irish supporters.

'It was the first time Hernández had been behind in the whole tournament and I knew my plan of attack was working,' remembered Carruth. A public warning, however, for holding in the second round was a setback but he was determined not to let his first round advantage slip away and he continued to go forward, slipping inside the Cuban's long left jabs and solid right crosses and scoring points.

To shouts of 'Keep it up Michael' and 'Don't let him off the hook' from the corner, the Drimnagh boxer was not afraid to mix it with the Cuban, who looked a bit concerned going back to his stool. He had not expected such stiff competition from this Irishman, and the scoreboard showed that they were still on level terms at 8–8 after two rounds. It was looking good for Carruth, however close.

Before going out for the crucial third and last round, he felt he wanted to have a real go at Hernández and told his father as much. But Carruth Senior was horrified. 'Are you crazy?' he barked. 'You have this fight and the gold medal. Don't be a damn fool. Stick to your game plan by forcing him to come to you and sneak inside.' Cruz pointed to Hernández's corner. 'Tempers are flaring,' he said. 'Frustration and panic are starting to show. You have him, Michael. Mark my words.'

Hernández upped his game in the final round. He felt his chances were slowly ebbing away and he needed a good finish, a solid three minutes, to make certain of the decision. The Cuban boxed well, both going forward and on the retreat but Carruth was landing the sharper, cleaner punches. The suspect right hand, a big secret naturally kept from the Hernández camp, was holding up well.

'I was ahead and the Cuban had obviously not been prepared for this situation and was unaware how to fight me,' Carruth recalled. 'I thought to myself that I must hold on as I was clearly in front. I frustrated him and held on for dear life. He was coming at me but I was able to land counter punches on the break and they were counting.

'I remember glancing up at the clock and noting that there were only twenty-three seconds to go, twenty-three seconds between me and a win that the experts said was impossible and here was dad going wild in the corner, shouting at me to dance and stay out of trouble. Then the bell went and truly, no sweeter music has ever reached my ears. It was all over and now Hernández, for all his mountainous reputation, couldn't get to me. I was safely back in port and the gold medal, which I was sure was mine. I looked over at Hernández and I was certain I saw the face of a loser.'

Carruth realised of course the hard, inescapable truth that there is nothing certain in boxing, and the Olympic Games was no exception. His mind raced back to the welterweight final of 1956 in Melbourne when his fellow Dubliner Fred Tiedt was shamefully robbed of victory.

'The referee called both of us to the centre of the ring. It was a moment I had dreamed of since I first entered the Greenhills club as a toddler. Then came the dramatic announcement – I had won by 13–10.'

Carruth had won the last round by 5–2 and jumped for joy as the arena reverberated with the cheers of the ecstatic Irish followers. Hernández was so disgusted at losing that the moment the decision was announced, he whipped off his headguard and threw it into his corner in anger. Despite his great disappointment, was this the way an Olympic loser should really behave, especially as it was a decision beyond dispute and agreed by neutral observers?

Still, all that mattered was that Michael Carruth, twenty-five years of age and the outsider, had won the gold medal, the first to come Ireland's way in any sport since Ronnie Delany's spectacular run in 1956. Carruth had joined the list of other famous Olympic gold medal winners including the likes of Floyd Patterson, Joe Frazier, Sugar Ray Leonard, George Foreman, Teofilo Stevenson, and the most celebrated ex-Olympian of all, Muhammad Ali, known as Cassius Clay when he won the Olympic lightheavyweight title in Rome in 1960. The Drimnagh boxer's sensational victory made headlines in all the Irish newspapers.

Tom Cryan, reporting for the *Irish Independent*, called the win 'fabulous' and said that with all the commotion over Carruth's spectacular victory Michael did not have time to have his injured right hand X-rayed again, what with the mandatory drug test, television interviews and a bottle or two of champagne to celebrate. Cryan also pointed out that Carruth had only caught up on two hours' sleep. 'Why bother about something as trivial as injury when the hand would not be needed for serious action for some time,' Cryan told his readers.

Gerry Callan in the *Irish Daily Star* likened Carruth's win to what he called 'never-to-be-forgotten moments in Irish sport. Moments like Ronnie Delany thundering through the field to steal the Olympic 1,500 metres gold in Melbourne in 1956. Or Barry McGuigan removing the world featherweight crown from the lofty and distinguished head of Eusebio Pedroza before twenty-five thousand fanatical fans in a London football stadium in 1985. Or Stephen Roche getting the jump on cycling's elite to win the world championship in Austria in his all-conquering year of 1987.

'Moments involving a selection of Irish sporting heroes including Denis Taylor, Alex Higgins, Eamonn Coghlan, Eamonn Darcy and John Treacy. But the notion that any of them defied the odds like Carruth did has to be challenged.'

'Quite honestly, I just couldn't believe it,' Carruth recalled in an interview with this author. 'It was a dream come true, it really was. I've been through that moment a million times in the intervening years and nothing could ever touch it. I'm not a particularly religious person and I was going to get down on one knee and bless myself, although not trying to copy Ronnie Delany on the track after winning in Melbourne. But that plan went out the window.

'I jumped high in the ring. Someone once described me that moment as a gymnast in pain. You know, I think that Hernández would probably beat me ninety-nine times out of a hundred, but not on that day. That day was mine. Having said that, I think I was one of his bogeymen and the Olympic win was meant to be, because I had a game plan and he hadn't. What an occasion. Incredible.'

The celebrations by the Irish in Barcelona were nothing compared to what went on back in Dublin. Driven through the streets of the capital in an open-top bus, drivers hooted their horns and there were open celebrations all over the city, with local bars dropping the cost of beer to 1956 prices when Ireland last experienced Olympic gold medal success. However, the mother of all parties was at his home in Drimnagh where family and friends celebrated and army helicopters flew overhead.

Carruth had left the city on the Liffey as a corporal and within a few hours he had a telephone call from the Junior Minister of Defence Noel Dempsey to say he had been promoted to the rank of sergeant. The local boy had made good on the biggest stage of all, a Rocky Balboa saga come true.

Jimmy Magee, the RTÉ boxing commentator, remembered: 'Before we left Ireland for Barcelona, I said that I felt Carruth would get a medal, though I would be cheating if I claimed I thought it would be gold. Hernández was the unbackable favourite and indeed, I think he lost only one or two bouts since being beaten by Carruth. I watched Michael come through the ranks. Don't forget, he was a bronze medallist at the 1989 World Championships in Moscow. He was a good operator and was beautifully coached, first by his father Austin and then by Nicholas Cruz. They really handled him well in the final.

'Michael's natural instinct was to go in and attack his opponent. Such an approach, however, would have played into Hernández's hands. So it was a question of Carruth backing off and picking his shots with care, and it worked. The funny thing was, Carruth had only made the Olympic team by the skin of his teeth. It was a very close call between himself and Billy Walsh from Wexford, now the national coach.

'There was only a punch or two between them at the Irish championships earlier that year, as there had been in the previous season also. It was almost a re-run of the Ronnie Delany story, when it took a casting vote to ensure he got the opportunity to run in Melbourne in 1956. But what a magnificent victory for Carruth in Barcelona.'

Like so many Olympic gold medallists, Carruth made up his mind to turn professional. The switch happened a year and a half after Barcelona. Three months before he turned to the paid side of the sport, and having had surgery done on his right hand, he said in an interview in the *Evening Herald* in November 1993: 'The decision to turn professional ate away at me. I talked it over with my wife Paula and the rest of my family and in the end I knew it was time to move. There was nothing left for me in the amateur game.

'I should have taken this decision six months after the Olympics but I was still tortured by the prospect of leaving the amateur game, which has been such a big part of my life since I was a boy. In the end I decided, however, that I'm not going to spend the next twenty years of my life wondering what would have happened if I hadn't turned professional.'

Taking leave from the army, he was given his opportunity in the professional ring on the undercard of a big double-header at the Earls Court Exhibition Hall in London on 26 February 1994. Topping the bill were super-middleweights Nigel Benn, the Dark Destroyer, against Henry Wharton, and Steve Little against Michael Nunn, won by Benn and, in a major surprise, Little.

With the former two-weights world champion and fellow Dubliner Steve Collins in his corner as trainer, Carruth clearly outpointed London's George Wilson over six rounds, referee Roy Francis marking it 60–56½ in the days when the confusing fractions in scores were used. The Dubliner had plenty of support from the crowd but he got a shock at the start of the first round when he walked straight onto what was nothing more than an outstretched arm and went down, more embarrassed than hurt.

Carruth ended 1994 with six wins, four inside the scheduled distance, and no losses or draws. He suffered his first defeat in January 1995 when he was outpointed over six rounds by Gordon Blair in Glasgow. The Dubliner's south-paw jabbing and left crosses controlled the early stages, despite being cut over the right eye in the third, but the Glaswegian came on strong towards the end, particularly in the fifth and sixth. Referee Lee Mullen, rather surprisingly, gave Carruth only one round and he kicked his gumshield away in disgust.

Carruth got his winning record back on track two months later when he travelled to Worcester, Massachusetts and stopped Vernice Harvard in three rounds. Seven victories followed, notably the biggest victory of his career to date, an impressive stoppage in ten rounds over the former British champion Chris Saunders in Nottingham in June 1996. The local was down three times from fast, hard combination punches before referee Dave Parris called it off.

The fight was a final eliminator for the vacant International Boxing Federation's inter-continental welterweight title, not a major championship but a win could lead to bigger things. It did, but not to the inter-continental title. Carruth got his big chance, a world welterweight title fight against the holder, Michael Loewe, an unbeaten Romanian based in Hamburg and a former world amateur junior welterweight champion.

It would be a golden opportunity for the Dubliner to add a world title to his Olympic medal, but he would have to travel to Germany to get it. The match was set for the fifteen-hundred seater Tivoli Eissporthalle in Aachen, a medieval city on the borders of Belgium and the Netherlands, on 20 September 1997.

Carruth, winner of all but one of his fifteen professional fights, against Loewe's twenty-seven straight victories, put in over a hundred rounds of sparring at Steve Collins' camp in Jersey. Before leaving the island, he told reporters: 'I'm feeling fitter and stronger than I've ever been and ready for the fight of my life. I've been waiting for this chance for maybe over two years now and I'm as ready as I'll ever be. I aim to bring the world welterweight title back to Ireland.'

Played into the ring to the sound of U2's *I Still Haven't Found What I'm Looking For*, Carruth looked very confident going out for the opening round in what turned out to be a gruelling battle, with one and then the other gaining the initiative. The Dubliner, however, was considered unlucky to lose a split decision. Judge Denis Nelson had both men level on 114 each, with the unrelated second judge Mark Nelson giving it to Loewe by 114–113. The casting vote was by referee Tomas Vasquez, who caused gasps from even neutrals when he announced it as a wide 117–111 for Loewe.

It has always been accepted, then and now, that to win in Germany, a visiting boxer generally has to knock his opponent senseless, and that might even be disputed. Going to a decision, and it's the roll of the dice. This seemed to be one of those occasions.

Carruth said in the dressing room: 'I was sure I had won. In my eyes I am the world champion. I definitely want a rematch and I hope my promoter Frank

Warren can get it sorted out. I thought I won by two rounds. I outworked him. Maybe I could have kept up the pressure a bit more but this was my first twelve-rounder and I had to pace myself.'

Loewe said he felt he was always in control and never at any stage thought he was losing. Warren, who wore a green shirt and tie into the ring, said: 'I though Michael won it by a couple of rounds, but it was always going to be hard for him to win it if it went to a decision. I think the middle rounds were where it slipped away from him.'

Gerry Callan wrote in the *Irish Daily Star*: 'It can only be described as a very, very debatable decision. The main problem with it was that every round was so close as to be extremely difficult to call. Pretty much everybody here had it equally close except referee Vasquez from Puerto Rico. God bless him and his eyesight, he made Loewe the victor by the insanely – even criminally – unfair six points. Which merely serves to show that while Puerto Rico may not be on a different planet, Senor Vasquez certainly is.'

Paul Howard in the *Sunday Tribune* reported: 'It will come as little consolation to Michael Carruth this morning that in another town on another day the result might have been quite different, but last night should have come as little surprise. He had always known the enormity of the challenge in trying to beat a world champion in front of a partisan crowd without possessing a knockout punch. He knew he needed to produce something special to wrest the title from Loewe, and for all his aggression in coming forward he never looked capable of it.'

Bob Mee said in *Boxing News*: 'Carruth's inexperience probably cost him victory. I thought Loewe edged it as Carruth failed to impose himself early enough, and let it slip in the early rounds. His late round aggression and pressure narrowed the gap to one point but it was not enough to turn around Loewe's early lead. He may well defeat Loewe in a rematch.'

Alas, the rematch never happened. Promoter Warren opened negotiations with his German associate Klaus Peter Kohl for the bout. But the British champion Geoff McCreesh was the mandatory challenger and the Dubliner would have to wait his turn, which could take months. In the end, Loewe announced his retirement through injury and the title was declared vacant.

Loewe would later become a national motor racing champion and also go into politics. McCreesh would soon be out of the running after losing a European title fight but despite a strong case put forward by Warren on behalf of Carruth to box for the vacant title, the opportunity never materialised.

Out of the ring for a full twelve months as he waited for news from Warren, Carruth did get a title fight, and in Dublin in September 1998. Not for the world championship but for the World Athletic Association title, although the WAA, a very minor US-based organisation on the international boxing scene, somewhat euphemistically billed the fight as being for the world welterweight title.

At the National Basketball Arena on the outskirts of the city, and making his first appearance as top of the bill, Carruth narrowly outpointed unbeaten Scott Dixon on a promotion by businessman Syl McClean. Conceding several inches in height and reach to his Glasgow rival, Carruth did just about enough on his better boxing and sharper punching to win the decision, despite a strong late surge by Dixon. Referee Fred Tiedt, the 1956 Olympic silver medallist and the lone official, marked his card 117–116.

The fight scenario came in for strong criticism from Paul Howard of the *Sunday Tribune*. 'The WAA's claims to being a legitimate world governing body are too preposterous even to waste column inches on,' he wrote. 'How could it be when the man who refereed and judged it was, like one of the boxers involved, an Irishman?

'There is no suggestion that Fred Tiedt is anything other than an impartial and competent official who did a good job of refereeing the fight and arrived at a fair decision at the end. The fact is that he has known Carruth from his early amateur days, is on friendly terms with his family and should never have been placed in the position where he had to make a decision that could ultimately have ended Carruth's professional career.'

When Larry Mullins, president of the WAA, was asked why a neutral referee was not used, he said: 'I have to admit that it's my one regret about the show. I wish now we'd had a referee outside of Ireland.' Asked how many 'world' champions the WAA had, he hesitated for a moment and said: 'We are having trouble with our computers but I think we have champions in about half of the weight divisions.'

The WAA soon faded into the obscurity from which it came, and with it went Carruth's label of being a 'world' champion. The Dubliner, who had now left the army after a thirteen-year spell, meanwhile continued on with his career and had three wins, two in the fifth round and one in the first, before getting a chance at the vacant International Boxing Organisation lightmiddleweight title at the York Hall, London in April 2000. His opponent would be Adrian Stone, born in New Jersey but based in Bristol.

Earlier there had been plans to match Carruth in a legitimate world title fight against Spain's Javier Castillejo, holder of the world lightmiddleweight title. After arrangements had been finalised and contracts signed for the fight to take place in Madrid in March, Castillejo pulled out two weeks beforehand with a damaged rib. The fight with Carruth never happened as while he was recovering it was announced that the Spaniard had signed a lucrative contract with the American promoter Don King.

Carruth came in eight pounds overweight for the Stone fight on a show being screened live by Sky Sports but the contest went on without the IBO title tag as boxers must come in at the required poundage for a championship fight. Trailing on points against his aggressive opponent after four rounds, Carruth quit on his stool at the end of the fifth, claiming a damaged right hand. In the dressing room, he said he had only nineteen days to prepare and should never have taken the fight in the first place. 'A proper Michael Carruth would have beaten him,' he insisted, 'but the proper Michael Carruth wasn't out there tonight and I'm to blame for that.'

Carruth announced his retirement from the ring in June 2000 but still retains his deep interest in boxing. As he says: 'The three concerns in my life are my family, my boxing and the Dublin senior hurlers.' In his roles as a team masseur and trainer with the current hurling team, he points out: 'I'm a true blue Dub.' It is not his first involvement in the inter-county set-up, having previously worked with the Westmeath team.

While there have been many critics of Carruth's professional career, saying that he should never have turned to the paid ranks, the facts were that he lost just three times in twenty-one fights and pushed a world champion all the way to a split decision, and before a partisan crowd. Yet he was never able to recapture the glory of his amateur days and that fabulous Olympic gold medal success on a hot summer's day in Barcelona. It was always going to be a hard act to follow.

13. WAYNE McCULLOUGH

The lady and the champ

No disrespect to Cheryl McCullough but old time boxing managers and promoters must have turned in their graves at the choice of Wayne McCullough's wife as Boxing Manager of the Year for 2002 by SecondsOut.com.

Cheryl guided her man through the often murky waters of professional boxing following a hugely successful amateur career, always negotiating contracts, looking carefully at the small print, arguing with promoters and matchmakers. But the old timers would have felt that a man could have done that, and done it better.

Confirmed sexists like Jack Dempsey's manager Jack 'Doc' Kearns recoiled at the news that the reigning world heavyweight champion was marrying the actress Estelle Taylor. Kearns was so upset at seeing himself losing control of Dempsey that he told the champion that while he held no animosity towards his proposed bride, he shouldn't marry her or anybody else for that matter, despite how much he loved her. Dempsey went ahead with the wedding, resulting in harsh words being exchanged, but the champion had the last say. Loyal to his new wife, he parted from Kearns.

Others of the same breed would have joined in the outcry over women looking after their boxers, including Rocky Marciano's manager Al Weill who was horrified when the world heavyweight champion told him that his wife Barbara was anxious for him to quit at the top – and he did. Another famous manager Joe 'Yussel the Muscle' Jacobs would have put it even more pointedly when women came into the scene by echoing his famous catchphrase – 'We wuz robbed'. Promoter Mike Jacobs, too, said women should stay out of boxing and let the men get on with it. 'What do they know about the game anyway,' he would sneer.

When you talk to Cheryl on being named top manager, she will explain that managers are dying out anyhow because she feels they are no longer needed. With two gold boxing gloves hanging around her neck like a veritable rope, she said without a trace of rancour or regret: 'It's the promoters who arrange the fights and do the big TV deals, Thomas. Ok, people say I'm difficult to work with but I don't do anything a man in my position wouldn't do.'

Wayne had no qualms whatsoever about his wife looking after his arrangements, and often said that he would not have reached the heights he did had it not been for Cheryl, who had known Wayne since they met through fan mail when she was sixteen and he was nineteen. 'Cheryl has been with me every step of the way,' he said. 'You know the old saying "Behind every success story is a woman", well, that's how it's been for Cheryl and me. I couldn't have done it on my own. I'm a wimp.'

Of course, he's not. How could he be, in a sport with its spartan lifestyle, dubious judging, financial rip-offs, the spivs, the dodgy dealers, the shady promoters, the petty jealousies and the inevitable casualties. On his own admission: 'A boxer risks his life when he climbs into a ring.' But Wayne always knew where he was at and where he was going, and Cheryl was with him all the way. Always the consummate pro, when this writer first met her and her husband to do an interview, she offered their business card at the end of the lunch and said with that winning smile: 'Keep in touch.'

McCullough's aggressive style of non-stop hitting earned him the nickname Pocket Rocket, given to him during his amateur days by his teammate Kieran Joyce from the Sunnyside Boxing Club in Cork. Wayne may have lacked the thunder punching of a Sugar Ray Robinson or a Marvin Hagler to end a fight instantly but make no mistake, he could hit hard. However, he is best remembered for his combination punching, his aggression and his fire, all of which got him to the top, which was all that mattered.

He could give and take a punch, and engaged in many wars, when his face would have accumulated a ghastly collection of lumps and both eyes had been almost reduced to narrow slits, as if he was wearing some particularly gruesome relic left over from Halloween. He was a fighter from first bell to last.

Wayne was born on 7 July 1970 and reared in the notorious Highfield Estate, a stone's throw from the loyalist Shankill Road in Belfast. It was the area where the Troubles in Northern Ireland were at their peak while he was growing up. Wayne remembers only too clearly British soldiers carrying rifles and patrolling the streets. It was normal, and the only life he knew.

'I could easily have been sucked into sectarianism but boxing was my only cause and saviour,' he remembered. 'I was a member of the Albert Foundry Boxing Club, which was nearby and always full of amateurs and professionals, and I loved it. It took your mind off the Troubles as growing up in the Shankill area was tough. Bombs and bullets were a regular occurrence and I'd witnessed a few shootings but I never had any interest in being involved with any parliamentary organisation. I liked boxing and going to the gym kept me out of trouble. There were nights when I would come home and find that some of my friends had been arrested.

'The Ulster Defence Association, known by their initials as the UDA, and the Ulster Volunteer Force, the UVF, were the main paramilitary forces in the area. A wall was erected as a security barricade to separate the two communities and there were riots between the kids on both sides of the Catholic divide every night. Friends in America talk about their cities' ghettos but I would expect they would class the area where I came from as a ghetto too.'

McCullough's boxing idol was Davy Larmour, a local from the Shankill Road and who, in the words of author and broadcaster Barry Flynn, 'became the darling of Belfast and beyond'. Larmour won a bronze medal in the 1970 Commonwealth Games and four years later brought home a gold in the same competition. He went on to represent Ireland in the 1976 Montreal Olympics and topped his professional career by winning the British bantamweight title in 1983 by outpointing another Belfast boxer Hugh Russell, who would later become a well-known photographer.

McCullough watched Larmour train, hitting the bag and the speedball and got to spar with him several times later on. In his 2005 autobiography *Pocket Rocket*, Wayne revealed: 'Davy may not have known it but I learned a lot from him. I found him very hard to hit. He would teach me new moves and I took it all in. I respected him for making the time for me.'

McCullough had an impressive amateur career, with a cabinet filled with awards and trophies. He was Irish lightflyweight champion in 1988, and moving up to flyweight in 1990, became national champion, Commonwealth Games gold medallist and World Cup bronze medal winner, all in the same year. Wayne won his third national title by taking the bantamweight championship in 1992 and was named Ireland's representative in that division in the six-man team for the Barcelona Olympics the same year.

Drawn against Fred Mutuweta of Uganda in his opening bout, McCullough forced a standing count in the second round and was never troubled in a 28–7 win. In his second fight he defeated the Iraqi hope Ahmed Abbood 10–2, but came out with an injured hand after a left hook smashed into Abbood's bicep muscle. He had treatment and as there were three days before his third contest, there was time to rest the hand. He remembered saying to the national coach, the Cuban Nicholas Cruz, that there was too much to lose to let a small matter like a dodgy hand get in the way.

Now into the quarter-finals, McCullough took on the Nigerian southpaw Mohammad Sabo, a gold medallist at the Commonwealth Games in Auckland two years earlier. The suspect left hand was standing up well and was no problem. Wayne won by a wide 31–13, which would turn out to be the highest-scored bout in the 1992 Olympics.

McCullough made it into the final with a 21–16 win over Gwang-Sik Li, a tough North Korean who had earlier beaten the Bulgarian and reigning world champion Serafim Todorov. Only one point ahead at the end of the second round, the Belfast boxer knew he had to convincingly win the third round to make sure of the decision. He did, winning 10–6 with a storming last three minutes. McCullough and the Dublin welterweight Michael Carruth were now the only Irish left in the finals.

With his fiancée Cheryl at ringside, having decided at a day's notice that she couldn't miss travelling from Belfast to see her fiancé boxing for the sport's ultimate prize, an Olympic gold medal, Wayne went out to face the talented Cuban hope Joel Casamayor in the final. Trailing 10–2 after two rounds, he complained to his coach Nicholas Cruz of severe pain on the left side of his face.

It turned out that a grazing blow to the left cheekbone near the bell had damaged a nerve in his cheekbone, and internal bleeding flooded into the outer corner of his left eye. He was in terrible pain whenever his cheekbone took the slightest pressure, and at one stage Cruz wanted to pull him out, only for McCullough to insist: 'No way. Not in an Olympic final. I'm going to see this one out.'

Despite the pain, he won the last round 6–4 but he had to keep his left hand constantly in front of his cheekbone. Alas, his supreme and brave effort was not enough to wipe out the Cuban's early lead, and the final score was 14–8. 'In finishing the bout,' wrote Sean Kilfeather in the *Irish Times*, 'McCullough earned the respect of the former world heavyweight champion George Foreman who said that if the fight had gone another round, he would have won. Foreman, himself an Olympic gold medallist in 1968, also drew attention to McCullough's courage and regretted that his fellow Americans were lacking in that quality.'

McCullough was our first silver medallist with the gloves for thirty-six years. One hour later Carruth defeated the Cuban, Juan Hernández in the welterweight final to win Ireland's first Olympic gold medal in boxing. Unfortunately, McCullough could not be in the stands with the fans to cheer him on. Officials would not let either Wayne or Casamayor leave the dressing room until they had taken their drug tests so he had to sit there watching, and cheering, on a monitor.

When it was time to leave Barcelona for home, their plane touched down at Dublin Airport in the middle of the night where thousands of fans greeted the boxing heroes. The next day they were taken in an open-top bus through the streets of Dublin where crowds estimated at over fifty thousand waved and cheered. Wayne got a similar reception in Belfast. Interestingly, Casamayor went on to have a successful professional career. Defecting to the US just before the Atlanta Olympics of 1996, he joined the paid ranks and went on to win world titles at superfeatherweight and lightweight.

McCullough recalled recently: 'The Irish Amateur Boxing Association wanted me to stay around another four years until the 1996 Olympics and they wanted to double the sponsorship I was already receiving, but I thought it was time to move on. I was tired of the amateur game. I wanted to be a professional boxer since I was fifteen and my mind was now made up. I was turning pro.'

It seemed the right time. McCullough was twenty-two, with a very impressive portfolio of achievements behind him. He had three hundred and nineteen contests, with only eleven losses. When his decision was made public, there were offers from Irish and British managers and promoters. McCullough and Cheryl studied all of them but with not much happening in Irish rings, Belfast or Dublin, and with no great urge to go to Britain, they planned to move to the US and set up base in Las Vegas, a busy town for big fights.

They had received some attractive American offers and in the end after considering the best ones, opted for a five-figure sum from Mat Tinley, a millionaire television executive and boxing promoter based in Denver, Colorado. Tinley would bring in the veteran Eddie Futch, one of the foremost trainers on the US fight scene and a highly respected figure in the sport. 'Futch is the best there is out there,' Tinley told the McCulloughs. 'You won't find anybody better.'

Tinley was not spoofing. Futch was a class act. Born in Hillsboro, Mississippi, his family moved to Detroit when he was eight. In the Motor City, he won a Golden Gloves lightweight title and in the 1930s trained with future world heavyweight champion Joe Louis, the Brown Bomber, in the city's Brewster Gym where a young Sugar Ray Robinson got his start. Futch was an amateur for four years but a heart murmur prevented him from turning professional.

In order for him to stay in boxing, a sport he loved, Futch started training boxers and in a long career as coach, he trained over twenty world champions including Joe Frazier, Ken Norton, Larry Holmes and Trevor Berbick, four of the five men to defeat Muhammad Ali. In October 1975, he famously pulled Frazier out of his brave, losing fight with Ali in the Thrilla in Manila when he refused to let Joe go out for the fifteenth and last round. As Frazier started to get up off his stool at the bell, Futch put his hand on his shoulder. 'Sit down, son,' he said. 'Nobody will ever forget what you did here today.'

Futch and McCullough was an ideal partnership. Eddie's philosophy was 'to leave the fighting to Wayne and the planning to me'. It worked. Futch, who died in 2001 at the age of ninety, remembered during a visit with McCullough to Dublin some years earlier: 'Wayne has always been a dedicated, loyal and hard-working fighter, Thomas. He has always followed instructions well and will go down in history as one of the best bantamweights to have ever entered a ring. The sweet science produces many a great fighter, but in this case, it also produced a very fine man.'

McCullough made a very good start to his professional career, winning his first ten fights, nine inside the scheduled distance, and holding out promises that good things were to come. He got his first title fight opportunity in January 1994 when matched with Javier Medina for the North American Boxing Federation bantamweight title, in Omaha, Nebraska. Javier, a tall, rangy stand-up boxer, was also undefeated, with nine wins and a draw and had forecast in a local newspaper that he was going to be so fast that the Belfast boxer would not be able to hit him, let alone hurt him.

It was McCullough's first twelve-rounder and not only was he able to wipe out Javier's boast but found the big punches in the sixth round by pounding him against the ropes, causing referee Ron Stander, who had unsuccessfully challenged Joe Frazier for the world heavyweight title twenty-two years earlier, to keep a close watch on matters.

With victory now in his sights, McCullough continued his assault in the seventh round. A straight right sent Medina to the boards and after he regained his feet, McCullough dropped him for a second time. He got up once again but the former Albert Foundry Boxing Club star was in no mood to prolong the agony and after a smashing right sent Medina staggering back on shaky legs with his eyes glassy. Stander intervened. McCullough was North American champion. It was a title, and a start, and would lead to bigger things. It did – to the most important fight of his career to date.

McCullough was matched in the main event at the Taj Mahal in Atlantic City on 19 June 1994 against the former world bantamweight champion and now leading contender for Wayne's NABF belt, Victor Rabanales from Mexico. There would be a lot riding on this fight as the winner was promised a shot at Japan's Yasuei Yakushiji for the world bantamweight championship. One of America's most famous referees, Arthur Mercante, would be in charge of the bout.

Like most Mexicans, Rabanales was a warrior, a tough, resilient battler who would fight on as long as there was an ounce of power left in his body. With the sounds of U2's *I Still Haven't Found What I'm Looking For* blasting through the venue, McCullough tried his traditional pressure tactics from the opening round but Rabanales met him in the centre of the ring punch for punch and scored with some solid body shots. A few strayed below the belt which caused referee Mercante to issue a warning.

In the second round the Mexican was catching McCullough with heavy rights to the chin which noticeably hurt but on Eddie Futch's advice, Wayne changed his tactics in the third round and started using his skill a bit more. He was able to frustrate Rabanales with fast, snapping left jabs and his far superior speed. As the rounds went by, McCullough was carrying the fight to his opponent but the Mexican was always dangerous. Mercante was kept busy warning both boxers to keep their punches up. Rabanales made a desperate rally to end proceedings once and for all in the twelfth and final round but McCullough was too elusive and kept that left jab snapping in the Mexican's face.

At the final bell, both boxers raised their hands in anticipation of victory but the unanimous decision went to McCullough on scores of 116–110, 117–110 and 115–113. Rabanales' manager Rafael Mendoza uttered the usual 'We wuz robbed' cry at the post-fight conference, in relation to the scoring rather than the verdict. He felt it could have been closer. Jack Hirsch, at ringside for *Boxing News*, had it 115–112 for the Belfast boxer and wrote: 'If McCullough goes on to win a world championship and have a memorable career, he will always remember this evening as the one that propelled him to such status. He was really tested.'

Wayne was nominated to meet the world champion Yasuei Yakushiji in the summer of 1995 but it looked as though it would be in Japan. McCullough and his manager Mat Tinley wanted the fight brought to Belfast but since neither side would agree on the exact location, the World Boxing Council, who were organising the fight, ordered a purse bid. This meant that any promoter could make an offer and stage it wherever they wanted to but the Japanese won the rights to put it on in the world champion's hometown of Nagoya. The date was set for 30 July 1995 and the venue was the Aichi Prefectural Gymnasium.

Japan had always been a very unhappy hunting ground for boxers from these islands. Scotland's Ken Buchanan had failed to regain the world light-weight title there in 1975 and the Liverpool-reared Welshman Alan Rudkin came back empty-handed ten years earlier in a world bantamweight title fight. Could an Irishman break the jinx? It was not going to be easy. The feeling was that McCullough would have to win by stoppage or not at all as Japanese world champions rarely lost decisions on home soil and a boxer like Yakushiji, who was on a winning run of twenty-one fights, had successfully defended the title four times in Nagoya, winning decisions.

With a capacity crowd of ten thousand in the hall, Yakushiji boxed in an upright, hands-up style but McCullough kept the pressure on him with his familiar two-gloved attacks to the head and body. The Japanese fighter was resilient, however, and walked through a minefield of jabs, hooks and upper-cuts without as much as a change of facial expression. First one and then the other gained the initiative and it was close as the rounds went by. On Futch's instructions, McCullough started rolling under the champion's left jabs and slamming away to the body. After ten rounds the Belfastman had a points lead but Yakushiji stormed back in the eleventh with good body shots to take the round.

It seemed to all hang on the final round but McCullough and his corner knew they would have to win it if the fight was close, which it was. Wayne now had a cut left eye to contend with, though it did not look too serious. At the bell Yakushiji came out with both gloves flying, determined to bring about a sudden end to the fight and guarantee his title but McCullough used his boxing skill, moving in and out and catching his opponent with long jabs.

The bell rang, signalling the end of the bout and both boxers raised their arms before McCullough fell to the canvas on his hands and knees and thanked God. The team was confident of victory but they anxiously awaited the decision. The ring announcer read out the judges' scores but it was all in Japan-ese. Translated, judge Barbara Perez voted for McCullough 118–110 and judge Kim Jaebong 116–115 in favour of Yakushiji. The deciding vote from judge Tom Kaczmarek clinched it for Wayne, 116–113. Tears, joy and pandemonium reigned. McCullough had pulled off the impossible. He was the new ban-tamweight champion of the world. One report called it a 'Shankill Samurai'. Yakushiji never boxed again.

In the dressing room with his arm around Cheryl, McCullough said the only time he knew he had won was when the announcer said his last name but he was outraged at the scoring of the South Korean judge Jaebong. 'I'm disgusted that he gave the decision to the champion as I clearly won,' he said. 'At the same time I'm obviously delighted that I'm the new champion as I'm in this game a long time now. Yakushiji was a good, tough pro and I knew it was not going to be easy.'

McCullough returned home to Belfast five months later for his first title defence when he stopped the previously undefeated Danish challenger Johnny Bredahi in eight rounds on an atmospheric night at the King's Hall. The intervention by Mexican referee Guadalupe Garcia surprised Bredahi's corner but the visitor was under sustained pressure and heavy fire throughout and there was no longer the slightest chance that he could pull off a win.

Wayne's second defence was in March 1996 against the Mexican Jose Luis Bueno at The Point, later the O$_2$, in Dublin. Despite a struggle to make the 8 st 6 lb weight limit, the Belfast boxer won a split decision before a five thousand crowd. Bueno, a former world flyweight champion, looked the stronger of the two but Wayne was always the better boxer with his fast, snapping left jab.

The Mexican got through the twelve rounds virtually unmarked whereas McCullough finished with his face a distorted mass of bruises and swellings, with blood coming from his nose and a perforated left ear. Judge Jose Lazaro had it 118–114 for McCullough while judge Rolando Barravecchio marked it 116–113 for Bueno. Judge Marty Sammon eased Irish anxiety with 116–112 for McCullough.

It was now clear that Wayne's days at bantamweight were at an end and feelers were being put out for a challenge to the world superbantamweight champion Daniel Zaragoza. At thirty-eight, the southpaw Mexican was the oldest world champion at his weight in boxing history but he was still a formidable battler and had taken part in eighteen world title fights. McCullough's manager Mat Tinley cabled Zaragoza's people for a Belfast fight in September 1996 but they insisted 'Mexico or the US'.

The venue and date were finally named, the Hynes Convention Centre in Boston on 11 January 1997. McCullough relinquished his bantamweight belt and this time there would be no struggle for him to make the weight. Indeed, he came in at two pounds under the 8 st 10 lb limit, with Zaragoza making it at 8 st 9½ lb. The combined purse monies would be a record for the superbantamweight division, with both men splitting a million dollar purse down the centre. The $500,000 Zaragoza pocketed was the biggest pay cheque of his busy sixteen-year career and when he got to Boston, he stayed in a hotel for the first time in his life.

Zaragoza was one of Mexican boxing's all-time greats. Born in the teeming streets of Mexico City two weeks before the Christmas of 1957, he had an impressive amateur career at home and abroad, and represented his country in the 1968 Olympics in Mexico, outpointing Dubliner Phil Sutcliffe and Britain's Ray Gilbody before losing to Michael Parris of Guyana in a stoppage in the second round of the quarter finals. On returning home Zaragoza turned to the paid ranks and ran up a record of sixty-three fights, consisting of fifty-three wins, seven losses and three draws, with twenty-seven of his victories either by countouts or stoppages.

A former world bantamweight champion, the rugged Mexican had the experience of having taken part in nineteen world title fights so he had the edge in experience over McCullough, who had started professionally in 1993 and was unbeaten in twenty contests, fourteen by the quick route. Nevertheless, the Irish camp felt that Wayne's youth and vigour, being the younger man by eleven years, would give him an advantage. Plus he would have the predominantly Irish crowd in Boston giving him plenty of vocal support. But this was not going to be a tea party.

'Eddie Futch and I had watched tapes of Zaragoza and we thought if I stayed on the outside and boxed him I would win easily,' McCullough recalled. 'So I began round one by boxing him. I was sticking my jab in his face and it was working. He was a crafty southpaw but I felt comfortable on the outside picking him off. Obviously, I like to brawl, and Zaragoza and I got into it a bit during the fight, but ultimately I thought I was controlling it.'

By the middle rounds, however, Zaragoza began to gain an advantage with his smashing body shots and the crowd, which had been shouting for the Belfast boxer early on, began to grow quiet. The cagey, experienced Mexican was bobbing and weaving, luring McCullough to the centre of the ring and cracking in hooks and uppercuts like a bullwhip. Nevertheless, Wayne always hit back with force and authority. Several times he motioned to referee Tony Perez to watch Zaragoza's head.

Over the last three rounds McCullough had the yelling crowd on their feet as he lashed into Zaragoza but the wily veteran ducked and dodged and rolled and punched back. There was a prized world title belt on the line here and nothing could be left to chance. McCullough caught the Mexican with a cracking left-right combination in the final session and Zaragoza stumbled but kept his feet and lurched back to match the Irishman punch for punch.

The decision was split. Judge Barbara Perez marked it for McCullough 115–114 but the other two judges, Chuck Hassett and Dick Flaherty, both called it 116–112 for the Mexican. Zaragoza, with his craggy face like an Aztec war mask, had his hand raised by referee Perez as winner and still superbantamweight champion of the world.

'I thought I did enough to win,' said McCullough at the post-fight conference. 'Sure, the early rounds were close and I thought I outpunched him two to one. The only thing I could have done differently was knock him out. Then they would probably still have given it to him.' In his autobiography in 2005, he said: 'I don't know how Zaragoza stayed on his feet in the last round. In that round the statistics showed he threw an amazing 119 punches but he had to because I had thrown 139. As we waited for the decision, though, I could tell it wasn't going my way. I found out after the fight that going into the eleventh, I was six rounds down on two scorecards.'

McCullough came out of the fight with a broken jaw, which, as he later discovered after watching the tape of the gruelling fight, happened in the second round when Zaragoza caught him with a big looping left hook. So he had fought for ten rounds with a serious injury. There had been rumblings in the lead up to the fight, too, that all was not well in the McCullough camp. Sure enough, it was soon announced that Wayne was parting from his manager, as Mat Tinley was now a promoter and had formed a promotional organisation called America Presents. It was an opportunity to have Cheryl manage his career.

Returning to the ring in the spring of 1998, a few weeks after Cheryl gave birth to a daughter, Wynona, McCullough had two winning fights, the first in Connecticut and the second in Texas before another world title opportunity came up. Naseem Hamed, the self-styled Prince, was prepared to defend his world featherweight title against Wayne. The fight would mean a move up in weights as McCullough was now a natural superbantamweight but he fancied his chances against Hamed. Besides, world title shots do not come too often and usually when they do come, you take them. The title fight was set for the Convention Centre, Atlantic City, on 31 October 1998.

Born in the Yorkshire steel town of Sheffield, the fifth of eight children of Yemeni parents who settled in England, Hamed was extravagantly talented, flamboyant inside and outside the ring, and a puncher of unusual power. He loved to box and always felt he had something to prove. His Dublin-born trainer Brendan Ingle said in a TV interview in 1998, the year Hamed fought McCullough: 'He asked me the other day what I would do if I were him and I said: "With £12 million in the bank, I personally wouldn't be in this game. I'd be at university or somewhere, getting myself some wisdom and education."'

But Hamed loved to box and felt he had something to prove. 'I want to be a legend,' he proclaimed from day one of his professional career in 1992. 'I want to win world titles at four weights, and retire with £40 million.' In the end, he won just one world title, at featherweight, and also fell short of his financial target, with £22 million according to the *Sunday Times* rich list, but he was one of the most exciting and colourful boxers of his day, and among the best.

The Prince's entrances were always spectacular, once being lowered into the ring in an elevator and often somersaulting over the top rope and into the ring. Complications over a work permit delayed Naseem's travels from his training quarters in Sheffield until four days before the fight. By the time he arrived in New York by Concorde he had missed the important promotional press conferences and handing out presents in a children's hospital in Philadelphia. McCullough had done his main training at Sugar Ray Leonard's gym in Nevada.

There was a dispute over the promotional rights between Britain's Frank Warren and America's Don King. Eventually Cedric Kushner, a South African based in New York, took over the promotion and all was set for the action. At a joint press conference in Atlantic City, McCullough said: 'I'm ready, I'm always ready, I'll take Naz. I will throw too many punches and I have a good chin.' To which Naseem replied: 'We'll see. I realise that Wayne throws a lot of punches but whether they land or not is another matter. Two years ago in Dublin, he came to my weigh-in and said he wanted to fight me. He kicked up a fuss. Now is his chance to prove how good he is.'

The show was at Halloween and it was billed as 'Fright Night'. As expected, the Prince made a spectacular entrance, coming to the ring through a mock graveyard resplendent with tombstones marked by the names of his championship opponents and which cost him £70,000. McCullough was cheered by the nine hundred or so Irish supporters among the crowd of eight thousand five hundred. He remembered walking along the boardwalk in the city and seeing posters in the windows of the many Irish bars with the words: 'Support Wayne McCullough.'

The Pocket Rocket knew too that Naseem was not going to be easy, with nine successful defences behind him. For the first time, too, Eddie Futch would not be in Wayne's corner. The veteran trainer had retired and former Los Angeles professional Kenny Croom was his replacement.

Naz started fast, firing punches from all angles and showboating by dropping his hands, inviting Wayne to hit him. But McCullough was ready and he was not going to fall into any traps as they exchanged fierce blows to the head and body. So it went for two rounds, with neither boxer gaining any clear advantage. Hamed had predicted he would knock out McCullough after two minutes and twenty-eight seconds of the third round. The Irishman landed a fast left hook in the third which grazed the champion's head and his glove touched the canvas at, amazingly, the precise moment the Prince said he would finish off McCullough. Referee Joe Cortez did not rule it a knockdown.

'Hamed was extremely hard to hit,' McCullough would recall in an interview in later years. 'He looked easier to hit on tape. When he was moving around doing nothing but running away from me, it was frustrating but I needed to keep my composure. Throughout the fight he was throwing backhand jabs, which are illegal in boxing. I'd felt he got away with every dirty trick in the book.'

A hard right from McCullough in the ninth sent spray flying from Naz's head but the Prince fired back in the tenth, along with doing some showboating, which annoyed the booing crowd. Wayne was behind on all scorecards going into the twelfth and final round, with the champion's harder punching and better all-round work coming through but the Belfast boxer was keeping the pressure on him all the way.

McCullough would say later that he felt he had done enough to win the title but that he would not get the decision because Hamed had lucrative contracts with the American TV people. So to the final bell and the result. All three judges marked it for Naz, with John Stewart scoring it 118–110, Nelson Vazquez 117–111 and Clark Sammartino 116–112. Several ringside reporters openly criticised the wide margins, saying it was much closer than that. Despite losing, McCullough received much praise for his gallant showing and for snapping Hamed's record of eighteen wins inside the distance.

Jim Watt, the former world lightweight champion working for Sky TV, told viewers: 'It's not often we have two winners in the one fight but I think that's what happened tonight. Naz won the decision but Wayne McCullough has won the credibility. Put up the fight of his life. The difference is that McCullough is used to having hard fights, and we forgot what a tough little number he is and how much pride he takes into the ring with him. We didn't give him credit for being the warrior he is.'

McCullough had by now patched up his differences with America Presents, and promoter Mat Tinley set up a world title challenge against Mexico's unbeaten Erik Morales for the superbantamweight title for 22 October 1999 at the Joe Louis Arena in Detroit, named after the legendary former world heavyweight champion who grew up in the city from the age of twelve. The lower weight would mean Wayne could return to his more comfortable poundage, and be stronger. But he knew this one was not going to be easy. In a warm-up ten-rounder in Las Vegas, McCullough won a unanimous decision over Len Martinez from Nebraska.

Known as El Terrible, Morales was one of the best boxers of his era. He would win world titles at superbantamweight, featherweight, superfeatherweight and lightwelterweight to become the first Mexican to hold four world championships. Remarkably, he was still a world champion at lightwelterweight in 2012, his nineteenth year as a professional. Morales came from the rough North Zone of the border city of Tijuana, and legend has it that he was born in a boxing gym.

He quickly excelled in the amateur ranks, with just six losses in one hundred and fourteen bouts, before deciding to turn professional at the age of sixteen. At first, his father Jose was strongly against it. A former pro himself, he knew just how difficult it was to be successful in such a tough sport. More importantly, Jose and his wife wanted young Erik to continue with his education but in the end it was his mother who gave her son her blessing to box professionally. 'What's the point in trying to stop him,' she said to her husband. 'He's going to box anyhow, even if he has to run away and we don't want that.'

Erik justified their confidence in him with a successful debut by a knockout in two rounds in Tijuana and would go on to be signed up by the prestigious Top Rank promotional organisation run by former lawyer Bob Arum. He was on the way.

Both boxers checked into the same hotel in Detroit, and when McCullough saw Morales, he went over and shook his hand. The Mexican had a shocked look on his face, as if to say, 'We're not supposed to do this.' They met again at the pre-fight press conference and this time Morales stood up and said he was going to knock out the Irishman. Wayne laughed and Morales said: 'You can laugh all you want to. I'm still going to knock you out.' Boxing writers could understand his reasoning. Hadn't he finished off nine opponents in a row coming up to this fight and wasn't his record studded with knockouts, twenty-eight in thirty-four winning fights?

Morales climbed into the ring a twenty to one on favourite but McCullough was not fazed. He had faced the odds before, and was determined to topple the Mexican, even though Morales had not let anybody past the ninth round in his seven previous defences and was determined to maintain that record. Enjoying advantages in height and reach, and more marginally in weight, Morales was constantly on the attack, coming in under Wayne's guard, although McCullough often caught him high on the head with left hooks. Still, no matter how hard McCullough whacked him on the chin, Morales kept storming back to trade blows.

After twelve rounds, the Mexican won a unanimous decision from the judges, with John Keane and Omar Mintun calling it 116–112 and Glen Hitch 118–110. It transpired that while McCullough threw more punches, 928–917, Morales landed 341 against 231 and that told the whole story. 'I've no real argument with the decision,' said Wayne later, 'but I didn't do too badly, did I, considering the critics did not think I'd be even there at the finish?'

In October 2000, McCullough returned to Belfast for a homecoming fight against the Hungarian, Sandor Kaoczek at the Ulster Hall. It would be his first appearance before his home fans in almost five years and he was very much looking forward to it. Two days before the bout was scheduled to take place, on a routine visit to the Royal Victoria Hospital, he was told he had a cyst on his brain and that he could not fight again as one blow on the head could kill him. The Northern Ireland office of the British Boxing Board of Control immediately slapped a ban on McCullough from entering the ring.

Wayne dashed to the offices of the Boxing Union of Ireland in Dublin where it was arranged he would have an MRI scan. This turned out to be negative, and they gave him the all-clear. 'We can find nothing life threatening,' he was told. McCullough showed the findings to the Northern Ireland officials and they sent on the X-rays to the British Board medical officers in London. But they came back and said they still had no alternative but to continue to refuse him a licence.

Wayne flew back to Las Vegas and was advised by the Nevada Commission to go to California and visit the neurosurgery department of UCLA for a more thorough examination. Within a few weeks the doctor at UCLA, Neil Martin, called McCullough to say that he had consulted with some of the leading neurosurgeons in the US and they had come to the conclusion that the cyst was not in fact on his brain but in a space between the brain and the skull, known as the arachnoid mater, and that he saw no reason for Wayne to give up his boxing career.

Nevertheless, the British Boxing Board of Control was sticking to their findings. McCullough was subsequently re-licenced in Nevada. He returned to boxing, after being out of action for over two years with a knockout in two rounds over Alvin Brown of Kansas City in Las Vegas in January 2002. With public pressure mounting on the British Board, they could no longer deny the Irishman a licence and he was back in a British ring in September when, on a Frank Warren promotion in London, he stopped the South African, Johannes Maisa in four rounds. Two months later, his long-awaited Belfast re-appearance took place when he finished the Russian, Nikolay Eremeev, also in the fourth round, at the Ulster Hall.

In October 2002 McCullough went to Glasgow as part of the Sky TV commentary team to see the local Scott Harrison challenge Julio Pablo Chacon for the Argentinian's world featherweight title. Chacon, a hard hitter, was favoured to win but Harrison kept the pressure on him for the full twelve rounds and walked off with an unanimous decision to become the first Scot to win the title in the one hundred and ten-year history of the nine stone division. Nevertheless, McCullough fancied his chances of relieving the Scot of the title and the match was set for 22 March 2003 at the Braehead Arena just outside Glasgow.

With Harrison's manager Frank Maloney, whose mother came from County Wicklow and his father from County Tipperary, making somewhat extravagant claims that his man was the best boxer Scotland ever produced and promoter Frank Warren boldly predicting that Harrison would become over the following twelve months the richest sportsman in Scottish history, all the hype was centred on the champion. But Wayne was quietly confident that the world title would change hands, even if the strong Scot had an impressive record of eighteen wins and one defeat.

It turned out to be a bruising battle. The partisan crowd booed McCullough as he climbed into the ring, drowning out the cheers from Wayne's supporters who had travelled over from Belfast. Harrison used an effective left jab and overhand right to break through McCullough's defence. 'My body and head shots were having no effect on him,' McCullough recalled. 'He was walking straight through them.' Harrison had a complete disregard for the rules and was repeatedly warned for low punching and hitting with the open glove, and not always reprimanded by referee John Coyle.

McCullough got his left jab going in the eleventh but he was still well behind on points. His corner knew he needed a knockout or stoppage and in the twelfth, with his fans keeping up their encouraging chant of 'Here we go, here we go, here we go', Wayne fought back and a right to the body made the Scot touch the canvas. But Harrison was still ploughing forward and the two men engaged in a slugfest. The crowd was now on their feet, cheering the visitor instead of booing him. The decision was a formality with the judges. Ruben Garcia had it 120–108, Andre Van Grootenbruell 119–109 and Mickey Vann 119–108. Scott Harrison was still featherweight champion of the world.

Wayne took a break from boxing for the next eighteen months or so, but he insisted he hadn't retired: 'The boxing world hasn't seen the last of Wayne McCullough, not by a long shot.' Nevertheless, he was kept busy with high-profile media work as well as television including a remake of the 1970s BBC show *Superstars* and a documentary about his old hometown called *Bits of Belfast: Up the Shankill*. He also opened his own gym and became *Ring* magazine's Las Vegas correspondent.

Yet like so many former champions, the lure of the ring proved too great. Following a conversation Cheryl had with the American promoter Dan Goossen, who had given McCullough his first professional fight eleven years earlier, Wayne was offered a deal to get his stalled career re-started, beginning with an eight-rounder against Nebraska's Mike Juarez in Temecula, California in September 2004. His purse would be $100,000, bringing his total ring earnings to over $4 million.

McCullough had little trouble with the American, who had been in with half a dozen world champions, and won on a stoppage in two rounds. 'It was a bit like starting all over again,' he said in the dressing room. The Pocket Rocket had been re-launched, at thirty-three.

When Goossen came up with an offer of a world superbantamweight title challenge to the Mexican, Oscar Larios, he accepted, even though the tall Larios was a younger and super-fit opponent who threw punches virtually non-stop and could do it for the full twelve rounds. Larios, billed as the Mexican Warrior, was at his peak at twenty-six and had been named Fighter of the Year by *Boxing News* in 2002 when he first won the title. He had since made five successful defences before now going in against McCullough at the Palace Indian Gaming Centre in Lemoore, California in February 2005. Wayne rightly pointed out that he himself had the edge in experience.

A packed house of eighteen hundred cheered as McCullough, fighting out of a crouch, set a brisk pace, especially in the early part of the bout as he fired what George Kimble of the *Irish Times* described as 'a buzzsaw of punches'. However, as the rounds went by, the Mexican's power started to tell as chants of 'Mexico, Mexico' filled the air. Larios was using a fine left jab, catching the challenger coming in over the closing stages, and while the two TV commentators, Sean O'Grady and Barry Tompkins, had it even at the last bell, the all-important judges saw it differently, all giving it to Larios by wide margins. Marty Sammon scored it 116–111, Kazvo Abe 118–110 and Marcos Rosales 118–109.

'The scoring was wild and I don't know how the judges could have been looking at the same fight,' McCullough said at the post-fight conference. 'I felt I had done enough against a tricky opponent.' It is a view he still holds. Larios' manager Rodrigo Gonzalez said that as the Irishman had fought so well that they were prepared to give McCullough a return fight.

The rematch was set for the MGM Grand in Las Vegas five months later. It had always been McCullough's dream to box on a big fight card in Las Vegas, the capital of the boxing world and now it was finally happening. He was now trained by Freddie Roach at the famous Wild Card Gym in Hollywood as Kenny Croom had moved on to coaching other boxers. Roach, of Irish extraction, was one of the most respected trainers on the American boxing scene and had learned his trade under McCullough's former mentor Eddie Futch.

The fight started at a fast pace but McCullough's plan to out-punch Larios seemed doomed to failure from early on as the Mexican used his height and reach advantage to land the cleaner shots and keep the thirty-five-year-old Belfast boxer at bay. Wayne rallied in the middle rounds but the Mexican fired back in the eighth and ninth with heavy shots to the head and body.

While Larios eased up in the ninth, both Roche and referee Richard Steele were already dithering on whether to stop the fight to save McCullough further unnecessary punishment. At the end of the tenth round, the ringside physician Dr Margaret Goodman walked around the ringside, up the steps and told Wayne she was stopping the fight. When McCullough protested, she shook her head: 'You've had enough. I can't let you ship any more punishment. It's all over.'

Amid emotional scenes, the doctor's orders were the final blow for the gutsy Belfast warrior, as McCullough's dreams of another glory night ended in tears, and losing for the first time inside the distance. It must have also been painful for the good doctor. She had played a significant part in resurrecting Wayne's career after he had been refused a licence to box by the British Board. It was Dr Goodman, too, who recommended him to a Californian specialist and who headed the assessment in Nevada. The doctor was now placing him on an indefinite suspension. 'It's a long way back from here,' she said.

The signs were there in front of his eyes. It was time to walk away and to leave the likes of Morales, Hamed, Zaragoza and the rest. The courageous warrior would have to make the bravest decision of his life. Alas, the lure of the roped square proved too much and he was back in action, this time well outside the jurisdiction of the Nevada Commission. He fought Juan Ruiz of California in Georgetown, Cayman Islands in June 2008 but the result merited only a few paragraphs in newspapers and barely one or two lines in boxing magazines – with the Belfast boxer retiring in the sixth round. How the mighty had fallen.

McCullough never officially announced his retirement but he never pulled on the gloves again, except in the gym. Nevertheless, fight fans everywhere, not only in his native land, will remember Wayne's fantastic two-fisted work-rate, his granite chin, his incredible bravery and in particular his noteworthy achievement in going to Japan, taking on the world champion in his opponent's own backyard and coming home with the title. That was indeed something very special.

14. KATIE TAYLOR

Warrior Princess with God on her side

In the ring at Bray Boxing Club, near the harbour in the seaside town in County Wicklow, Katie Taylor goes through a sparring session with her dad and coach Peter. They wear the pads and he lets his daughter punch away with jabs, hooks and uppercuts. They do four fast two-minute rounds before having her gloves and headgear removed, and taking a short break.

Talented, modest and unassuming, the twenty-six-year-old is a true champion in every sense of the word. Consider her achievements. Besides her gold medal success in the 2012 London Olympics, she has won medals of a similar colour in four World Championships, five European Championships and, what is often overlooked, four in European Union Championships.

These feats have never been achieved before, and are unlikely to be even matched, let alone beaten. Taylor, who boxes in the lightweight division, has been collecting medals the way a philatelist gathers stamps. As well as these major championships, she has brought home a collection of ten gold, four silver and two bronze medals from other international tournaments in Europe and Asia. It is a remarkable record whichever way you look at it. Record books provide cold statistics and nothing more, but when she climbed out of the ring at the ExCeL Arena in East London after her Olympic final success in August before a capacity crowd of ten thousand, she had lost only seven of her one hundred and forty bouts.

On her Olympic performances alone, Katie has with one deft blow dispelled much of the misgiving and controversy surrounding women's boxing by showcasing the grace, skill and dignity that comes with the sport, and even succeeded in turning around non-boxing fans. Weighing between 9 st 6 lb and 10 st in competition, she has made women's boxing acceptable by her exceptional all-round skill and clever footwork, always on the balls of her feet for perfect balance and positioning.

Moreover, she has attracted more women to the sport, not only those who do the training solely for fitness but also many eager to get into the ring once they have mastered the skills. 'If for nothing else, it's a fantastic way of getting fit,' said former Irish Olympian and professional boxer Cathal O'Grady, 'and for many, much more engaging than just counting down a timer on a treadmill.'

Petite and attractive, with enviable skin and intense brown eyes, the soft-spoken, slim, 5 ft 5 in young lady with the golden gloves, the Warrior Princess, was a poster girl for women's boxing not only in Ireland but around the world

213

long before her Olympic achievements. Boxing has been her way of life, the only life she has known, for as long as she can remember. Growing up, Katie had her bedroom adorned with pictures of Muhammad Ali, Sugar Ray Leonard, Roberto Duran and Marvin Hagler at a time when other teenagers pasted up posters of pop stars.

Before the Olympics, her most significant performance was in the northern Chinese city of Qinhuangdao in May 2012 when she won her fourth consecutive gold medal in the World Championships. The victory earned her the Olympic ticket as it was the only qualifying tournament for London 2012. On the way to the final in China, she defeated Tunisia's Rim Jouini 19–6, stopped Saida Khassenova of Kazakhstan in the fourth round, had a walkover against Romania's Mihaela Lacatus and had a 16–6 win over Mavzuna Choirieva of Tajikistan.

In the final itself she was up against the girl she would beat in the Olympic decider, the Russian southpaw Sofya Ochigava, a twenty-five-year-old former World Championships gold medallist at flyweight and bantamweight. They had boxed twice before, with a win apiece, but this time Katie wanted to make no mistake. In a tense and tactical contest, the score was even at 4–4 after two rounds. But Katie held her nerve and composure to come on strong and gained an 8–6 advantage in the third before claiming the fourth by 3–1. She had her hand raised as winner on an 11–7 score.

'I always knew it was going to be a tough fight against her in China,' she recalled. 'She was so tricky, a counterpuncher, and the fight was a cat-and-mouse affair. I always thought it was going to be close but my dad in my corner told me to just keep my nerve. He's always very encouraging.

'I was naturally delighted with the win, and my fourth gold in the championships. It gave me great encouragement for the Olympics. I also felt it was a great showcase for women's boxing because I think the goal is to bring out the best in one another. There were over three hundred boxers from seventy-seven nations in the tournament, breaking all records for the previous six World Championships.'

Then came London, and on the memorable afternoon of 9 August 2012 Katie achieved her ultimate ambition when she struck gold in the lightweight division. It was fitting that she achieved her greatest success on that historic occasion when women's boxing made its official Olympic debut. Eight years after the Olympics of the modern era began in Athens in 1896, men's boxing became an official Olympic sport. In those 1904 Games in St Louis, Missouri, women boxers did make an appearance but it was only as a demonstration. London 2012 was the first time they boxed competitively.

Had it not been for Taylor's success internationally, women would not be boxing in the Olympics at all. Dr Ching-Kuo Wu, president of the Amateur International Boxing Association, was continually impressed by her performances and persistently lobbied the International Olympic Committee and eventually convinced them to bring in the ladies at three weights, flyweight, lightweight and middleweight. Now women's boxing will be part of all future Olympics.

Katie always looked the favourite to win out, and justified that status. A decisive win over Britain's Natasha Jonas by 26–15 earned her a bronze medal. 'I could have thrown the kitchen sink at Katie and it wouldn't have made any difference,' said Jonas in the dressing room. 'Whatever I did just would not work. She'll go on to the gold medal.'

In the semi-final, Katie reached the silver stage by defeating Tajikstan's Mavzuna Choirieva on a 17–9 score. She would now come face to face with her old foe, Russia's formidable southpaw Sofya Ochigava, a former kick boxing champion. For the first time in her career Katie felt nervous, and was too worked up to have breakfast, but she went out and did what she had to do.

After a tense first round which finished 2–2, Ochigava edged 2–1 ahead after the second. Taylor stormed back in the third which she won by 4–1 and he sealed an historic victory, her third in four meetings, in a pulsating fourth round to gain a 10–8 decision amid absolutely joyous scenes in the docklands venue. She later received the Best Female Boxer of the Olympics Award.

Looking back on the tournament, Katie recalled: 'I felt we wanted to shock the world and I think that's exactly what we did. I was the most nervous I've ever been before a fight and I had a knot in my stomach all day. It was my dream since I was a child to represent Ireland and win an Olympic gold medal and I wasn't going to pass up the big chance. We knew the final against Sofya would be such a tough fight. It always is. That was the fourth time I boxed her and every time it was cat-and-mouse between us. It was always going to be that kind of fight so there was nothing surprising.

'It was going to be a game of patience. I knew I had to stay calm, even if I was a couple of points down after the second round. My dad and Zaur Antia didn't push the panic button in the corner. The last thing you want to do is panic. In the last round she caught me with a few shots but I caught her too, and I thought I landed the cleaner punches. The crowd, even the English fans, played a big part in the victory. They were cheering like mad. It felt like a home fight for me. At the last bell I didn't know what the scoreline was. I felt I had done enough to win but you never know for certain, especially in the Olympics with so many disputed decisions.

'There was a long delay before the decision was announced and I thought it was going to go to a countback, and as you know, you can never be sure of anything with a countback. I was hugely relieved when the announcement came that I won. This was better than all the World Championships, all the European titles, everything. I still haven't got over it. I thought the support was going to be good but I didn't realise it was going to be the way it turned out. It was incredible.

'I wouldn't have made it had it not been for the funding I received over the last few years in the High Performance Programme. And as a result of that funding I was able to train as a full-time athlete. Hopefully the young girls who will have watched the Olympics and have an interest in boxing will have been inspired to take up the sport and try to become Olympic champions themselves, but they need the funding and we have to make sure that the money is there to look after the next generation.'

Katie is as likeable outside the roped square as she is competitive inside it. She is the quintessential girl-next-door and always comes across as genial in interviews, whether for television, radio or the print media. On the many occasions that this writer has met her, or called her, she has always been pleasant and open, and never reluctant to talk.

Born on 2 June 1986 to Peter and Bridget Taylor in Bray, she is the youngest of four, two boys and two girls. They have five grandchildren. Peter came with his father from Leeds, Yorkshire in 1979 to help him work on the seaside amusements. His life then changed when he met a local girl, Bridget Cranley, in a Bray nightclub and the couple instantly fell in love. Peter decided to stay behind when his parents returned to Leeds, married Bridget and worked as an electrician.

Peter won an Irish junior title in 1986 but with his career beginning to wind down, he was starting to drift into the coaching side of the sport at Bray Boxing Club, then known as St Fergal's. One particular night, Peter was scheduled to oversee a training session in the gym, then little more than a converted boathouse, but a little problem arose. Bridget had an arrangement to go somewhere else that night and Peter was stuck for a babysitter for his eight-year-old daughter Katie.

'I solved the dilemma in what I thought was the most practical way possible,' he recalled. 'I took Kate along with me to the gym. Just to keep her occupied I put a pair of boxing gloves on her and stood her in front of a heavy punchbag and let her whale away. Not only was she content but she seemed to be hooked on the sport there and then. She was really enjoying the atmosphere of the club.'

Katie added: 'That is true. Indeed, you could say the sport is in my genes. As well as my dad being an Irish junior champion, my mom would become Ireland's first female judge. I loved it there and then. Watching him train brought me closer to the sport as well, although he never actually encouraged me to lace on the gloves, or planned for me to become a boxer. He always said it was up to myself, and my mom felt the same way.

'It just happened. I enjoyed being in the club and he kept bringing me back. I don't think he thought anything was going to come of it really. There were no other girls in the club then so I started sparring with the lads. I still spar with them, and that early sparring gave me a head start. Some of the other girls on the international scene are starting to do that now. What I've always liked about boxing, and still do, is that it is an individual sport and success is not totally dependent on other players as in other sports.'

For years the Taylors had to battle their way through barriers of discrimination for Katie to make progress in boxing. When Peter first approached the Irish Amateur Boxing Association in the 1990s to set up contests for his daughter with other girls, he was met with stony silence. Women's boxing was taboo, he was told in no uncertain terms. It was a sport for males and nobody else. By early 2001 there was a groundswell of public opinion that girls should be allowed to box, and the IABA set up a committee to examine the situation. It was headed by Sadie Duffy from Buncrana, County Donegal, a prominent referee and judge at championship tournaments and internationals.

Sadie had already made something of a breakthrough against discrimination and bias when in March 1999 at the National Stadium she became the first woman to referee a contest in the Irish Senior Championships – a featherweight final at the National Stadium between Bernard Dunne, who would go on to win a world professional title, and Terry Carlisle, won by Dunne.

'There was definitely a big interest in getting women's boxing off the ground,' remembered Sadie, 'and we decided to gather as much information as possible from clubs all around the country. We got a positive response. After all, women's boxing had caught on all over the world, including the US and Canada and there was no reason why it could not be successful here. In 2001 the Women's European Amateur Championships were held in France and the first Women's World Championships in Pennsylvania, as well as the first Asian Women's Championships in Bangkok so the interest worldwide was there.

'I was certainly in favour of women's boxing and encouraged the girls to take part in the sport. The problem was that there were a lot of girls keen on the sport but because nothing was happening as far as competition was concerned, they just fell away. Katie Taylor changed all that, and now girls compete in Irish championships.'

This writer was fortunate to be at ringside when Katie made her debut at the National Stadium, Dublin on 31 October 2001. It was a night when Halloween bonfires blazed in the suburbs and exploding fireworks lit up the night sky. However, boxing fans were more interested in the sparks which crackled at the South Circular Road venue. The occasion was an Ireland–England male international, with three women's bouts on the card. It was an historic event as it was the first time in the association's ninety-year history that girls had swapped jabs, hooks and uppercuts in open competition: 'A momentous day for Irish boxing,' as Dominic O'Rourke, IABA Director of Boxing, now refers to it.

The first girls into the ring were Taylor, then a fifteen-year-old schoolgirl, and her opponent Elanna Audley from the Sandy Row Club, Belfast. Katie was the main focus of attention as she had shown most promise. With Sadie Duffy as referee, the Bray girl dominated the action over the three ninety-second rounds and won a popular decision by 23–12. The result received good coverage in the Irish and British media. Irish women's boxing was off to a great start.

Two years after her auspicious debut, she was brought into the IABA's High Performance Programme enabling her, and some of her male counterparts, to receive generous grants from the Irish Sports Council. It spurred her on to greater success. In 2005 Katie won the first of an unprecedented five European Championships gold medals and the following year she gained the first of her four World Championship titles; another record. All this before going on to win a record-breaking four European Union gold medals. 'Still, the recognition in Ireland was always the hardest part,' she conceded. 'I had to win my third European title before I started getting my picture in the newspapers on a regular basis.'

Katie is coolness personified. The night before a fight, even in the Olympics, she wouldn't find it hard to sleep. 'The next morning after I attend the weigh-in, my dad and I would have a routine where he talked to me about the fight and then I go for a walk to try and keep my mind off the fight as much as possible,' she said. 'I read the same Bible verses, and even walking up to the ring I'm always silently praying. When the bell rings I would be totally focussed, my mind on the job in hand.

'I know all about the risks in boxing but if you didn't take risks, you would never get out of bed in the morning. I take the risks in boxing because I love the sport and I love the training. In any event I think amateur boxing is a safe sport. It's three or four rounds and you have the referee there. The referee can stop a fight if you are taking punishment or you are in trouble. That's why boxing is such a hard sport. You have to give one hundred per cent because you have to avoid getting hurt.'

Katie said that being a female in a traditionally male sport has been a challenge, but it is a challenge she has always been up for. 'There probably were negative attitudes around but my family kept all that away from me,' she said. 'These people who were against women's boxing have probably never even seen an amateur fight or a women's fight. They don't understand the difference between the professional and the amateur sport. I've had more injuries playing soccer than I've ever had in boxing.'

Her mother Bridget agreed: 'I would honestly feel more worried about my daughter getting injured playing soccer, and remember she is an international soccer player. Yes, it's tough being a boxer and I suppose there is an element where people wonder if she is missing out on parts of life because of her schedule or regime but nobody would be good at anything if they did it half-heartedly. Where would greatness come from otherwise? If you want to play the piano you have to practice the whole time. To succeed at anything, whether it's boxing or anything else, you have to be disciplined.'

Katie has always kept her weight in check, and attributes a lot of it to a fear of flying. 'That's how I make the weight so easily,' she said. 'I do so much sweating on the plane that the weight just falls off me. I feel every bump when there is turbulence.'

What did Katie herself think has given her the edge over the past number of years? 'I don't know,' she said. 'Maybe it's because I'm a lot more focussed than a lot of the girls out there. Because of my lifestyle as well, I suppose. I'm a Christian, and God is in my life. That gives me strength. Things like that make you feel really strong and confident. I train very hard. I've got a great coach, a great family. I think that all these things add up and make you who you are.'

On St Patrick's Day in 2010, Katie achieved a personal ambition when she visited the White House in Washington and met President Obama. The invitation had come from the First Lady, Michelle Obama, who had heard of Taylor's great achievements in the sport. 'It was an honour to be invited to meet President Obama and the First Lady,' Katie recalled. 'She told me she did a bit of boxing herself in her young days and, like me, she was trained by her dad. It was a tremendous experience and I never dreamt my boxing career would present me with opportunities like that.'

Besides boxing, Katie has also proven herself at soccer. The first girl to play in the Wicklow Schoolboys League, before the name was changed to include 'girls', she lined out for Ardmore, winning over forty caps for Ireland at all levels right up to senior, and claiming nineteen caps for the women's international team. Indeed, she could have made a career at soccer. Before she sat her Leaving Cert, a number of US colleges had noted her talent. Universities like St John's NYC and Hofstra in Long Island, where women's soccer is big, offered her scholarships.

Arsenal and Birmingham City also sought her services to come across for trials. However, she turned all offers down, concluding that if she accepted, it would have meant leaving boxing, and her dream, after all, was to win an Olympic gold medal. She had also completed one year of a health and leisure degree in University College Dublin but once again, boxing came out on top.

Katie went to Sallynoggin College of Further Education in County Dublin to study leisure management and fitness instruction. As the boxing took over, she dropped out to focus on the sport. 'It's something I would like to go back to,' she says.

Sport has always been her thing. It was athletics and Gaelic games in the early days too but boxing was always in the background. The sport appealed to her competitive nature. 'Even when I was small, my parents used to say to me that you have to be able to enjoy your sport.' It is clear she really enjoys boxing.

Katie's training routine for major championships, including the Olympics, has always been a mixture of lifting weights, sparring, running and physiotherapy sessions along with a balanced diet which includes lots of fruit and vegetables, and some porridge for breakfast.

Outside the ring, she lives a very quiet life and can often be seen taking her Staffordshire terrier for a walk in Bray. He's called Hagler, after the great American middleweight boxer Marvin Hagler. She also likes to catch up with friends. 'Naturally I don't get to see much of them when I'm training,' she said. 'But when I'm on a break I like to have a good time by going to a concert or the movies.' A teetotaller but a self-confessed chocaholic, she said: 'People often say I missed out a lot by being dedicated to boxing but I never thought about it that way.

'Winning the Olympic gold medal surpassed all my dreams and made everything worthwhile – making up for no social life, no boyfriends, no parties after school exams, all that. There was no time for a social life and that's the way I wanted it and I have never felt like I missed out on anything. I am very happy with my life. Winning the Olympic gold medal, and the other medals, were incredible moments for me and my family, who have always been so supportive.'

Like all boxers, Katie has to keep control of her nerves, before and during the fight. Some boxers play cards in the dressing room, others take a short nap while some listen to music. Katie has her iPod and listens to carefully chosen Christian rock music, reciting specific extracts from the Bible, such as Psalm 18. It begins: 'The Lord is my rock, and my fortress and my deliverer; my God, my strength, in whom I will trust; my buckler, and the horn on my salvation, and my high power.'

Along with her family, Katie's Christian faith is a surprise to nobody. Having known her now for eleven years, since she had that first official bout at the National Stadium, it is quite clear to this writer that prayer plays a central role in her life. She has never made any secret of her deeply-rooted beliefs. 'Apart from those in my corner, it is God who helps me when the first bell rings,' she will explain.

The family go to St Mark's Pentecostal Church on Pearse Street in Dublin's south inner-city, usually the noon service, every Sunday when they are at home. A former Church of Ireland building where Oscar Wilde was baptised, there are no images of Jesus or scenes from the Bible there. Instead, oil paintings of lighthouses hang on the walls. Flat screen televisions are placed at the front, and a drum kit rests in a place where one might find a tabernacle in a Catholic church. The rousing Psalm 18 is known as Katie's Psalm.

A creature of habit, Katie sits in the same seat, three rows from the front, to the pastor's left, flanked by her parents. She believes God trains her hands for battle, makes her feet nimble as a deer and shields her from the punches of her opponents. It's a belief that was shared by Joe Louis, the former world heavyweight champion. It was Louis, the Brown Bomber, who famously told President Roosevelt during World War II: 'We'll win 'cos we're on God's side.'

In the weeks leading up to an important fight or tournament, she prays that she will fight to the best of her ability and prays for her own safety and that of each of her opponents. She also asks Pastor Peter Mullarkey to pray for her, and before a bout, she contemplates all those prayers offered up to her, from those she knows and those supporters she has never met. After her Olympic final victory, she said: 'I may be Olympic champion but Jesus is a champion of champions. With him, nothing is impossible.'

Such heartfelt sentiments are rarely heard publicly in the increasingly secular Ireland of the modern age, especially from a celebrity, but Taylor has much of the same single-mindedness about Christianity that she does about boxing. On Katie's green robe are the words: 'The Lord is my strength and my shield.'

On the day of her Olympic final win, St Mark's opened its doors to anybody who wanted to share a few moments in her spiritual home. More than two hundred people jammed themselves in front of the big screen in the church to pray for Katie and cheer her on as four hundred green, white and gold balloons hung from the ceiling and the railings outside as passing motorists sounded their horns. A large poster on the outside wall read: 'Praying for you Katie! We believe!' Inside the church, 'The Family', as Pastor Mullarkey affectionately calls his flock, watched the fight and were jubilant when she achieved her goal.

Katie said she will never forget the mother of all welcoming parties on the seafront in Bray when over twenty thousand people turned out. As she stood on the old Victorian bandstand against a picturesque backdrop of Bray Head and a calm blue sea and gazed out at the cheering faces, the tears in her eyes spoke more than words ever could. It was good to be home again. It was a moment that made up for all the sacrifices, all the long, lonely and arduous years of training. 'Incredible' is how she remembered it. 'I was just over-whelmed, really I was.'

One of her big thrills on returning to Bray was to meet again her eighty-year-old maternal grandmother. Kathleen Cranley was not able to travel to London to cheer her on but she watched the contests from her living room in Bray. They had a lovely get-together. Another exciting moment in the week she returned was when the Oscar-nominated actor Liam Neeson, who was born in Ballymena, County Antrim rang the Taylor home and asked to speak to Katie.

'When I took the call, I couldn't believe it,' recalled Peter. 'When I told Katie that Liam Neeson was on the phone, she laughed and thought I was having her on but I wasn't. He talked to Katie for three or four minutes. He congratulated her on her Olympic win and said that he'd been in New York and the bars were full of people watching her. He said she brought America to a standstill and that she made him proud to be Irish. It was just amazing.'

As this narrative comes to a conclusion, the performances of Katie's male counterparts in the London Olympics also deserve a mention, not only because of their medal successes but also because of their passion, drive and Irish fighting spirit. Mullingar bantamweight John Joe Nevin, who boxes out of the Cavan club, brought home a silver medal and there were two bronze from

Belfast lightflyweight Paddy Barnes from the Holy Family Boxing Club and flyweight Michael Conlon, also from the northern capital and who boxes for St John Bosco.

It was Barnes' second Olympic bronze, to go alongside the one he won in Beijing in 2008. He is the only Irish boxer to do the Olympic double. It is worth recording too that all three lost to the eventual gold medallists. They deserve full credit for their endeavours in creating our best ever Olympic boxing medals haul, beating the previous best at Melbourne in 1956 when one silver and three bronze were brought home.

The other two male boxers, Wicklow welterweight Adam Nolan, from Katie Taylor's Bray club, and Kilkenny middleweight Darren O'Neill, the team captain attached to Paulstown Boxing Club, went out earlier yet performed to the best of their ability on the toughest and most prestigious stage of all. Olympic places are hard to come by, and won by relatively few. Ireland's six-strong squad in London was the smallest panel of any of the nations in the top ten.

It was, however, the sensational success of the only girl on the team that grabbed most of the interest and the headlines. Besides her natural ability with the gloves, Katie Taylor effortlessly endeared herself to the wider world, courtesy of her modest charm and natural personality. The Warrior Princess with the golden gloves, the woman with God in her corner, was once again a knockout, inside and outside the roped square.

Bibliography

Books

Anderson, Roger, *The Fighting Irish*. Edinburgh: Mainstream Publishing, 2005.

Bunbury, Turtle and Fennell, James, *Sporting Legends of Ireland*. Edinburgh: Mainstream, 2010.

Byrne, Peter and Carruth, Michael, *Ring of Gold*. Dublin: Blackwater Press, 1992.

Callan, Gerry and Mullan, Harry, *Barry McGuigan, The Untold Story*. London: Robson Books and Arrow Books, 1991.

Carney Jr, Jim, *Ultimate Tough Guy: The Life and Times of James J. Jeffries*. Ohio: Achill Publishing, 2009.

Collins, Steve with Howard, Paul, *Celtic Warrior*. Dublin: O'Brien Press, 1995.

Donnellon, Matt, *The Irish Champion Peter Maher: The untold story of Ireland's only World Heavyweight Champion and the records of the men he fought*. Indiana: Trafford Publishing, 2008.

Dunne, Bernard, *My Story*. Dublin: Penguin Ireland, 2010.

Dunne, Bernard, *The Ecstasy and the Agony*. Dublin: Liberties Press, 2009.

Flynn, Barry and Brown, Jean (ed.), *Legends of Irish Boxing: Stories Seldom Told*. Belfast: Appletree Press, 2007.

Gallimore, Andrew, *A Bloody Canvas: The Mike McTigue Story*. Cork: Mercier Press, 2008.

Hannigan, Dave, *The Big Fight*. London: Random House UK, 2002.

Heller, Peter, *In This Corner: Forty World Champions Tell Their Stories*. New York: Dell Publishing, 1973.

Johnston, J.J., and Beck, Nick, *Babyface and Pop*. Indiana: Bustout Books/Xlibris, 2011.

Lewis, Greg and Sharkey, Moira, *I Fought Them All: The Life and Ring Battles of Prize-fighting Legend Tom Sharkey*. Cardiff: Magic Rat, 2010.

McCafferty, Dan, *Tommy Burns: Canada's Unknown World Heavyweight Champion*. Toronto: Lorimer, 2000.

McCullough, Wayne, *Pocket Rocket*. Edinburgh: Mainstream, 2005.

McGuigan, Barry, *Cyclone: My Story*. London: Virgin Books, 2011.

223

Mee, Bob, *The Heavyweights: The Definitive History of the Heavyweight Fighters*. Gloucester: Tempus, 2006.

Myler, Patrick, *Regency Rogue: Dan Donnelly, His Legend and Times*. Dublin: O'Brien Press, 1976.

Myler, Patrick, *Dan Donnelly 1788–1820: Pugilist, Publican, Playboy*. Dublin: Lilliput Press, 2009.

Myler, Patrick, *The Fighting Irish: Ireland's Role in World Boxing History*. Dingle: Brandon, 1987.

Myler, Patrick, *Gentleman Jim Corbett: The Truth Behind a Boxing Legend*. London: Robson Books, 1998.

Nicholson, Kelly Richard, *A Man Among Men: The Life and Ring Battles of Jim Jeffries*. Utah: Homeward Bound Publishing, 2002.

O'Hara, Eamonn, *Rinty, The Story of a Champion*. Belfast: Brehon Press, 2008.

Taub, Michael, *Jack Doyle, The Gorgeous Gael*. London: Stanley Paul. Dublin: Lilliput Press, 2007.

Newspapers, magazines and record books

Boxing Illustrated
Boxing Monthly
Boxing News
Evening Herald
Evening Press
Irish Boxing Yearbook 2002
Irish Daily Star
Irish Examiner
Irish Independent
Irish Press
Irish Times
Ring Magazine
Ringside Yearbook 1975
Sunday Independent
Sunday Tribune
Selection of US and British newspapers
The Boxing Register